The School
as a Safe Haven

The School as a Safe Haven

ROLLIN J. WATSON AND ROBERT S. WATSON

BERGIN & GARVEY
Westport, Connecticut • London

Library of Congress Cataloging-in-Publication Data

Watson, Rollin J., 1941–
   The school as a safe haven / Rollin J. Watson and Robert S. Watson.
      p.   cm.
   Includes bibliographical references and index.
   ISBN 0–89789–900–8 (alk. paper)
   1. School accidents—United States—History—20th century.   2. School violence—United
States—History—20th century.   3. School crisis management—United States—History—
20th century.   I. Watson, Robert S.   II. Title.
   LB2864.6.A25W38   2002
   371.7′82′0973—dc21   2001052795

British Library Cataloguing in Publication Data is available.

Library of Congress Catalog Card Number: 2001052795
ISBN: 0–89789–900–8

First published in 2002

Bergin & Garvey, 88 Post Road West, Westport, CT 06881
An imprint of Greenwood Publishing Group, Inc.
www.greenwood.com

Printed in the United States of America

The paper used in this book complies with the
Permanent Paper Standard issued by the National
Information Standards Organization (Z39.48–1984).

10 9 8 7 6 5 4 3 2 1

*For our wives, the teachers Norma Osborne Watson
and Linda Reeves Watson,
and for our beloved children and grandchildren*

Contents

Preface:
Metaphor and Myth

Writing this book has been a sad assignment in many respects. For anyone who loves children, it is very difficult to look for prolonged periods at the dark side of the American school, the tragic side, the side that in our hearts we don't even want to know about. Some of the things that have happened in schools tear at the heart of a parent or grandparent. And yet, some essential truth must be found if we are to see things truly. Tragedy is part of life, and organizations are like organisms of any other kind in nature: through the course of their lives they have pleasant and dreary times, happiness and sorrow. We are committed to the idea that school is a salubrious and altogether positive part of our lives as Americans. So in order to turn the school inside out, to do what is contrary to our nature as educators, we had to develop the idea that the metaphor of the school only works if seen in its entirety; we cannot know the truth about our schools unless we learn things about them that have harmed children, things that must be worked on so that future generations of children will not have to experience them. Thus, we have taken the metaphor "the school as a safe haven" and tried to examine it closely. Sadly, in many respects, it is a myth.

An old professor of ours was fond of using Plato's "Allegory of the Cave" to impress upon us the subjective, culturally relative nature of sensory impressions, using myths to illustrate how various cultures have handled the same or similar ideas, thereby showing us how the scientific, objective worldview itself should be questioned.

In other words, the mental picture we have about something, he stressed, is not necessarily always uniform and consistent and cannot always be precisely measured. Sometimes we want to believe in a concept even though our rational side tells us that a contrary idea may be true. Throughout the history of civilization, man has been guided by the flickering images he sees on the wall, synthesized into the ideas that form the myths around which he structures his life.

In the case of the safety of the school, we have wanted to believe in the myth of the inviolate nature of the place where our children are sent to be nurtured in peace and safety, and we hold onto this myth in spite of many indications that it is a naïve misperception of reality, lacking the refinement experience should bring.

When we decided to develop a comprehensive study about school safety that would balance research with the practitioner's working knowledge of the subject, we began to realize that what we believed would be tested by historical facts and statistical realities, sometimes to the detriment of the things we preferred to believe. Like most of the rest of American society, we wanted to believe in the historically sacrosanct nature of our places of learning, their pristine purity, like our first memories of them: clear and sure and safe.

There has been very little historical perspective developed or written on the safety of the American school. Without that kind of perspective, it is impossible to see how the subject of safety cuts to the philosophical heart of American education: children must be able to learn in an environment that is safe and secure, one that allows them the freedom to grow and express themselves. Almost all studies of school safety are undocumented, anecdotal accounts rather than documented, factual renderings; this is primarily because school people many times had no reason to write about or document safety concerns and incidents until relatively recently when they were required to do so, and often it was only journalists or administrators who made records of the most noticeable violations and threats to schools.

Then, too, for outsiders to come in and document that a particular school is endangered seems to contradict the prevailing and dominant ideology about the schoolhouse.

In *The School as a Safe Haven,* we have tried to utilize both historical and anecdotal methods to consider in how many different ways the safety of schools has been compromised, especially in the era after World War II, and then to contemplate how serious or meaningful that may be when set in the context of the vast enterprise of K–12 education. When we began our research, we did not expect to find what we did. There is such a vast amount of material available that we found ourselves selecting only representative incidents to try to illustrate our points.

While we hoped to see the interrelatedness of all the various conceptual facets and components that go into making safe schools on an everyday basis, we knew that it would be difficult to tie them together in the absence of good theoretical principles. Very little well developed theory exists on school safety. One of our primary objectives, therefore, has been to provide a sound theoretical basis that ties together disparate and often contradictory ideas about school safety. We realize that in order to be valid, this body of theory must be derived from both the historical background of the American school and from the knowledge garnered from those who have spent many years of active work in "the field"—out in the thousands of schools where children learn and teachers teach.

The time right after World War II when we were young and safe in school seems in retrospect truly to have been an age of innocence, for us certainly, for the American school, and perhaps for the country as well.

There are shaping influences or watershed moments in the lives of educators, occasions when something instrumental changes in one's thinking about the way the school environment can be threatened or corrupted, how intrusion of all kinds is perceived and reacted to, and what significance better preparation could be taken in preventing tragedy, avoiding trauma, and in saving people's lives.

In the nascent year 1950, we lived in a southern town where the distinction between rich and poor was quite evident, even though we did not think of things in those terms then. We accepted our family's humble economic condition as a fact we could find ways to live with. If one takes the philosophy that the uses of adversity are sweet, there are many things to be learned from being poor in rural America, even in a little rented house with no indoor plumbing on a dirt road beyond the outskirts of town.

That day when we were eleven and nine began with the neighbors' huge white frame farmhouse in the background distance, juxtaposed against the diminutive dwelling which we had just left, the two of us, our jeans splotched with mud from the swimming hole—a beaver pond about a half mile from our house where the country boys swam—as we started down the dusty dirt country road to school after having taken an early morning swim, dodging to the side as a passing gray 1950 Mercury convertible left a cloud of dust over us. A girl, flush with the innocence of youth, tendrils of soft brown hair flowing about her playful, piercing black eyes in the sweet symmetry of her face, walked along behind us—she was called Puff, like a little burst of wind swirling about. She and our little brother Harry came with us because Dad thought it could be dangerous for a girl and a boy Harry's age. We would walk to the school bus stop a half mile away and wait with them there. Later, Doug, Don, and Sal would also go into the little country town on a school bus.

As we look back on the 1940s and '50s, we realize that there was concern on the part of educators and support staff for the safety of children while they were in school, but not a heightened awareness of threats and dangers to safety. Our parents probably worried more about the school bus than they ever did about the school, for they took it for granted that schools were safe. The more protected children, the upper-middle-class kids who did not have to walk the unprotected streets or wait in the cold for the school bus were usually free of the dangers faced by the others who traversed the dirt roads, dodged cars, fended off attacks from wild dogs, got soaked in the rain, and so on. But in a way, all of us had more freedom from malevolent dangers than school children do now.

Our association with schools has lasted from that time until now, and that is why we wanted to concentrate our study on the post–World War II era. A different world of perception exists between the time when we were in school and the environment of fear and danger some people think is pervasive in certain schools now. The primary concern of this book is to find incidents that show how we went from where we were in the late '40s and early '50s to where we are now. It is the incremental development of threats to the safety of schools and the way people perceive those threats that are of particular interest in this book.

As teachers and as administrators, we have had our times of trial in schools and colleges. There were times when children brought guns to school, times when young people were killed and we had to tell their parents, there were fights, there was the invasion of a thousand threats, and there was the turbulent era of the 1960s and 1970s when the whole world was changing. There was the time in 1988 when an intruder walked into one of the schools in Bob's district and shot eleven people, killing two. From that incident, Bob and his staff of administrators realized that they had to develop contingency plans so that that could never happen again.

Even though one incident such as the 1937 gas explosion in Texas, discussed in Chapter 4, killed more individuals than are killed in any one year of violent school killers, people are frightened by the Columbine experience more than by anything else threatening the schools. Most schools are safe—we know that—and we do not wish by writing this book to scare anyone and put false impressions in their heads. But we would like to present a realistic portrait of the schools and the dangers that can threaten them. We hope this book selects a good combination of well-researched and thoughtful incidents that help illustrate that.

Chapter 1

The Sanctity of the Schoolhouse

THE MYTH

In America, they say, perception is reality. In the popular imagination, there are very few institutions that sustain the same kind of image as has the American school. The school as an enduring ideal is almost sacrosanct for the masses of Americans, for it epitomizes something sacred in the mythology of American culture. The notion that the schoolhouse is a "safe haven," separated from the world purposefully so that America's young will learn in a protected environment, nurtured by caring adults, is one of the enduring aspects of the myth.

Out of harm's way and free of the intrusions of uncontrollable cacophony and clutter that so characterize society outside, the school is a quiet reserve, a sanctuary. While proclaimed "academic," it never pretends to be a bastion of intellectualism; that might suggest trouble-making; nor does it encourage activism. Rather, it is comfortable, as it maintains the status quo, focused on well-roundedness as its goal, content because it is the *sine qua non* in the American myth of success. A primary part of the folklore surrounding the school, and perhaps accounting for a great deal of its charm, is the permanence of this mythic ideal about learning as an indispensable precursor to a productive adult life. Most of its allure for parents who have so fervently believed in the notion of success through education, so thoroughly embedded in the American dream, so clearly articulated by Thomas Jefferson ("If a nation expects to be ignorant and free, in a state of civilization, it expects what never was and never will be"), has been that the schoolhouse provides a clear, safe way to achieve success—the one proven ideal, a straight path in a confusing and contradictory culture. Had not generations of parents thought their children safe in the pristine environment of the school each day, they would not have had let educators serve "in loco parentis" to begin with. Therefore, the phrase "safe haven" is a term commonly applied to the school as an integral part of the language of the myth.

THREATS TO SCHOOLS

In how many ways can the work of the school be interrupted by disturbances emanating from either inside or outside the classroom and school building, jeopardizing the "safe haven"? For the most part, neither educators nor members of the general public know about the many unwanted intrusions into the sanctity of the classroom in our schools, nor are they aware of the many threats to safety that are present on a daily basis. Hopefully, most schools have never had a major incident, and some administrators get by with only routine incidents of interruption. Up until a few years ago, most educational administrators probably gave little or no thought whatsoever to safety concerns. The threats were not clearly defined, and some were denied because they were not expected. Safety is still seldom a part of the training provided in most teacher training institutions and has only recently begun to be evident in the courses offered for aspiring administrators.

Now invasions into the work of schools have seemingly become an epidemic, a deluge of violations of safety ranging from accidents to mischief to torts, all the way to full-blown cases of criminal conduct—some of the worst kind—all calling into question the ideal of the school as a "safe haven." Each violation of the sanctity of the school seems more heinous than the last, and because of Columbine and other deadly incidents of student-inflicted violence, school safety has in recent times become a nation-wide concern. The role of "media hype" in all of this remains to be seen—are there truly more threats to school safety than in previous decades, or is the perception such because the media has overplayed the phenomenon, as some claim?

Thought of in its broadest terms, school safety can be threatened by alien elements such as disease—conveyed through air borne pathogens and blood borne pathogens, car accidents—in which some 600 students a year are killed, food poisoning, proximity to hazardous materials, instruments of (mass) destruction (gases, radiological dangers, explosives, chemicals), stored chemicals, drugs of choice, and so forth. Safety is also occasionally jeopardized by uncontrollable events such as dangerous weather conditions.

Unfortunately, sometimes it is easier to understand safety by looking at those negative elements that jeopardize safety, just as it is easier to arrive at a definition of a thing by naming its opposites.

Some of the threats to the school have included accidents, fires, environmental dangers, building problems, and many other factors. Ever since the advent of the school bus, for instance, there have been accidents. When schools were built with wooden frames, school fires were common. Environmental dangers exist. Shop classes in schools have always been a potential hazard. The list of potential threats is a very long one. However, student discipline, while always a concern to educators, has never been until recent decades the major focus of school safety.

Schools are full of remedies—physical and procedural—developed in response to defined threats. In recent years, state and national governments have taken an interest in dealing with the threats to school safety and have helped define threats in the language of laws. Unsafe schools are now part of local, state, and federal governments' "public concern," and while no doubt politics plays a role in the "concern" expressed by these officials, there is a true alarm running through the rhetoric and actions of leaders in all three sectors of government. Violent intruders and student perpetrators have proven that they are not bluffing in many cases, so every potential disruption must be taken seriously. The federal government has taken an increasing role in school safety:

> In addition to disseminating statistics, the federal government often offers possible solutions to local school problems. Regarding school violence, Secretary of Education Riley announced in June 1998 that the Department of Education was contracting with the National Association of School Psychologists to write guidelines for identifying possible violent students. In addition, the Department of Education receives Congressional funding under the Safe and Drug-Free Schools and Communities Act to fund antiviolence programs. In response to

the rash of student massacres, the director of the safe and drug-free program, William Modzelski, said, "The federal government is not the savior for communities' drug and violence programs, but we want to provide schools with the information to craft solutions." Modzelski announced that his office was assembling a team of experts to provide guidelines for dealing with school violence.[1]

Most states have set up school safety training offices to deal with the subsequent rash of problems associated with recent incidents of school violence.

The different kinds of threats to school safety can be categorized or grouped according to their seriousness, their danger, and in some cases, their deadliness, their type, and—as was mentioned above—their point of origin either within the school or from outside it. Natural disasters, such as earthquakes, tornados, and floods have always been a major intrusion factor for schools. Fires are a major problem, constituting a category, as do accidents of all kinds, including bus accidents. Intentional man-made intrusions, including hostage taking, bombings, murders, rape, and kidnapping are crimes that have been perpetrated both by intruders and by students. Suicides have become an increasing problem category. So have teacher-initiated incidents of all kinds, including assaults, pornography, carrying guns, and so on. Mischief such as vandalism is a major category. Outside school disciplinary problems, such as gangs and bullying, have intensified of late. Interior disturbances such as the disciplinary type have always been part of school life, as have certain types of ever-present threats such as school fires and school bus accidents. Some types of exterior threats may appear to be of fairly recent origin, such as the danger posed by intruder-killers, although we shall see that this particular threat is not necessarily a new one and that in fact it has a long and pernicious history, going well back into the early twentieth century.

PUBLIC OPINION

We began by remarking about the importance of perception; certainly, public opinion plays an important role in safety. The actual safety conditions of a school are sometimes not so important as the perceived conditions. That is, perceptions that students, parents, and the general public hold about the safety of schools may in fact be more significant than the actual safety conditions. If, for instance, a school is governed by an environment of fear that something terrible will happen, the fear has the same effect it would have if there had been an actual accident or act of violence that brought about the element of fear in persons there. To ascertain the overall safety of a school, both real and perceived conditions must be considered.

And as Ascher has said, "Too often in urban schools across the country, both students and teachers feel unsafe."[2] A poll by *Time* showed that parents and teens feel differently about safety—fewer teens feel very safe from violence in schools today while more parents believe teens feel safe, with half of the teens in the poll saying that they have been insulted or threatened in the past year, but only 22 percent of the parents believe their kids have experienced that situation. So,

> The vast majority of schools in the United States are safe places for children to learn and grow. Most injuries that occur at school result from accidents, not violence, and most school crime is theft, not violent crime. In addition, U.S. schools are becoming even safer. Between 1993 and 1997, the overall school crime rate for students ages 12–18 declined, and the percentage of high school students carrying weapons or engaging in physical fights on school property decreased significantly. Notwithstanding this encouraging news, the recent shootings in the United States have clouded the public's perception of school safety. Many parents wonder whether their children will be victimized by school violence. Many educators question the adequacy of their school's security measures. And if the trend that displayed itself during the first half of the 1990's continues in the same direction, many children feel less safe at school now than they did in the past.[3]

STUDENT VIOLENCE

Once the least imagined of school atrocities, student-initiated violence is now the most dreaded, if not the most common, violation of the harmonious environment of the school. There are many other ways the peaceful process of schooling can be interrupted, but violence perpetrated by students gets the most media attention and draws the most concern. Some argue that the magnitude of school violence is overplayed: one group of researchers points out that "The best data on the very specific threat of school-associated violent death reveals that children face a one in a million chance of being killed at school. Other research shows that the number of school shooting deaths has declined since 1992. To give the reader a sense of the idiosyncratic nature of these events, the number of children killed by gun violence in schools is about half the number of Americans killed annually by lightning strikes."[4] In contradistinction to that approach, which relies on statistics for the force of its argument, there is a perspective relying primarily on anecdotal and or analytical elements to prove its point. In discussing reasons for the increased violence in schools, Carol Ascher points out that

> The celebration of violence in movies, television, and in popular songs has turned into an epidemic of personal tragedies for people living in our Nation's cities. Exacerbated by the ready availability of drugs and weapons, violence has become a public health issue of immediate concern. Yet the sources of violence are deep and long-standing, for ours is a country sharply divided between haves and have-nots; and areas of high poverty concentration have long been susceptible to all forms of violence, from vandalism, robbery, and rape, to suicide—the ultimate violence of despair.[5]

Other writers have suggested that parents, more than any other influence, bear responsibility for children's attitudes. Of course, the availability of drugs, peer influence, and the media are all culpable contributors. One conservative commentator said this about American children:

> I am struck by four factors: first, students don't believe in very much and are unwilling to make moral judgments; second, they have artificially inflated opinions of themselves and are unwilling to tolerate criticism; third, they are poorly educated; and finally, they hated their high school experience. The result is an explosive mixture of nihilism, narcissism, ignorance, and resentment.[6]

The point here is the same as made by the authors above—the school has to deal with problems endemic to and inculcated by the greater culture. One study pointed out in 1977 that

> The climate for all kinds of unwanted behavior by students in the public schools of America has changed radically during the last generation. Not only has violence increased, but also much of what is now taken for granted would have been shocking twenty years ago; that is, the character of violence has undergone dramatic changes. The actions and viewpoints of school administrators in dealing with violence have also changed; there is some indication that these altered

actions and viewpoints may in turn have influenced student violence or may influence it in the future.[7]

Today, safety may be an administrator's primary concern. The growing tendency towards terrorism, violence, and the disruption of the school is, in its many forms, a reflection of the problems of the greater culture—for which the school often takes blame—changing the way schools are managed and teachers teach. Indeed, the alarming number of children carrying guns to school, the increase in fights, gangs, accidents, and violent deaths in schools over recent decades has marked a decided change in the way others perceive the school. A more threatened school is viewed differently now by prospective teachers, by parents, and by other agencies in society, such as the police, EMS, and fire departments. Fear has made safety more important than academics in many schools. The entire school is being impacted by fear and trauma: "teaching practices; children's readiness and capacity for learning; hiring and retention of teachers, administrators, and other school staff; the openness and accessibility of the campus; student rights to privacy; the physical building and grounds; and the quality of the learning environment more generally."[8]

The public perception of violence in the schools has shifted dramatically. From 1982, when 3 percent of adults in a national poll identified crime and violence as the most important problem facing the country to August 1994, when more than half identified crime and violence as the nation's leading problem, there was a major opinion shift. In 1994, violence and a lack of discipline among students were identified as the "biggest problems" in American schools. The public blamed deficiencies or dysfunctions in the family, public schools, and the criminal justice system for this condition.[9]

The Centers for Disease Control and Prevention's Youth Risk Behavior Survey for 1997 found that 8.3 percent of high school students carried a weapon in the thirty days before the survey, many of them carrying it on school property. Another 7.4 percent of high school students were threatened or injured with a weapon on school property during the 12 months preceding the survey. Approximately one-third of all students nationwide had property stolen or deliberately damaged on school property one or more times during the 12 months preceding the survey.[10]

Many people think school safety relates only to student violence—but school safety is not limited to student-initiated violence. It is about the overall well being of schools. Safety is larger than and encompasses security, which is a means to the attainment of safety.

Threats to school safety almost always derive from one of seven areas: environmental conditions, school design, equipment, technology, procedures, training of staff, and student personnel. Schools also find remedies to offset threats from these same areas. The successful integration of these remedies determines the extent to which a school facility may be safe and secure.

THESIS AND PURPOSE OF BOOK

The thesis of this book is that the ideal of the American school as a safe haven has always been challenged by the realities of American culture and that, at least since the beginning of the post–World War II period—which is the period covered by this study—the reality, if not just the perception, of safety in our schools has been changed by the events and social forces of each succeeding era. The threats to safety may change with each new decade, and the dangers to schools may or may not remain the same. Thus, this book attempts to place the idea of safe schools within the context of social forces and philosophical currents at work in the greater culture.

This book has several purposes. The first is to present a balanced view of school safety and all of its related concerns, which comes out of the conviction that public opinion should be based in facts as well as impressions. The second purpose is to present an historical basis for analysis of the school safety question. Third, we think it is important to provide a basis for future scholarly inquiry by presenting facts about events that have not been pulled together before. In doing so, we want to move from the totally anecdotal approach, which characterizes most works so far, and move to a factually based discussion. Fourth, we also want to try to determine what the states have done to make their schools safer. Fifth, we want to try to show what impact historical disruptions of the schools—as well as other factors such as public opinion—have had in shaping the federal, state, and local laws, as well as court decisions, which relate to school safety. It would not be an understatement to say that there has been a plethora of new state laws since 1990. Finally, since the authors are educators, we hope to demonstrate how complicated it has become for teachers and administrators to respond to the myriad of new requirements and administrative tasks the need for safe schools has placed on them. (For instance, one could cite the fact that only a small percentage of marriages these days have two parents living in the household who are lifetime parents. Many times the persons authorized to remove a child from school are boyfriends, former spouses, and so forth, and it is difficult for school personnel to keep up with the changes in people's lives—it takes a great deal of constantly updated record keeping.)

RESEARCH METHODS AND LIMITATIONS OF STUDY

The methodological basis of this study is in four primary tools: historical evidence, statistical and survey-based information provided by national agencies, some anecdotal evidence, and analysis of the data the authors have encountered. While the book does not try to be a totally comprehensive history, it uses a generous amount of historical evidence.

We have limited the study to the safety of public and private schools in the United States. While we find it extremely interesting to compare the problems American schools are having with those in Great Britain, Canada, Japan, and Western Europe, where it appears that there is an epidemic of violent behavior,[11] the scope of the study would be too large to adequately handle this interesting and probably very informing contrast. Another measured limitation of the study is that the authors have focused on the time after World War II because it is during this era that schools face an increasing burden of invasive disturbance from the outside culture. Incidents cited before the World War II era help set the stage for the study, but are discussed only in the first four chapters. Some of the same difficulties exist today that were troublesome for Rubel's study in 1977:

> to collect data that give a quantitative assessment of these changes is extremely difficult—because the methods for recording disruptive incidents are nonuniform. Many people observed or read about increasing violence in the schools. But to prove such increases, to collect data; some offenses are not reported, whereas others are over reported; and reporting procedures involve overlapping categories that precludes drawing hard, precise conclusions from the available data.[12]

The evidence that is presented here is merely the tip of the iceberg. We want the reader to understand that our research has turned up literally hundreds of incidents that have not been used in this book. We certainly want it to be known that we do not include every intrusion ever made; in fact, we have very selectively used incidents to make our points—there are hundreds, if not thousands, of others that could be cited. We are also aware that there are many incidents we have not uncovered because they are available only if the researchers were to go to every school and school system in the United States and look through old records. This of course is impossible. Joseph J. Ellis quotes this passage from Lytton Strachey's *Eminent Victorians* to show that an historian does not always have to use a strictly chronological story line:

> If he is wise, he will adopt a subtler strategy. He will attack his subject in unexpected places; he will fall upon the flank and rear; he will shoot a sudden revealing searchlight into obscure recesses, hitherto undivined. He will row out over the great ocean of material, and lower down into it, here and there, a little bucket, which will bring up to the light of day some characteristic specimen, from those far depths, to be examined with a careful curiosity.[13]

We believe that there are watershed themes in the history of the school of a safe haven. By following Strachey's advice, we can probe themes, and perhaps develop them in a selective way that sheds light upon the whole history of American school history.

Also, the authors want to stress that very few indices were computerized before 1979. No index to a daily periodical is as complete as that of the *New York Times*. Because the *Times* is so well indexed, and because it is one of the world's most respected journals, we have relied heavily upon it.

It is not our intention in this book to frighten school professionals or parents—or the general public—with the facts we are going to discuss. Some people may be unaware that events so deleterious can have had such a long history in American life. In fact, it is our hope that by describing what has happened in the past, people will realize that threats and violence are not a new phenomenon and that they can be reduced, and possibly prevented. We do not advocate that every school official and parent rush out to see the myriad of "experts" who have emerged since the Columbine incident. Rather, we advocate that persons use good common sense and demonstrate support for intelligent and committed educators, police, fire, and emergency personnel who are working to devise ways to prevent further episodes. This is a matter that calls for the wisdom and action of all concerned: it is not going to go away because someone writes a simple handbook or because the federal and state governments take an interest in it.

It is important to reiterate that the first purpose of this book is to show that a balanced perspective on school safety is necessary. Educators and parents must develop an awareness that safety can easily be compromised and that teachers and principals in the schools and parents at home are the first line of security, but that all other members of the community must join them if we are to make our schools safer. At the same time, communities and citizens should know that good work has already been done in making schools safer and that by and large American schools are relatively safe, certainly at least as safe as most other institutions of our society. We do not, however, dismiss a commitment to school safety as "hype," as some have argued, and we will provide a more extended discussion of the reasons why after we have presented an historical survey of violations of safety in American schools.

Some good work has been done in studying responses to crises in schools, which is a part of school safety. A school and community's response to crisis can mean the difference in lives saved, for "A school emergency has an immediate and powerful impact on the school, the district, the families of students and staff, and on the local and extended communities."[14]

Unfortunately, incidents demonstrating the tenuous nature of the "safe haven" ideal—although they came slowly at first—grew exponentially in the era after World War II, with more incidents in each decade than in the one before. The focus of this book is on the post–World War II period, but we want to look at a few incidents that happened prior to that era in order to show the kinds of things that can disrupt the work of schools and would later with great frequency.

EARLY THREATS TO SCHOOLS

For instance, it was in the Cleveland suburb of Collinwood, which is now part of inner-city Cleveland, on March 4, 1908, that children between ages 6 and 14 were in school when a janitor saw smoke coming from beneath the front stairwell. When he sounded the alarm, the children, who were well trained in fire drills, prepared to march down the stairs toward the front exit. As they assembled there, the front stairwell became blocked by flames, and the children at the front broke from the lines and tried to fight their way to the floor above while those behind them coming down shoved them mercilessly back into the flames, according to witnesses.

Some children made it to the rear exit, which was locked. Outside rescuers unlocked it but found that it opened inward, making it impossible to push against the press of the panicked young people. After breaking the door down, rescuers found what a bystander described:

> We thought the work of getting the children out would be easy, but when we attempted to release the first one we found it was almost impossible to move them at all. We succeeded in saving a few who were near the top but that was all we could do. The fire swept through the hall, spreading from one child to another, catching their hair and the dresses of the girls. Their cries were dreadful to hear.

The school's janitor was accused of setting the fire, even though he lost four children in the fire and was badly burned trying to rescue one of them. The sheriff's men had to detain him in protective custody to keep mobs from lynching him.

The death toll in this disaster was estimated at 176. Uncertainty over the fire's cause left the survivors with mixed feelings over whether children were safe in public institutions. An editorial writer said that this was a base betrayal of childhood by its natural protectors. The site of Lake View School is now totally obliterated by the expanding city.[15]

On May 17, 1923, in Kershaw County, South Carolina, about six miles southeast of Camden, about 300 people—mostly parents and their children—gathered to watch the play *Topsy Turvey,* the last event scheduled at the school, which was to be closed the following year. The large room where children, their parents, and members of the community were seated to watch the play had only one entrance/exit and was on the second floor of the wood frame building. A narrow staircase provided the only way to reach the second floor; this staircase did not lead directly to the front entrance to the school, but instead began in a cloakroom on the first floor.

During the first act of the play, an oil lamp fell to the stage from a post, spreading kerosene so that the flames rapidly ignited nearby pine straw and cheesecloth curtains and then spread suddenly. Panicked people rushed to the one exit, and their weight caused the stairway to fall. Those people were trapped in the fire, as the door outside opened inward. Many other persons jumped from the second story windows.

Seventy-seven people were killed that night—28 pupils and 49 adults. They were buried the next day in a mass grave at the Beulah church. Every family but two lost a member in the tragedy. A survivor described the chaos in the second floor room after the fire rampaged as she took care of her little sister:

> In that short time the room was filled with smoke and it was difficult for me to breathe, much worse for Leila. She had been sick that winter with pneumonia and kept saying "I can't breathe" over and over, crying all the time. I pushed our way from the stairwell (we had not yet reached the steps) and we finally reached the window. I lifted her up so she could hold her head out the window and I told her to breathe deep. While I was holding her a man with his musical instrument pushed both of us aside and dropped it down. He then got into the window opening and dropped down. I looked down and a man caught him. Then a lady with a child pushed us aside and she dropped the child and it was caught also. The man on the ground kept saying to me, as I held Leila up for air, "drop the little girl down."

The girl and her sister both jumped to the ground to be saved from the fire. The next day she learned that her other sister and brother had been killed.

The school's tin roof increased the intensity of the flames by hampering the escape of fire from the building; no fire departments were located in that area of the county. Among the dead were 47 people under the age of 18, including three one-year-olds.

Because of the school fire, the South Carolina legislature passed the School Building Code (May 1924) that required adequate fire exits for two-story buildings. The fire also had an impact upon revised national fire codes. A large memorial to the victims of the fire stands in Kershaw County, South Carolina.[16]

> At the scene the smell almost overcame me. I do not remember praying or asking God's help, I was in deep shock, but I'm sure God was with me. Papa then told me that the American Red Cross was there and workers were there and asking family members to help identify bodies so they could be tagged and put aside. Then the family could decide if they wished to bury their own in their family cemetery plot, or have them buried in the big mass grave that was being prepared at Beulah Methodist Church. Papa said that he had looked all the bodies over but could not find either Ora Belle, or J.C. At that time I could go out in our back yard and smell the odor of burned flesh and Papa said it was much worse at the school site. He said to me "you

know your Mama cannot leave Hattie at the hospital in her condition. Claude tried to identify them but could not do so, now, I'd like you to dress and go and I'll stay here with the children." I told him I'd rather not go but he insisted, saying "I know it's hard, but some one has to go." Reluctantly and prayerfully I dressed to go and as I approached, there were many already wrapped and tagged and placed some distance from the others. As I approached the unidentified section I saw a body dressed in green and lying in a very grotesque position. As I neared the body I knew it was she. I could not stop crying. There was no sign of burning on her except on a little spot of hair that showed some singe. This was my beautiful sister, Ora Belle. . . . I had more trouble finding J.C. and I would not have done so had I not known what he wore the evening before. As I write this, the horrible memories come back to me. There were a number of partial bodies in one area, and he was one. He had no arm, or legs, just a body and part of a head. I recognized his teeth and his new shirt, with thin brown stripes. Silenced forever was this happy little boy with his sweet disposition and his cheerful little whistle and sweet smile. (Clara Elizabeth Woodson, age 88, remembering the Camden fire)

AN EARLY ACT OF TERRORISM

But fires were not the only devastating threat that could cause mass suffering. One of the most insidious episodes of intrusion in the history of the American school happened on a sunny day in May 1927. May 18 was truly a somber day in what are stereotyped as the carefree and gleeful days of the "roaring twenties," because on that day an embittered school board member gave the town of Bath, Michigan, a small farming town near Lansing, its brief moments of fame, recorded the next morning on the front page of the *New York Times*. A 55-year-old farmer and treasurer of the Bath school board, mad because the Bath Consolidated School had been funded by a tax increase that would threaten his farm with foreclosure, decided to blow up the town's three-story brick schoolhouse. Andrew Kehoe set off a series of bombs inside the school that killed 45 people, including 38 children.

Kehoe wired the basement of the school with more than 500 pounds of dynamite. When it went off, the explosion produced by the dynamite buried the teachers and pupils under tons of debris. The principal of the school, E.E. Huyck, rushed to confront Kehoe, who was attaching another wire to more explosives inside his car. As the two men grappled, the bomber fired at his car, setting off another explosion, killing both of them. Before he had set the explosives in the school, Kehoe had killed his wife and horses and had blown up his home. Reporters of the day interviewed Kehoe's neighbors to attempt to find what might have motivated the man. They said his lands were well kept and his buildings well furnished. They reported that he appeared intelligent, but he had a "tendency toward being pugnacious." Apparently, the controversy with the school board had made him "morose."

The incident is notable for the magnitude of the crime committed. But it is a precursor to later events because it was so difficult to understand why a seemingly ordinary person would attack what must have been the most innocent and peaceful persons in a community: the children, as they studied at school. Like many later episodes, there apparently was no way this behavior could have been foreseen or prevented, and like so many others in later decades, this all took place in a rural area, where things like that "just do not happen."

In spite of the horror of this event, acts of terror, then and now, were the least frequent of threats to schools.[17]

THE IMPORTANCE OF THE HISTORICAL PERSPECTIVE

A culture is an organism whose life unfolds over time. The school is a part of American culture, and it can only be understood within the context of the broader culture. Events unfolding in the life of the culture, whether they are mainstream movements—such as the Civil Rights Movement, or underlying implicit currents such as are discussed in Chapter 7, "The Demise of Discipline"—are integral to understanding the safety and well being of the school. The authors prefer to make the assumption that American schools are different from schools in Europe or South America or Japan, and although the same kinds of forces may be at work in all post-industrial societies, the way an event—even a violent intrusion in a school—is received and reacted to may have subtle differences depending on the place in which it occurs. Only after American schools are studied and then compared with those of other countries will we be able to juxtapose the uniquenesses of one culture with another. Because of the authors' belief in the importance of placing this study within the context of the history of the larger culture, the chapters will be seen to study sociological phenomena in a chronological way as much as possible. At the same time, of course, each chapter has a thematic basis, so the historical current is traced through the context of that particular theme. Some of the chapters carry the story all the way from 1945 to the present. Others have a more limited time period.[18] After the introductory chapter, the book opens in Chapter 2 with a description of post–World War II America and the place of the schools within that context. Then the book proceeds to problems faced by the schools in a rapidly developing population. The story is then carried forth through the 1950s, '60s, '70s, '80s, '90s, and up to the present. At the end, some conclusions are drawn, and the authors try to project where the safety of schools will be in the years ahead.

NOTES

1. Joel Spring, *American Education* (New York: McGraw-Hill, 2000), pg. 220.

2. Carol Ascher, "Gaining Control of Violence in the Schools: A View from the Field," *ERIC,* ED377256, 1994. Jodie Morse, "Looking for Trouble," CNN.com. April 17, 2000. "School Safety: A Collaborative Effort," *ERIC Review,* 7: 2000. http://www.accesseric.org/resources/ericreview/vol7no1/ltrfrmed.html.

3. "School Safety: A Collaborative Effort," pgs. 1–2.

4. Elizabeth Donohue, Vincent Schiraldi, and Jason Ziedenberg, "School House Hype: School Shootings and the Real Risk Kids Face in America," *Justice Policy Institute,* 1–15, 2000. http://www.google.com/schoolreport.html.

5. Ascher, pg. 1.

6. C. Bradley Thompson, "Our Killing Schools: Public Schools: Intellectual and Moral Wastelands that Destroy America's Youth." Ayn Rand Institute's *Media Link,* 1–2, 2000. http://www.aynrand.org/medialink.

7. Robert J. Rubel, *The Unruly School* (Lexington, Mass.: D.C. Heath and Company, 1977), pg. 1.

8. Delbert S. Elliott, Beatrix A. Hamburg, and Kirk R. Williams, *Violence in American Schools: A New Perspective* (New York: Cambridge University Press, 1998), pg. 9.

9. Ibid.

10. "Facts About Violence Among Youth and Violence in Schools," CDC *Media Relations,* 1–5, April 21, 1999. http://www.cdc.gov/od/oc/media/fact/violence/htm.

11. See the Associated Press story "A Dutch School Shooting: Student Opens Fire at High School, Wounding Four," ABC News.com, December 7, 1999. http://abcnews.go.com/sections/world/daily news/dutch99/207.html> or Sue Masterman, "Two Tiny Hostages Freed," ABC News.com, June 1, 2000. http://luxembourg000601_hostages.html.

12. Rubel, pg. 1.

13. Quoted in Joseph J. Ellis, *Founding Brothers: The Revolutionary Generation* (New York, Alfred A. Knopf, 2001), pg. xi.

14. Robert S. Watson, Janice H. Poda, C. Thomas Miller, Eleanor S. Rice, and Gary West, *Containing Crisis: A Guide to Managing School Emergencies* (Bloomington, Indiana: National Education Service, 1990), pg. xi.

15. Ray Jablonski, "The Neighborhood Never Forgets," October 8, 1998. http://www.sunnews.com/news/1998/1008/collinwoodfire.html.

16. Materials sent by the Camden Fire Department, Camden, South Carolina, including a *Newsletter* of the Kershaw County Historical Society, an old newspaper clipping, and other typed and printed information about the disaster.

17. "Maniac Blows Up School, Kills 42, Mostly Children; Had Protested High Taxes," *New York Times*, May 19, 1927, pg. 1. "School Massacre Not Worst," *Los Angeles Times*, April 23, 1999, pg. A30. Robert S. Johnston, "Events Stir Memories of Dark Day at Michigan School," *Education Week on the Web*, June 18, 2000. http://www.edweek.org/ew/vol18/34bath.h18. "1927 School Bombing Killed Nearly 40 Children," *Boulder News*, April 25, 1999. http://www.bouldernews.com/shooting/4251927.html.

18. We have used our own arbitrary time periods to frame a thesis about a certain force in the greater culture acting upon the school. Granted, in many cases they show only the beginning of a social movement.

Chapter 2
Postwar Innocence (1945–1950)

The cessation of years of fighting World War II gave the world a chance to begin anew, again. For Americans the possibility of a renewed innocence would occur as soldiers returning from the battlefields in Europe and the Pacific theaters exchanged the unbearable banality of war for the exhilarating sameness of peace. During the years 1941 through 1945, American schools, like every other component of the culture, went quietly about their work while thinking of little else besides the war. The apparent lull of inactivity during those years would soon be followed by a frantic storm of change in the postwar years.

Schools generally reflect societal changes very slowly, but the changes made in American society in the years following the war were profound, impacting the schools more quickly than they usually would—soon those changes had an enormous impact upon the size, curriculum, management, and safety of schools.

A new set of social forces at work in the postwar world would have a dynamic impact upon the development of the school. The baby boom resulting in part from the return of the soldiers would greatly increase the population and create a demand for more schools and more teachers. The number of soldiers taking advantage of the GI Bill to attend college would mean that there would be a greater number of college-educated people. The advent of the Cold War would eventually put great pressure on American schools to increase academic rigor and enhance the curriculum, with special emphasis on math and science.

The suburbanization of the entire country would shift much of the tax money paid by the white middle class from the cities to the suburbs, thus making suburban schools wealthier and more desirable than urban schools. Additionally, this meant that urban schools would be less safe as the aging school buildings deteriorated, the cities' infrastructure crumbled, and the urban landscape degenerated further, with slum areas on the increase and all of the problems associated with them keeping ahead of new urban renewal efforts.

Other changes related to demographic shifts and infrastructure needs would affect schools. The population would see a demographic shift to the rapidly growing sun-belt states. In all areas, the many new roads constructed to accommodate pressures from the automobile, tire, and petroleum industries—and the suburban American driver—would increase the demand for transportation of children to and from school.[1]

In the time from the end of World War II to the end of the century, adolescence itself changed greatly. In 1955, 60 percent of U.S. households consisted of a working father, a housewife mother, and two or more children. By 1980, that number had decreased to 11 percent, and by 1985 only seven percent of families were so characterized. Additionally, by the turn of the century, children reached puberty earlier and were confronted with issues far beyond those concerns considered "normal" in the 1950s.[2]

PRESSURES ON SCHOOLS AFTER THE WAR

Most significantly, enrollment in public schools climbed relentlessly during the baby boom years. From 25.1 million students in 1950, enrollments rose to 46.1 million in 1971, which meant that a great many schools had to be built quickly. Almost one-half of American schools at the turn of the century were built in the 1950s and 1960s, and 29 percent more were built in the 1970s and 1980s. Because nearly half of the nation's schools were built between 1950 and 1970 and because of the need for fast construction, the focus was on quantity, not quality. That meant that many safety, as well as maintenance, problems would plague school districts for years to come.[3]

In 1995, the U.S. Department of Education estimated that schools in America had long been suffering from deferred maintenance or no maintenance and that conditions were not always safe for those reasons. The average age of a public school building in 1999 was 42 years old, and the mean age ranged from 46 in the Northeast and central states to 37 years in the Southeast.[4]

Furthermore, schools were allocating less and less money to maintenance. President Clinton said in 1995 that one-third of the schools needed major repairs and more than one-half had major building problems. The General Accounting Office reported that 14 million students attend schools in need of extreme repair or replacement and half of America's schools—housing about 46 million students—had unsatisfactory environmental conditions.[5]

SCHOOLS IN USE AFTER THE WAR

This was the situation in the post-war epoch: in 1930, there were 150,000 one-room schoolhouses in the United States, and most were beginning to disappear as more centralized facilities to which children could be bused increased efficiency.[6] After the war, there were many old school buildings still standing, and there were many more new ones being built. But both new and old schools were not adequately constructed or equipped to deal with enhanced safety dilemmas presented in this new era. By the 1950s, there was a plethora of schools under construction—most built in an eclectic style under hurried conditions with questionable construction techniques and materials—and then there was another group of older schools, which had been constructed around the turn of the century, that were facing the period of their heaviest use. New schools were built with economy and efficiency in mind, with little regard given to beauty or safety.

The scene included many older, stone, Gothic structures, such as the once-spacious and architecturally beautiful City College in Baltimore and the magnificent four-story Scranton Central High School in Scranton, Pennsylvania, which had been constructed in 1894, and which still had a boys' entrance on one side of the building and a girls' entrance on the other side. It also included, not many miles away (usually in areas away from the downtown) new one-, two-, and three-story brick structures, such as the then recently built, rambling South Scranton Junior High School on the south side of town, which represented a new wave in high school buildings at that time.[7]

Design seems to have played a much greater role in the older schools. They were often built to be part of a city's architectural heritage, or at the least they were constructed to fit the cityscape. Both Central High and Elyria High in Elyria, Ohio, built during that era, are bordered with sidewalks and rise impressively above the civic and commercial buildings that surround them.

Seeming as impenetrable as a stone fortress, Scranton Central's four stories of classrooms form a rectangle around the inner core of the building, which is occupied by an auditorium and a gymnasium. Solid hardwood and brass adorn the main entrance and corridor in the front of the school. Similarly decorated, the Elyria school is the oldest school west of the Alleghenies; more than one hundred classes of students have graduated from Elyria High. Throughout the years, there have been numerous additions, so the edifice now occupies almost all of the space once available around it. Student parking lots at Elyria, which were not part of the original scheme, are not easily accessible. (Scranton Central had no student parking lots.)

SCHOOL ARCHITECTURE AND SAFETY FACTORS

These sturdy old buildings—and many that were not as well constructed—had a number of safety and maintenance circumstances that did not meet the needs of the society of the 1950s and later. Many of these older schools were built in the centers of cities, where urban problems—including traffic and vandalism—were at their worst. Other problems of the older buildings included inadequate lighting on the outside of the buildings and on walkways between buildings. Inadequate drainage often caused flooding and electrical problems; overburdened electrical systems posed fire hazards and dangers of electrical shock. As plastic windowpanes replaced broken glass, visual access was further reduced. Asbestos in floor and ceiling tiles, and sometimes in the walls, caused many problems in the post-war era. (Children often spend up to 40 hours a week in school buildings and were routinely exposed to environmental hazards known to trigger asthma, affect verbal perception, cause motor and behavioral disabilities, and bring on a number of other dangerous maladies.)[8]

The architecture of the older schools was often called "classical" because of its emphasis upon order and balance. However, school buildings traditionally were usually simple in design, with classrooms set outside the center core, along the windows of rectangular buildings, with halls, gymnasiums, and auditoriums occupying the center areas. Doors were usually left unlocked during the day, and main offices on the first floor seldom had a clear view of the classroom halls. The outer doors were the only barriers to control access from the street; fences usually did not protect the schools, as they were built close to the streets. Many of the older schools often had more than one building, and as the number of students increased, later buildings were set near original buildings, so many school districts had high schools with numerous buildings, usually designed differently, making up hodge-podge campuses that presented numerous safety problems.

Critics have argued that architecture has not been fully employed in the design of schools. For school architecture, there were only a few imperatives: "An impenetrable roof, school walls, and an adequate mechanical system continue to be standard even when designing new facilities."[9] Between World War I and World War II, eclectic styles of school buildings were built. These often-creative styles were the first signs of a romantic era in school design that emphasized free expression over order. Romanticism dominated school design until after World War II and well into the post-war era, as schools often possessed an airy feel with asymmetrical patterns.[10] Yet, as time went on, school systems needed more and more buildings, so they later opted for more standardized designs and cheaper building materials.[11]

Usually the new schools were built to accommodate a certain number of students and then quickly became outmoded as numbers far exceeded the plans for the buildings. It has long been thought that smaller schools are safer, cleaner, more manageable learning environments. But the consolidated school districts of the post-war era called for large, centralized county schools. Schools sprawled over more and more acres as the number of floors were reduced to two in most cases.

The very fact that a school has multiple floors increases management problems, and the more space a school occupies, the fewer the vantage points available to observe and monitor the behavior of students. It became obvious during this era that many security problems were a result of a lack of visual access, and that because of this, supervisory personnel were prevented from directly viewing persons entering the school or seeing the behavior of those already in the school. Restricted line of sight can make controlling access to a facility difficult and supervision of students nearly impossible. Increasingly, hidden threats, such as weapons, drugs, bullying, and sexual harassment, all made the need for openness to visual inspection more pressing.

Officials soon found that schools that have many hiding places, narrow hallways, and poor lighting were open invitations for misbehavior. Bullying and sexual harassment, which have always been problems in schools, worsened because of the way schools were constructed. Even before Title IX and Supreme Court rulings made sexual discrimination in the form of harassment illegal, schools found a pressing need to deal with the problem. Narrow halls, crowded spaces, and dim lighting exacerbated these problems.

School officials used several remedies available to them when school design contributed to misbehavior. Buildings were remodeled, and better lighting was installed. Additional supervision in the hallways and the use of video cameras, as well as the implementation of safety procedures and the training of students and staff about their rights and responsibilities, helped to alleviate behavior problems. Many schools developed a disciplinary code under which those students engaging in inappropriate behavior were consistently punished, followed in some instances by additional interventions, if deemed necessary. Many schools in the 1990s resorted to metal detection devices such as are used in airports to detect weapons hidden in loose-fitting clothing.

In addition to the restriction of visual access in narrow hallways, the danger of fire or other threats can cause panic among students. Additions to schools often resulted in lengthened hallways; long, narrow hallways account for both real and psychological danger points for students.

The visual access problem and the way in which school boards and their architects dealt with them sometimes brought criticism from those who said that schools were being turned into prisons. The easiest buildings to monitor are designed like spokes of a wheel—this is sometimes called the "penitentiary model." From one spot, by turning one's head or body, each hall may be visible in its entirety if there are no secured areas or alcoves built into them.

Visual access from the hallways or walkways into the classroom is important. Most classroom doors have some type of observation window, but frequently teachers block the view by covering the window space. This is especially true in high schools because students in the halls may appear in the windows to distract students in the classroom. While visual access into the classroom is important, visual access inside the classroom is crucial. In recent years, with the advent of computers and workstations, mischief has occurred even while the teacher was present (as when students in a Birmingham school were raped when the teacher was present in the room). Post-war overcrowding often created the same situation (see Chapter 8). Cluttered classrooms where some spaces were obscured from view became more common as schools became more crowded.

Visual access problems are usually caused by poor design. In an effort to overcome the limitations of restricted line of sight, many schools now employ some variation of video cameras to cover areas where students may get into trouble. This feature can be useful to schools to overcome the limitations of design. The extent to which these devices are utilized depends on their capability, their maintenance, and the ways schools use equipment. There are three purposes for video surveillance: prevention, intervention, and apprehension. Cameras are not barriers to access, but they can provide a warning or a record of events, which otherwise might have gone unseen.

When the history of school architecture is told, no doubt there will be revelations about the mistakes made in the post-war era, including the construction of pod-shaped buildings, where principals complain that visual access is nearly impossible. Open-space schools sounded very democratic when they were built in the 1960s and 1970s. With one glance, the principal could see the entire school. However, the designers forgot about noise and the distractions available in open-space areas. Open-space schools are frequently reconfigured with walls. Teachers themselves construct barricades between classes with bookshelves, portable equipment, or anything else available to them to seal off their teaching areas.

CAMPUS PERIMETERS

Most schools have three perimeters: the edge of the property, the outside doors, and the classroom doors. Each of these perimeters may be used to control access, depending on the nature of the barriers. Barriers may be of different types, but the main purpose is to control access to the campus or facility. If a school has a fence and a guard at the gate, access to the campus from the outside may be controlled to a certain degree. If at the second perimeter the outside doors can remain locked from the outside, the school has further control over access. Some schools are self-contained; during the day, all but the front doors are locked. For schools without a fence, the system may be adequate. Multiple buildings complicate security because often doors must remain unlocked to allow staff and students to move about freely.[12]

Controlling access from a security point of view must be accomplished at the first and second perimeters in open-space schools. Freedom High School in Burke, North Carolina, is an open-space high school with a complete chain link fence and a guard who controls all entry and egress from the campus. For some high schools, students leaving the campus without permission constitutes a major safety and discipline problem. Sometimes, overgrown fences or broken fences that border residential or industrial areas give students an easy way off campus, or intruders an easy way in.

Fences have value in the security of schools at all grade levels. When schools are built or when fences are added to schools, they should be set in from the property line so that custodians or yard workers can mow behind the fences and keep vines off them.

On the interior of a school, classroom doors are an integral component of security protection. Some schools still in use today were designed without doors. Beyond being a noise problem, this situation makes security difficult if someone in the building is creating a disturbance. Locked doors sometimes save lives, and with no barriers between the classroom and the outside world, safety is compromised.

Because schools are public places, the efforts to make them more secure are hampered by the tradition of openness and the expectation of parents in a community school that they have the right to make contact with their children at any time or place in the school.

The difficulties of tightening security in the school are heightened by 1) teachers' and parents' lack of awareness about threats, which amounts to an indifference about danger; 2) the absence of equipment such as fences or property locking devices; 3) multiple doorways that remain unlocked and accessible; 4) multiple buildings with unlocked doors not surrounded by fencing; 5) the design of the building that restricts visual access; 6) the location of the school in a dangerous neighborhood; 7) a lack of space around the school; 8) inadequate policies and procedures for security; 9) a lack of staff training in safety and security; 10) a lack of proper equipment and technology for daytime and nighttime security and communication; 11) a lack of faculty and staff documents that govern the school's efforts in prevention and intervention.[13]

Studies have established the relationship between the condition of schools and student achievement. When calling for a modernization plan, President Clinton cited a number of these studies:

- A District of Columbia study found that students in schools in poor condition had achievement that was 6 percent below schools in fair condition and 11 percent below schools in excellent condition.
- A 1993 study of rural Virginia high schools found that student scores on achievement tests were found to be up to five percentile points lower in buildings with lower quality ratings.
- A 1996 study of urban Virginia high schools found achievement was as much as 11 percentile points lower in substandard buildings as compared to above-standard buildings.

It has been shown clearly that smaller schools are safer schools. Other studies found correlations between school conditions and the health and morale of the school staff.[14]

In "The Evolving Role of the American Schoolhouse," Bradley demonstrates that in each stage of the evolution of the American school there were additional complications that could have added more risks to pupils' safety. The first schoolhouses were one-room, sparsely furnished structures that lasted well into the twentieth century. As a population outgrew its school, a second room was added. Soon, two smaller recitation rooms separated the two larger rooms. When students were placed into grade levels, schools grew to four stories, with each "grade" occupying a full floor. Boston's Quincy Grammar School served as the model of this type of school. By the end of the nineteenth century, schoolhouse design was becoming centralized and standardized.

The Gary Plan was adopted by many school districts between 1912 and 1928. It involved a "work-study-play" model that had basic instruction, gymnasiums, workshops, playgrounds, and auditoriums. Even as it accommodated this more specialized instruction, the exterior of the school did not change much and was not guided by architects, who did not become involved in school design until after the Great Depression.

In 1940, the Crow Island Elementary School in Winnetka, Illinois, was one of the first schools to use architecture as a way to enhance teaching and learning. This progressive school replaced the three-story box with a one-story, residential scale school with classrooms in wings. Each wing of the school was self-contained, presenting a "warm, personal, and intimate" learning environment. As World War II began, further efforts to expand on the Crow Island idea were abandoned.[15]

SCHOOL DISCIPLINE IN THE 1940s AND 1950s

A great deal about teachers' feelings concerning the safety of schools can be inferred from opinion surveys regarding the top disciplinary problems in schools. Unfortunately, one of the most famous lists comparing teachers' concerns in 1940 and in 1990 appears to be a hoax that trivialized concerns of the earlier era, although the scholar who uncovered the specious origin of the comparative list suggests that some lists of teachers' concerns in the 1940s did indeed rank talking and gum chewing high as disciplinary concerns. Certainly, teaching became much more difficult in the time between 1940 and 1990, and teachers' perceptions of their work would show that society's problems were indeed the main problems of the schools.[16]

Perhaps teachers' perceptions of disciplinary problems were more innocent than was warranted by the circumstances of the times, although the activities of wayward boys seemed to progress from mischief to vandalism to violence in the post-war period, and thus perhaps events seemed to be comparatively innocent, at least at first. In 1945, for instance, three small nine-old boys, who broke into a public school in Brooklyn and hacked away at the desks and other furniture, pictures, and windowpanes with fire axes, wrecked a school. Then they set small fires with waste paper, chopped at keys, and snapped the wire strings of a grand piano. Damage to the school was so extensive that it took five pages single-spaced to list all of the items that were damaged. Because of the boys' weekend fun, the school for girls had to be closed on Monday.[17]

In another incident on the same day, two eleven-year-old boys tried to burn down the school they attended.[18] And the school-wrecking business was not confined to New York. In Springfield, Massachusetts, in the following year, three boys entered a school, broke every window, and caused such damage that the investigating officer said, "it was the worst example of vandalism I have seen in twenty-odd years of police experience."[19] In December 1946, a gang of boys set a fire in one of New York's oldest schools, causing a five-alarm blaze.[20]

INCREASING VIOLENCE

The juvenile delinquents who jeopardized school programs seem to have gotten more violent during the late 1940s and early 1950s. A fifteen-year-old boy in Newark, New Jersey, for instance, brought a gun to school in March 1947 and fired three shots at his teacher. The boy told classmates in the morning that he had a "Christmas present" for his teacher and later suddenly began firing shots at the teacher, who ran out in the hall only to be pursued by the boy, who fired a third shot at the fleeing teacher.[21]

In the following year, four boys came seeking revenge on a teacher for a reprimand he had given them. The teacher had admonished two younger boys for disturbing his class in the morning, and they were heard to threaten that they would bring someone back "who'd take care of" the teacher. At 1:00 P.M. the two showed up with two older boys and all four pounced on the teacher. The teacher stood his ground, and other teachers soon came to assist him. The oldest boy was 17 years old.[22]

Enough dynamite to blow up a city block was found on the roof of a Jewish school in August 1949. Four boys had taken 38 sticks of dynamite from a construction camp in New Jersey, hitchhiked across the George Washington Bridge, and then ridden the subway back to Brooklyn, where they threw the dynamite onto the roof of the school. The investigating lieutenant said, "If this dynamite went off it could have blown up a whole block."[23]

Bombs in the hands of juveniles apparently became more of a problem as the decade of the 1950s opened. We continue our story of juvenile delinquency in the 1950s in Chapter 3 of this book.

ORGANIZATIONAL CONCERNS FOR SAFETY

The largest teachers' organization, the National Education Association, showed an early interest in school safety, even before the term "juvenile delinquency" was invented. Together with the National Safety Council, the NEA had an impact on a new emphasis on school safety after World War II. Even as early as 1913, the National Safety Council, organized in that year, had established training centers where trained teachers showed how safety programs could be taught. Due to the influence of these two groups, by 1929 well-developed safety programs were having an impact in the schools, as fewer school-age children were killed by motor vehicles, even though total deaths from cars were on the increase: "The programs of safety education in the schools unquestionably made the difference. A variety of methods were used—demonstrations of the right and wrong way, dramatized stories, safety games, posters, slides, and motion pictures."[24]

Robert MacMillan published his doctoral dissertation, *Safety Education in the Public Schools of the United States* in 1936. MacMillan noted the unevenness among the states in the way in which they pursued safety education. He concentrated his interest on "the accident problem," but did advocate a safe schools approach—in this respect he was one of the first.[25]

The war seemed to increase the need for safety education in the schools. In 1943, the NEA authorized the National Commission on Safety Education under the leadership of Frank W. Hubbard. This commission began its work in 1944 with the direction of the first secretary, Robert W. Eaves. The commission and the NEA began to issue bulletins and leaflets, later adding films, posters, and bulletins dealing with fire, home, bicycle, and bus safety and driver education.[26]

SCHOOL BUS SAFETY

Chapter 5 of this book is concerned with school buses, and the kinds of jeopardy caused to schools and parents by the use of school buses. The history of the school bus cannot be separated from the history of the development of America after World War II, with increasing migration to suburbs surrounding the cities, moving farther and farther from the downtown areas of cities. The modern school bus began in a conference in 1939 called by Frank W. Cyr, the "Father of the Yellow School" bus, who was a professor at Teachers College, Columbia University. At that meeting, Cyr urged the standardization of the school bus. Participants came up with the standard yellow color and some basic construction standards. Cyr had studied school transportation and found that children were riding in all kinds of vehicles—one district, he found, was painting their buses red, white, and blue to instill patriotism. In Kansas, children were taken to school in one district in horse-drawn wheat wagons. School bus manufacturers wanted standardization because they could not produce the myriad colored vehicles on an assembly line. The attendees at the conference voted on a total of 44 standards, including body lengths, ceiling heights, door specifications, and aisle widths. Almost everything but the color of the buses has changed since then. Among his other accomplishments, Cyr helped set school transporation policy during wartime.[27]

School buses were important first in rural areas, especially after schools were consolidated after World War II.

The "innocence" of a country, fresh from the triumph of the greatest war in history, was more a refreshed sense of possibility than it was naiveté. The country was truly coming into the mature period of its development, as it changed over after the war, first from a dynamic industrial economy to a post-industrial one later in the century. In the meantime, the American school had to absorb all of the social problems and adapt, just as the American people did.

NOTES

1. Mike Kennedy, "A Century of Progress," *AS&U,* December 1999. http://www.asumag.com/magazine/archives/1299century1.html.

2. Judith A. Brough, "Changing Conditions for Young Adolescents," *Educational Horizons,* Vol. 68, No. 2, Winter 1990, pgs. 78–81.

3. John B. Lyons, "K–12 Construction Facts," U.S. Dept. of Education, Number 1, May 1999. http://www.ed.gov/inits/construction/k-12facts html.

4. Ibid.

5. "Hard Hat Area: The Deteriorating State of School Buildings," *Education World,* 1999. http://www.education-world.com/a-admin089.html.

6. "Bell Tolls for One-Room Schoolhouse," CNN, FYI. Com>Teacher Resources, June 12, 2000. http://www.CNN.com./2000/fyi/teacher.resources/education.news/06/12/schoolho. . . . /index.html.

7. Many school systems and high schools have web sites of their own on the Internet.

8. "What is an Unhealthy School?" http://www.hsnet.org/unhealthy.html.

9. William Bradley, "Expecting the Most From School Design," paper presented at the University of Virginia, July 10, 1999. http://curry.edschool.virginia.edu/curry/edlp/800/papers/prmaples/principles-intro.html.

10. In William Bradley's article, "The Evolving Role of the American Schoolhouse," he gives this account of schools built since the 1960s: "Since the early '60s, the "open-plan" was imported from England and interior walls in many schools were knocked out to encourage self-directed, student-motivated learning. In the '70s, the "community-school" surfaced in the wake of demands of a broader, more efficient use of school plant facilities. After schoolhouse construction slowed in the '80s, "home-based" schools partitioned into "communities," "neighborhoods," and "families" began

appearing in the '90s. William Bradley, "The Evolving Role of the American Schoolhouse," 2000. http://curry.edschool.virginia.edu/curry/edlp/800/papers/history/history.html.

11. "100 Years in the Tennessee Valley: Designs Reflect Social Times," *Decatur Daily News,* January 3, 2000, online edition. http://www.decaturdaily.com/decaturdaily news/00103/schools.shtml.

12. See Robert S. Watson and Rollin J. Watson, "A Realistic Approach to School Security," 1999. http:// www.safeschoolsamerica.com/article.html.

13. Ibid.

14. "Hart Hat Area: The Deteriorating State of School Buildings" and Carman J. Lee, "Smaller Schools are Safer Schools, Experts Say," *Post-Gazette*.com, August 29, 1999. http://www.post-gazette.com/regionstate/19990829bbuild4.asp.

15. William Bradley, "The Evolving Role of the American Schoolhouse," 2000. http://curry.edschool.virginia.edu/curry/edlp/800/papers/history/history.html.

16. Barry O'Neill, "The History of a Hoax," *New York Times Magazine,* (March 6, 1994), pgs. 46–49. The list comparing teachers' attitudes in 1940 and 1990 was created by a fundamentalist Christian and used by dozens of conservative commentators, including William Bennett, former secretary of education. The list was also circulated by educational leaders like Derek Bok and popular writers like Ann Landers.

17. "School Wrecked by 3 Small Boys," *New York Times,* March 28, 1945, pgs. 1, 24.

18. "Fire in Another School," *New York Times,* March 28, 1945, pg. 24.

19. "Boys Wreck a School," *New York Times,* October 28, 1946, pg. 14.

20. "Fire Laid to Boys Damages School," *New York Times,* December 10, 1946, pg. 21.

21. "Boy Fires at Teacher," *New York Times,* March 1, 1947, pg. 17.

22. "Teacher Attacked by Four in Classroom," *New York Times,* May 26, 1948, pg. 27.

23. "Enough Dynamite to Blast a Block Found on a Jewish School," *New York Times,* August 24, 1949, pg. 27.

24. Edgar B. Wesley, *NEA: The First Hundred Years—The Building of the Teaching Profession* (New York: Harper and Brothers, 1957), pg. 312.

25. Robert MacMillan, *Safety Education in the Public Schools of the United States* (Philadelphia: Temple University, 1936).

26. Wesley, pg. 312.

27. "Frank W. Cyr, 'Father of the Yellow School Bus,'" *News Bureau, Columbia University,* June 24, 2000. http://www.tc.columbia.edu/-newsbureau/news/cyr.html.

Chapter 3

Juvenile Delinquency and the Schools (1950–1975)

THE FEAR OF THE JUVENILE DELINQUENT

Juvenile crime was a frightening prospect for Americans in the 1950s, and when it affected the schools, it did so profoundly. As in the case of other mass movements that radically changed the American school, the nation's fear of juvenile delinquency—and the often too real manifestations of juvenile crime occurring in the cities—brought about alterations in the way American schools conducted school business, defended themselves, and perhaps overreacted to the threat of juvenile delinquency.

The finest scholarly explication of the phenomenon traces the country's fear of juvenile delinquency to three main sources:

The first is an immeasurable but probable increase in the incidence of juvenile crime, attention paid to crime, or both. The second is a probable shift in the behavior of law enforcement agencies, probed by government and private pressure groups and public opinion to assert authority over the behavior of young people. The third includes changes in the behavior of youth that were susceptible to interpretation as criminal. These, in turn, were imbedded in both long- and short-term changes in youth culture that became especially apparent after World War II. To make matters graver, these changes coincided with other larger fears about the reliability of traditional American institutions such as the family and the tensile strength of American society under the duress of the Cold War.[1]

It was in the interest of certain government agencies, law enforcement officials, and social scientists to foster the fear of juvenile delinquency so that they could enhance their own prestige and efforts to fight it. This caused parents and agencies, especially schools, to try harder to regulate behavior. Parents and agencies thought they saw the growth of a new adolescent culture that was largely alien to middle-class mores and fashions. The principal scapegoat charged with causing juvenile delinquency was the mass media.[2]

Two of the most famous films about the lives of urban youth dramatized the situation to the alarm of the American people and came to illustrate some of the sociological changes that were taking place in the nation's big cities during the 1950s. Both movies brought to public attention the dangers inherent in a multicultural urban environment during a prosperous but conservative era. Published a year before the historic Supreme Court ruling of 1954—the Brown decision—a novel by a former teacher, Evan Hunter, entitled *Blackboard Jungle,* was taken by some as a foreshadowing of things to come in American education. A few years later, in 1961, *West Side Story* was released in theaters. Ironically enough, the period between the two movies saw the development of new patterns of juvenile misbehavior, the use of bombs and bomb threats as means to intimidate the authority of the school, and new and often violent attacks upon teachers by juveniles.

The novel version of *Blackboard Jungle* was later made into an influential movie about school life, which the Eisenhower administration and Claire Booth Luce considered a "shocking film" and kept from being shown at the Venice Film Festival. Several cities banned it. Young people of both black and white races were part of gangs in the movie, which starred Glenn Ford and Sidney Poitier. One of the most shocking elements of the film was the attempted sexual assault of a female teacher. For teachers and parents in small town and rural areas, the movie must have represented all of the evils of gangs and interracial schooling in urban areas, both of which portended a frightening specter of things to come.[3]

Those early representations of the integrated urban school, with realistic portrayals of racial tension, perhaps were the most foreboding celluloid dramatization of out-of-control discipline in American city schools in the 1950s and seemingly served as a precursor to the kinds of undesirable behavioral circumstances that would characterize the American school for the next several decades, especially after the Brown decision of 1954.

A concomitant uneasiness about the safety of schools was beginning to be represented in the media. For instance, a *Life* magazine cover story charged that students in American cities "terrorize teachers" and declared that it often takes physical courage to teach.[4] A new perception about the danger of urban schools on the part of teachers and parents would soon become widespread, largely because of an increased number of media reports.

EXPLANATIONS FOR JUVENILE DELINQUENCY

A contemporary psychologist, P.M. Smith, suggested that the school as an agency contributes to juvenile delinquency and listed a number of factors that bring about conditions making schools conducive to fostering delinquency in their students. The first factor, he said, was the severe shortage of adequately trained teachers, and the second most important factor was the "Serious deterioration of physical plant, equipment, and facilities, resulting in the use of obsolete, unsafe, and overcrowded classrooms in many areas."[5]

Facts could be presented to bolster Smith's argument. Schools built in the 1920s and 1930s were beginning to fall apart in some cities by the late 1950s. For instance, in one school built in 1921, just as third-grade pupils were about to take their milk break, their teacher and another pupil were hurt when the ceiling fell in on the children. A 29-year-old teacher suffered a concussion when plaster fell on her head and neck. She and an eight-year-old boy were taken to the hospital, and seven of the other children were injured as well. The school, which was built in the 1920s, had not been repaired because of a lack of funds.[6]

Whatever the reason, incidents of delinquent behavior against schools on the part of junior and senior high school boys either increased or were given more attention by the media during the fifties. For instance, as 1950 opened, three Brooklyn boys, all under 12 years old, who "didn't like teachers" set fire to their school after throwing books and chairs about.[7] Boys who entered from the roof of the school's one-story extension vandalized another Brooklyn school. The vandals damaged 25 of the school's 42 rooms.[8]

But it seems that "nearly harmless" incidents of vandalism were accompanied by some other more frightening incidents. In one school in Queens in 1951, an eleven-year-old killed another boy with a T-square.[9]

In a case in which two boys, for no apparent reason, assaulted a teacher in the corridor of Benjamin Franklin Junior High in New York in March 1954, the magistrate reprimanded the delinquents in a passionate tone: "Instead of showering devotion and gratitude on these teachers, you abuse them. It is high time somebody realized the seriousness of this problem. You've been mollycoddled too much. You're just bums to me." The two Bronx boys were given indeterminate sentences at the Elmira Reception Center.[10]

One authority figure felt the sting of revenge. Two boys got up early in the morning to set fire to the principal's office at 3:00 A.M., and even though they were caught by police, the act of vandalism was notable for the time of day in which it occurred.[11] In another case, boys who broke into school offices ripped up all the records in four offices. In the principal's office, they set fire to a large bundle of clothing intended for needy students.[12]

It was common for acts of vandalism and arson to occur when schools were closed. In one Brooklyn case, three boys were charged with arson after they set fire to a public school on Sunday morning and caused $10,000 worth of damage.[13] Such arson and vandalism in schools often seemed less tendentious than insouciant. In another instance, four teenage boys were arrested after police caught them ransacking classrooms in a school in Brooklyn.[14] Clearly, random vandalism and attacks upon teachers were on the increase, and it was not only boys who were committing the crimes. At about the same time, two teachers were attacked by three schoolgirls after the girls had consumed a pint of whiskey. One girl was 16 and the other two were 15.[15]

Several incidents in Detroit in 1958 seemed to indicate that student tempers out of control were turning violent. At McMichael Junior High School one 15-year-old boy was stabbed twice in the back and a 17-year-old student was slashed on the side of the head in the basement of the school.[16] At another site, a 31-year-old teacher was refereeing a baseball game when four boys pelted him with rocks and attacked him. In still another case, a 45-year-old teacher who stopped two boys loitering in the hall in a high school was beaten by the youths. The Detroit Federation of Teachers said that it had asked the

Detroit police to provide protection for teachers at all 42 of the city's high schools. The Detroit Board of Education had turned down a previous request.[17]

When a teacher scolded a 14-year-old boy in Brooklyn in 1958 for interrupting his class and then turned toward the blackboard, the boy broke a soft drink bottle and slashed the teacher with it. The teacher turned to grapple with him as other students ran for aid.[18]

BOMBS AND BOMB THREATS

Most students attending school during the 1960s and 1970s remember that bomb scares became so frequent at times as to become disruptive. By the end of the century, the disruption caused by bomb scares was worse than ever, as many schools were shut down by the threats made by anonymous callers. But bomb scares, at least in metropolitan areas like New York, were becoming a nuisance as early as the 1950s. On Long Island, a bomb scare in a high school on March 24, 1954, caused all 900 students to be evacuated from the building. It was the second bomb scare the school had had in a two-week period. What added a bite to this particular incident was that 20 sticks of dynamite and 38 blasting caps had been stolen from a nearby fertilizer plant just two days before the first call.[19]

Two days after the second bomb scare, officials were prepared to take action against what a judge called "teen-age tyranny." A rash of bomb threats had disrupted schools. A high school principal found one threat on a note in his car. Before classes began, police searched the school and found nothing. A second scare took place at an elementary school, with the bomb note found in the nurse's room. Judge Levine of Nassau County warned that "All convictions in the future will bring jail sentences. Teen-age tyranny in Nassau County will not be tolerated."[20] School officials in other parts of the New York metropolitan area were equally as concerned; in Brooklyn, all high school principals met with law enforcement officers to try to find a solution.[21]

A crude homemade bomb exploded in an alcove off the cafeteria at New York's Lafayette High School where 800 students were eating lunch on December 6, 1955. The bomb caused no injuries. The police bomb squad found a piece of half-inch copper tubing about seven inches long with traces of explosive powder.[22] Bombs and bomb scares continued in the ensuing months and years, sometimes paralyzing a whole town or city at a time. In New Rochelle, New York, in November 1956, eight schools were evacuated on the same day. At 8:11 A.M., police were told over the telephone that a bomb had been placed in a high school and that "it will go off before noon." In the recent past, two unexploded bombs had been found in an abandoned theater, so the police were taking no chances. Joining the policemen in search for the bomb were firemen and hundreds of teachers in both public and parochial schools.[23] In White Plains, New York, five days later, a bomb scare halted classes for 130,000 pupils in public and private schools in Westchester. There had been a bomb scare in the schools every day for five days straight.[24]

Whether bomb scares and even bombs were pranks, malicious vandalism, intended murder, or violent acts of racial hatred (see Chapter 5) was often unclear to police. When a bomb went off in a school, as one did in Buffalo when a high school student opened his locker, the motive seemed to be some sort of deadly prank. The 15-year-old boy, who was not injured, told police he had no idea who set the bomb or why it was set.[25]

A bomb blast that killed six at a Houston school in 1959 seemed reminiscent of the lunacy of the Bath, Michigan, incident (1927; see Chapter 1) because the work was clearly that of a deranged person with a personal motive. A man walking by a school playground tossed a bomb into the schoolyard. The explosion killed the bomber, three children—including his son—and two other adults. Nineteen children and the school principal were injured and were taken to the hospital. The bomber was identified by one of the teachers. The explosion from the bomb rocked the entire residential area near Rice University.

The principal later recounted the story: a man with a suitcase came to her office that morning with a seven-year-old boy. When the principal told the man the child would have to be registered before he could go to class, the man did so and then walked out to the playground. The principal followed him to the playground, where there were three groups of children with their teachers; she told him he would have to leave the play area, or she would call the police. He replied that the police could not do anything to him.

When the bomb exploded, the man's child, Dusty Orgeron, was one of the ones killed. Near the area where the bomb went off, police found a rifle and a pistol—they believed the bomber had triggered the blast with a pistol shot.

The man's estranged wife later reported that he had left her a note threatening to kill her and the children. The note was found in the vicinity of the blast. Also, in a station wagon nearby, six explosive detonators and a plastic sack, which had held explosives, were found. Another note intended for the principal was found on the man. Among other things, it said, "I'd like to talk about God while I'm waiting for my wife."

Children rushed to the streets when the blast went off. A fire drill bell evacuated those inside the school. Many frantic parents rushed to the school; those who could not find their children went in search of them at the local hospital.[26]

GANGS AND THE SCHOOLS

Schools would continue to be interrupted by gang activity, as in a 1955 incident in which a band of teenage boys forced their way into a Bronx high school and beat two students in a classroom. On the previous Friday, a fight between a black boy and a white boy culminated in a free-for-all after classes two blocks from the school. The gang of raiders, all blacks, was seeking revenge on the white boys when they entered the school; apparently, they carried out their work so quickly that several different stories emerged about the incident, including the number of boys in the gang. Estimations of the size of the group ranged from five to eight. The teacher had her back to the class when the boys entered her classroom. Unfortunately for the two boys who were attacked, the gang had mistaken them for other boys, as they had not been involved in the original fight.

The police said that this particular incident was not a "race fight." Apparently it was often very difficult to determine whether gang activity had racial motivation. Police caught the nine boys in the attacking gang, and they admitted entering the high school. A later newspaper report said that

> Five of the youths, all of whom are Negroes, entered the classroom and hit two white youths with a bayonet scabbard, while the three others remained in the school corridor as look-outs, the confession story said. . . . The scabbard-wielding ringleader said that while he was watching [the original] fight a white boy hit him. He rounded up his companions on Monday and they rode up to the school seeking revenge. When they could not find the boy they wanted, they decided to attack others, the leader said.[27]

While violent, this gang activity was not nearly so disastrous as later actions would be, the danger becoming obvious in subsequent gang activities that involved stabbings and the use of bombs.

Post–World War II gang membership was younger, largely non-white, used or sold drugs, had well-organized street fighting techniques, used fire arms more often, had a more rigid organizational structure, and aroused more attention from society at large.[28]

After World War II, most urban gangs were ethnic or racial in composition, and most of their members' ages were getting younger and younger. Gang activity often centered on large-scale, well-organized street fighting, with frequent use of firearms. The structure of the gang organizations became more rigid as time passed. Partly due to the influx of African-Americans and Puerto Ricans into northern cities, and coinciding with it, the post-war period became the greatest era of gang activity in history, with gang fighting rising to an all-time high.[29]

On March 2, 1956, gang activity in a crowded gymnasium in Brooklyn endangered many lives.[30] Eight armed teenagers entered a crowded school gym, where a meeting was taking place on a recreation night, and fired five shots into the crowd. Carrying cleavers, pistols, and bats, and wearing garrison belts, the eight youths rushed into the gymnasium at 10:00 P.M. jostling boys who were playing at various games. Some were knocked to the floor. Two boys were then stabbed in a fight that followed. Detectives thought that the wounded youths were members of the Chaplains, a youth gang, and that their assailants were allies of the Bishops, the main rivals of the Chaplains.

Gangs often had an impact upon the attendance of other students in the schools of cities like New York. In one instance, it was simply rumors of gang violence that kept children from attending school. A board of education spokesman said that the rumors had a pattern that suggested an organized campaign, but the rumors were having an increasing effect.[31] The superintendent of schools applauded city teachers for their role in quelling the rumors, saying that they had to contend with "frenzied" mothers, and he told of a little girl who carried a knife to school to defend herself. The superintendent used the example of the teachers' diligence to provide an example of the "strains and tensions" faced by teachers. He added that teachers with a "religious conviction" were a major bulwark against "adversity and perplexity." [32]

But gang activity continued to spill over into the schools. Four members of a gang called the Arabian Sportsmen approached two boys just outside Metropolitan Vocational High School in New York and slashed them in the face with knives in 1958. Police reported that the four had been drinking wine and were "in a troublesome mood and looking for a fight."[33]

In September 1959, police in New York moved to set up a "gang fact file" in which all policemen on the force would feed in data on youths "in the continuing battle against juvenile delinquency." After Mayor Wagner had discussed the juvenile delinquency problem on television, Commissioner Stephen P. Kennedy sent a directive to all precincts. The mayor was particularly concerned about a series of stabbings on the West Side, which he called "full-fledged crime."[34]

Because much of the activity of gangs is surreptitious and at least sometimes criminal, the historical literature on gangs leaves much to be desired. The best studies are sociological and localized.[35] According to most accounts, while there was gang activity in New York and other cities during the 1960s and 1970s—much of it related to the racial conflicts of the time—gangs allegedly did not get into drugs in a big way until well into the 1970s. In some instances, drug-using members were forced out of the gangs in the 1950s and 1960s because they could not be relied upon in fights.[36] The *New York Times* published this account in 1973:

> In New York, the spawning ground for gangs has been the South Bronx, where low-income housing projects, like brick cliffs, hide the rotting tenements and storefronts of one of the nation's worst slums. Forty per cent of the neighborhood's residents are on welfare, 30 per cent are unemployed. Gang activity increased noticeably late in 1969, and by last summer [1972] had spread to virtually every neighborhood in the Bronx. . . . Police count 100 "fighting" gangs in the Bronx. Estimates of gang membership (about 70 per cent Puerto Rican, the rest, mostly blacks) run as high as 11,000.[37]

In order to make money, gangs used other methods besides selling drugs. In 1973, five members of a Bronx street gang were indicted for extortion. Members of the gang were threatening grocers and taking money and groceries so that they would not inflict harm upon the establishments or their owners.[38]

Like big business, the gangs apparently gave up one turf to have branches in other parts of the city. While it is obvious that gang life affected the public schools in urban areas, it is not clear how much they interfered with the programs and stability of schools. Some experts feel that gangs and schools evolved into a mutual respect for each other's territory, with gang activities staying out of the schools and schools in general leaving gangs alone.

Through the late 1960s and well into the 1970s, racially inspired fighting disrupted schools in almost every part of the country. (Some of these incidents are detailed in Chapter 6 of this book.) Clearly some of the activity was inspired by gangs, although it was recognized that few if any of the gangs were integrated and usually pitted one ethnic or racial group against another. In April 1972, a 17-year-old boy was clubbed over the head with a pistol butt and stabbed just outside a Manhattan high school. The stabbing followed a fight on the previous day between two Dominican gangs. City officials viewed this episode as the resurgence of youth gang violence in the city, and that estimation seemed to correlate with information from other large urban areas of the country. Police in New York said that 15 youths had been slain in gang "rumbles" in a five-month period.[39]

One incident at Canarsie High School seemed to have been typical of gang violence. An 18-year-old was fatally stabbed as he played ball in the school gym. He was approached by two youths wearing jackets with the emblem "Black Hawks," and then a third gang member joined the other two. They pulled knives and stabbed the ball player. A teacher who happened in at the time ran the three youths off, but they were caught and arrested.[40]

There is little doubt that gangland disagreements were resulting in more killing. In November 1972, it was reported that young assassins had committed more than 100 murders in one year in three American cities. In Los Angeles, there were 31 deaths caused by gangs. In Philadelphia, there were 37, and in New York there were 30 gang killings in the Bronx alone. In Los Angeles, gang members abruptly ended a football team homecoming with a volley of gunshots that left five teenagers wounded. It was an act of gang retaliation, the police reported.

The same report said that, in the meantime, gang activity seemed to have decreased in Chicago, with little gang violence in Cleveland and Pittsburgh. In San Francisco, a gang of Filipino-Americans had tormented the Chinese community. The report stated that during the period of racial confrontation in the1960s gang activity seemed to have subsided but that in some cities it was on the increase again in 1972. During the 1950s gangs fought mostly for turf and among themselves. By the '70s, gangs were more violent. White gang activities were confined to the poorest areas of the cities.[41]

In 1973, for instance, violence and terror by street gangs in Philadelphia aroused public outrage. Fatal incidents happened with such frequency that they were becoming weekly occurrences. Citizen groups began taking to the streets to protest the gang violence. While reports of increased gang activity were coming from all of the country's major cities, Philadelphia officials said that the problem seemed to be worse there. As of May 1973, ten people had been killed. Thirty-nine had been killed the year before, and 43 the year before that. Mayor Frank Rizzo, who campaigned for office on the pledge that he would wipe out the gangs, had not been able to do so. To contain the problem completely, Rizzo said, would require a virtual police state. Leaders of the black community, which bore the brunt of gang activity, believed that the problem had increased dramatically.

Officials reported that there were 100 to 150 gangs in the city, and possibly more, most of them black. They estimated that there were 8,000 members, ranging in age from eleven to the early twenties. Unlike the weaponry of the 1950s—which was largely switchblades and low-powered pistols, gang members in the 1970s were carrying high-powered automatic weapons, and warfare on the city's streets often killed innocent children. The average age of victims was a little over 16. Violence perpetrated by the gangs included both many prearranged fights and much random shooting.[42]

DIFFERENT TYPES OF DELINQUENTS

The emergence of the suburban, affluent delinquent in the early sixties was a departure from the stereotype of the juvenile delinquent as a tough, poor, inner-city kid. At a coming out party on Long Island in 1963, 125 young men, staying at a guest mansion for the debut of Fernanda Wanamaker Wetherill, made a wreck of the place. The boys broke over 1,000 windows, a chandelier, and furniture, tore up carpet and ruined other parts of the rambling 30-room home. Gin bottles and beer bottles littered the grounds. The owner of the house said, "It was shocking and terrible that the youth of our country do such wanton destruction. Yet it is not the destruction that worries me the most, but that the privileged youth of our country should set such a horrible example."

A commentator in his news analysis said that the pattern of destructiveness among affluent youth was becoming a trend. He pointed to other incidents in affluent suburbs. In Connecticut, a country club had been plagued by robbery and vandalism by affluent youth. The writer contrasted the decadent lifestyle of the youths with young people who were joining the Peace Corps and Civil Rights Movement. He suggested that the wealthy set an example for youth around the country. He said that access to alcohol and excessive drinking was one problem; unsupervised parties were another; a lack of discipline another. He thought that parents were giving too much to their children too soon. Finally, he thought money came too easy to them.[43]

The children of the affluent sometimes caused each other some trouble. On the same evening in 1963, the son of Walter Winchell, the columnist, pointed a rifle at a group of 15 boys who drove cars onto his father's estate in Scarsdale, New York. The boys placed charges against Winchell for his wielding of the gun, and the court held Winchell. The boys were almost all college students.[44]

This came at a time when many new suburban schools were opening, as enrollments at the outlying areas burgeoned. In the New York, Connecticut, and New Jersey suburban areas surrounding New York City, for example, many new schools opened with an increased number of teachers to meet the demand of increased numbers of students.[45]

In the later years of the 1960s, middle-class white teenagers who became hippies represented a new element in the tension between ethnic groups in New York and other cities. The hippies were affluent kids who gave up the good life for poverty. "These unwashed beatniks are terrible. . . . But don't be surprised when our people lose their patience with this dirty invasion," one critic averred. It was estimated that about 2,000 hippies had moved into the area.[46]

Increasingly, girls were becoming more involved with criminal behavior. A federal government crime report issued in April 1972 noted that juvenile delinquency among girls 10 to 17 years of age rose twice as fast as crimes involving boys the same age from 1969 to 1970. Cited as the reason was the "more aggressive, more independent" behavior of girls. In 1970, juvenile courts handled over a million cases involving male and female juvenile delinquents, but the rate of delinquency slowed for the first time in five years. The boy-to-girl ratio narrowed from four to one in the mid-sixties to three to one in 1970. Crimes covered in the statistical report included aggravated assault, burglary, larceny and auto theft, and the use of drugs and truancy.[47]

An incident in January 1973, in which two teenaged girls allegedly attacked a school principal of a junior high school after he suspended them from school, seems to have given some validity to the further involvement of girls in delinquent behavior. The principal of Grover Cleveland Junior High School in Elizabeth, New Jersey, reportedly was kicked, bitten, and scratched by two girls, as was a teaching assistant who went to the principal's aid. The principal later denied that the girls had physically attacked him.[48]

And yet at the same time, girls continued to be victimized. A ten-year-old girl was raped in the stairwell of a school in Brooklyn in 1974. She had just finished eating lunch in a first-floor cafeteria and was going up to the second floor when a teenage boy accosted her. Afterward, the little girl ran home and told her mother. She described the boy as about 16 years old, but he was not apprehended.[49]

INCREASING USE OF DRUGS

Concomitant with the increasing numbers of rowdy middle-class white teenagers was an increase in the use of marijuana and other substances. In some small towns and suburban areas, a concerted effort was made to fight the use of drugs by juveniles. In Maplewood, New Jersey, for example, the mayor announced a campaign against the "widespread" use of marijuana by teenagers. He said that police reported "an exceedingly high" rate of usage in high schools. "It could run as high as one out of every two children . . . ," he said. "It isn't happening to the kid down the street—the bad boy, the incorrigible. It's happening with the 'good' kids, good students from good homes who are encouraged by the underworld." Meanwhile, in nearby Montclair, two students were suspended from school for using marijuana.[50]

In March 1969, an 18-year-old senior at a Queens vocational school slumped over dead in his seat after having apparently injected himself with a narcotic. The student's death in school seemed to confirm reports that use of illegal drugs had escalated among students in the city's public and private high schools, reaching a point at which their open use in school buildings was steadily growing. The principal of the school said that the incident was a first, even though "We sometimes see students under the influence [of drugs], but we have never seized any pills or marijuana."[51]

Drugs take a heavy toll on American schools.

HIGH SCHOOL UNREST

A type of delinquency sprang up as a concomitant to the Civil Rights Movements of the 1960s, and this showed up as unrestrained uprisings in the high schools and junior high schools. Student protests in schools often spilled over into uprisings that caused damage to persons and property. "The high school principal is replacing the college president as the most embattled American," said an official of the National Education Association. Violent activities took place in 348 high schools in 38 states during one period. Most of the protests outside the cities were nonracial. "The central issue is the growing effort toward more student freedom and involvement in school policy" according to surveys taken by major newspapers. In many cases, of course, it became impossible to distinguish between reckless, rebellious, often destructive acts, and acts of protest against the war in Vietnam or in favor of the Civil Rights Movement.[52]

In October 1969, a child was seriously injured, losing at least three fingers on his hand, and three others were hurt when a blasting cap exploded in an elementary school classroom in Elmont, Long Island. At least 17 children had been given the blasting caps by an 11-year-old who had found the caps. The police said they had found about 70 caps possessed by the 17 children.[53]

Schools began to react to increased student insubordination and violence with tough, no-nonsense administrators. This was the case in Englewood, New Jersey, when a tough new principal came in and suspended 20 students, most of them black. Some of the students had been involved in a stabbing and a beating. Dr. Mildred W. Abramowitz had been a principal in South Bronx when she was hired to tighten up discipline in Englewood. Even students who did not think the suspensions were fair had to admit that there were fewer fights and better behavior in the school.[54]

With every indication that gun use by teenagers was increasing rapidly in the early 1970s, schools had to pay more attention to security precautions. New York reported that gun incidents involving students and outside intruders in the city's public schools doubled in 1973. A report sent from the school chancellor to the State Commission on Investigations said that 58 separate incidents had been recorded since 1968, with 25 of them coming in 1973, whereas there had been nine in 1972.[55]

By 1974, schools were dealing with violent episodes by increasing security. New York's school increased security by putting all security guards on overtime, renting vans for transporting mobile guard units, and establishing a command center for security that was open 24 hours a day.[56]

THE TOLL OF JUVENILE DELINQUENCY

The National Institute of Education did a study of the toll taken by juvenile delinquents, revealing that about one-fourth of the country's schools are vandalized monthly, that burglaries occur five times as often in schools as in businesses, that one out of every 100 schools experiences a bomb-related offense in a typical month, that each month nearly 282,000 students are attacked in schools, that 40 percent of the robberies and 36 percent of the assaults on teenagers occur in schools, with even higher percentages for children ages 12 to 15. Also, each month more than 2.4 million secondary school students are victims of theft, each month approximately 130,000 secondary school teachers have something stolen, and each month 5,200 teachers report being physically attacked, making teachers five times more likely than students to be seriously injured in attacks.[57]

The expense, both in monetary and human terms, that juvenile delinquency inflicts upon the schools and the community surrounding them should not be forgotten. Juvenile delinquents disrupt the work of the schools and traumatize their victims. They are not just kids raising hell; they are deviant boys (sometimes girls) who cause other people trauma. While there is always discussion about possible causes of delinquent behavior by juveniles, and most often parents or the media or the violent culture are blamed, the schools are not always held blameless. One need only see the lines of young children receiving daily doses of medication in nurses' offices in our schools[58] or witness the way in which a few teachers treat poor children to realize that perhaps some of the schools have in some ways contributed to the problem.

NOTES

1. James Gilbert, *A Cycle of Outrage: America's Reaction to the Juvenile Delinquent in the 1950s* (New York: Oxford University Press, 1986), pg. 71.

2. Ibid., pg. 79.

3. "Blackboard Jungle—Movie Review and Sounds," 2000. http://www.destgulch.com/movies/bjungle.html.

4. Richard Rothstein, *The Way We Were: The Myths and Realities of America's Student Achievement* (excerpts by the Century Foundation, pg. 3). http://www.tcf.org/publications/educational/way_we_were/Chapter 1.html.

5. P.M. Smith, "The School As a Factor," *Juvenile Delinquency* (Joseph S. Roucek, Editor), (New York: Philosophical Library, New York, 1958), pg. 155.

6. "Teacher, 3 Pupils Hurt," *New York Times,* March 27, 1952, pg. 33.

7. "Set Fire in Schoolhouse," *New York Times,* January 6, 1950, pg. 16.

8. "Vandals Damage School," *New York Times,* March 22, 1951, pg. 33.

9. "Boy, 11, Paroled in Death," *New York Times,* January 13, 1951, pg. 30.

10. "Two Students Held in Teacher Assault," *New York Times,* March 1, 1954, pg. 21.

11. "2 Seized in School Fire," *New York Times,* May 16, 1957, pg. 64.

12. "Vandals Set Fire in 4th St. School," *New York Times,* November 3, 1957, pg. 50.

13. "3 Held in School Fire," *New York Times,* June 11, 1957, pg. 70.

14. "Four Boys Arrested in School," *New York Times,* March 13, 1954, pg. 12.

15. "3 Truants Attack Student, 2 Teachers," *New York Times,* March 13, 1954, pg. 16.

16. "2 Students Stabbed in Detroit Violence," *New York Times,* April 3, 1958, pg. 24.

17. Ibid.

18. "Boy Attacks Teacher," *New York Times,* November 7, 1958, pg. 31.

19. "Bomb Scare in School," *New York Times,* March 24, 1954, pg. 24.

20. "School Officials Fight Vandalism," *New York Times,* March 27, 1954, pg. 19.

21. Ibid.

22. "Bomb Bursts in School," *New York Times,* December 6, 1956, pg. 41.

23. "Hoax Shuts School," *New York Times,* November 1, 1956, pg. 56.

24. "Bomb Scare Halts School," *New York Times,* November 10, 1956, pg. 40.

25. "Small Bomb Blast at School," *New York Times,* February 11, 1958, pg. 21.

26. "Bomb Blast Kills 6 at Houston School," *New York Times,* September 16, 1959, pg. 1.

27. "Youth Gang Invades High School," *New York Times,* March 29, 1955, pg. 1.

28. "Overview of Gangs: Post World War II." http://alphabase.com/westside/gangs.html.

29. There are many good books and articles about gangs. In addition, there is a plethora of information on the Internet. One good site is http://ojjdp.ncjrs.org/jjbulletin/9808/youth.html.

30. "2 Boys Stabbed in Gang Fracus," *New York Times,* March 2, 1956, pg. 8.

31. "Rumors of Violence Curtailing Schools," *New York Times,* November 10, 1956, pg. 40.

32. "Teachers Lauded in Panic Incident," *New York Times,* November 8, 1956, pg. 74.

33. "2 Students Knifed: 4 Youths Arrested," *New York Times,* May 28, 1958, pg. 42.

34. "Gang Fact File Set Up By Police," *New York Times,* September 8, 1959, pg. 1.

35. Books such as *Gangs in Schools,* issued in 1988 by Pepperdine University for the National School Safety Center are helpful in describing gangs to teachers.

36. James C. Howell and Scott H. Decker, "The Youth Gangs, Drugs, and Violence Connection," *Juvenile Justice Bulletin,* January 1999, pg. 2.

37. "The Fighting Gangs: Execution in the Bronx," *New York Times,* June 17, 1973, pg. 6.

38. "5 in Bronx Street Gang Indicted as Extortioners," *New York Times,* December 19, 1973, pg. 47.

39. "Stabbing of Washington High School Student Points Up a Resurgence of Youth-Gang Violence in City," *New York Times,* April 19, 1972, pg. 29.

40. "Youth is Arrested in Canarsie Killing," *New York Times,* January 5, 1973, pg. 29.

41. "Rise in Youth Gang Killing Alarms Police in 3 Cities," *New York Times,* November 27, 1972, pgs. 1, 53.

42. "Violence and Terror by Street Gangs Arouse Public Outrage in Philadelphia," *New York Times,* May 24, 1973, pg. 23.

43. "Youths in Brawl Face No Charges," *New York Times,* September 5, 1963, pg. 25. "Affluent Delinquency," *New York Times,* September 5, 1963, pg. 25.

44. "Winchell's Son Ends Complaint on Youths, But He Faces Trial," *New York Times,* September 5, 1963, pg. 25.

45. "New Schools in Suburbs Ready for 4% Increase in Enrollment," *New York Times,* September 4, 1961, pgs. 1, 8.

46. "Hippies Heighten East Side Tension," *New York Times,* June 3, 1967, pg. 16.

47. "U.S. Notes Sharp Rise in Delinquency of Girls," *New York Times,* April 12, 1972, pg. 36.

48. "Pupils Attack Elizabeth Principal," *New York Times,* January 19, 1973, pg. 70. "Principal Denies Attack by Girls," *New York Times,* January 20, 1973, pg. 67.

49. "A Girl, 10, is Raped in Brooklyn School; Teen-Ager Hunted," *New York Times,* September 24, 1974, pg. 45.

50. "Maplewood Starts Drive on Marijuana," *New York Times,* February 22, 1968, pg. 22.

51. "Student 18 Dies, A Narcotic Case," *New York Times,* March 19, 1969, pg. 31.

52. "High School Unrest Rises, Alarming U.S. Educators," *New York Times,* May 9, 1969, pg. 1.

53. "4 L.I. Children Hurt As a Blasting Cap Explodes in Class," *New York Times,* October 21, 1969, pg. 93.

54. "Englewood Students Praise Suspensions," *New York Times,* January 26, 1973, pg. 75.

55. "School Gun Incidents Doubled in '73," *New York Times,* April 8, 1974, pg. 39.

56. "Security at Schools Is Increased to Curb Outbreaks of Violence," *New York Times,* October 11, 1974, pg. 46.

57. James A. Rapp, Frank Carrington, and George Nicholson, *School Crime and Violence Victim's Rights,* (Malibu, California: Pepperdine University Press [National School Safety Center], 1986), pg. 2.

58. A suit brought by a group of parents in Taft, near Bakersfield, California, charged that school officials told parents that they must consent to their children taking Ritalin or be excluded from the school entirely or placed in sections for the mentally retarded. The suit was submitted on behalf of 17 children. "Suit Says School Forced Drug Use," *New York Times,* September 10, 1975, pg. 10.

Chapter 4

Fire Bell in the Schoolyard (1945–1992)

Of all of nature's dangers, other than man himself, explosion and fire have represented the greatest threat to the American schoolhouse. At the beginning of the post-war era, with modern technology, contemporary building techniques, and the finest training provided to school children, faculties, and staffs, fire still loomed as potentially the most deadly enemy of the sanctuary of the school. The decade of the 1950s would see some of the deadliest American school fires. There were others in the subsequent decades.

A great enigmatic force of nature, fire has often tricked people in some way or other. Sometimes fires have caused people to panic. Once in a while, people believe there is a fire when there is not. In the 1950s, the city of New York was still using a 91-year-old schoolhouse and a companion building built in 1908 in Greenwich Village to house classes for "problem boys." Ironically, that site had been the location of a four-story, stone and brick schoolhouse built in 1850 that was separated into the "Male and Female" departments. A teacher was sitting on a raised platform in her classroom on November 20, 1851, when she was seized with facial paralysis. Her pupils began screaming. Teachers and children in other classrooms thought there was a fire and began screaming "Fire!" Forty-five children were killed and sixty others were injured in the ensuing panic.[1]

A PRE-WAR CATASTROPHE

The worst disaster ever to befall an American school was an explosion that occurred on March 19, 1937. The unincorporated districts of London and New London, located in the northwest corner of Rusk County, Texas, were part of an oil region that was prosperous even during the days of the Great Depression. The campus of the consolidated London and New London school district covered several acres, had seven oil wells on it, and had a number of detached frame brick buildings. The junior-senior high school was the centerpiece edifice. It was built in 1931 with additions in 1934; it had a steel frame and was designed in the California Spanish style, with hollow tile and brick trimmed in stone. Built on sloping ground, it appeared from the front to be a one-story structure, whereas from the rear the basement was at ground level.

The "E"-letter-shaped building had a main front section and three wings covering 30,000 square feet. The structure was valued at $300,000 in 1937 dollars. Under the building was a large area of concealed space, bottled up and without ventilation, which was filled with gas pipelines and electrical circuits.

Grammar school classes had been dismissed by mid-afternoon on that fateful day. Some of the children waited for their parents, who were attending a Parent Teachers Association meeting in the gymnasium. Two hundred yards from them, in the junior-senior high school, students were about to cast ballots in a school election. At 3:00 P.M., the school day was almost over, with just ten minutes to go before dismissal.

A teacher in the basement workshop apparently unplugged an electric sanding machine at that time, and suddenly there was a flash of light and heat as an explosion blew the floors and roof toward the sky.

Workers in the oil fields and parents and staff attending the PTA meeting came out to see debris falling on a mound of rubble that had been the school. Outside the building, students in a physical education class ran for cover, and although some were injured by falling debris, they survived. The teacher, who had gone into the building, was killed by the blast.

Investigators later concluded that a leak had occurred in one of the concealed gas pipes. This had produced an accumulation of gas so great that it overflowed into the manual training shop where the teacher threw the switch. The explosion was of such force that it broke through an eight-inch concrete floor. An automobile sitting at some distance from the school was crushed like an eggshell under a two-ton slab of concrete that had been hurled from the building.

The famous newsman Walter Cronkite began his career by reporting on this tragedy in which 311 teachers and students were killed. Schools in other parts of the country found that they also had gas pipes running through concealed basement areas.[2]

POST-WAR SCHOOL FIRES

At the end of World War II, school fires plagued the nation. A fire that destroyed a school in Passaic, New Jersey on April 9, 1946, was the third fire to destroy a school in just over a year. In Passaic, 500 students watched their three-story school building burn to the ground. Twelve teachers had marched every one of the children to safety in what the children thought was a routine fire drill. The blaze started on the roof where a tinsmith accidentally ignited a pigeon nest in a gutter. A general alarm was sounded as the fire spread through the third and second floors. The school was 40 years old and one of the oldest in the school system.[3]

Later in 1946, another school in New Jersey was badly damaged when a heating system exploded in the basement, a few minutes after children had assembled in their homerooms for the morning. Windows in the three-story structure were blown out. Three children were injured in the Asbury Park explosion. In December 1946, another school was nearly destroyed in Belmar, New Jersey, when a short circuit caused the auditorium and several classrooms to burn.[4]

Just before the end of the war, in April and June 1945, fires had destroyed schools in Hackensack and Wildwood. Children were not in either school at the time of the fires.

In November 1946, in Baroda, Michigan, an explosion shattered two floors of a consolidated rural school while 280 children were in the building. One child was killed and 18 others were injured. One of the injured was in critical condition after the blast, which came from a boiler. Boys and girls in one classroom were buried beneath debris as their classroom dropped from the second floor to the basement. A score of children had left the classroom just above the boiler minutes before the explosion; had they stayed, they would have faced certain death.[5]

Writer Amy Porter wrote an influential article in *Collier's* magazine on October 2, 1948, called "Death in the Classroom" in which she made an impassioned plea for eliminating the dangerous schools around the country. She said that more than half of all the schools were firetraps and that there were seven school fires daily in the United States. While not wanting to be an augur, Porter said something that later came true: "by the law of chance, sooner or later one of those fires is going to bring wholesale slaughter. It has happened before and it will happen again."

Porter recounted a fire that happened on January 22, 1947, in Monroe City, Missouri, in which four boys were killed. Five others were badly injured. One of these lost both ears in the fire. The fire was caused when the spark from an electric welder jumped to an open pan of gasoline. One boy fell into the pan as he was trying to flee.

The writer then cited the following:

> In lots of schools you'll find rickety fire escapes covered with ice all winter long. . . . You'll find overcrowded third floor assembly rooms with only one exit and that exit partially blocked by stacks of chairs. . . . You'll find boiler-room doors, supposed to close automatically, wired back so they can't be closed. . . . And the risks keep multiplying, now more than ever, as the school population grows and grows, and as old buildings, often old firetrap dwellings are pressed into temporary service. . . . Fire experts keep pointing out that school fires are on the increase.

Porter told about a Weston, Massachusetts, three-story brick high school that had burned down. When it was built in 1931, the interior was not made fire-resistant.[6]

Six days after the Monroe City explosion, a Jersey City explosion in a parochial school nearly caused great damage, with an oil burner exploding just minutes before school opened. The nuns who were the school's teachers led the 100 students who had assembled on the second floor of the school to safety.[7]

THE EARLY 1950s

A blast that was heard five miles away destroyed a school in Morganville, New Jersey, in 1950. Reminiscent of the 1937 Texas gas explosion, the New Jersey school was at least partially blown up by a spark igniting escaping gas in the basement. The explosion, which occurred while children were absent from the school, injured the building superintendent and caused a fire that was later extinguished.[8]

Two fires early in the decade in which no children were hurt burned private schools and served as a foreshadowing of the worst private school fire ever to occur in 1958 in Chicago. A Jewish school in the Bronx chased all 500 students from the building as a fire began, but no one was hurt.[9] In Camden, Maine, flames roared through the main building of the Landhaven private school and destroyed the 630-room structure. No children were hurt.[10]

Vandals at a grammar school in a fourth-floor laboratory triggered one school blast in 1953. When the boys, who were students at the school, caused the explosion, they were spattered with burning rubber cement. They became hysterical, climbing out on a window ledge, then back into the burning room, where police and firemen rescued them. The boys were carried out of the building after their Sunday morning escapade.[11]

A tragic year followed these incidents in 1954. In a Roman Catholic school in Brooklyn, 550 pupils and teachers fled the building when a student discovered smoke pouring from the auditorium on the top floor of the school. Fire inspectors suspected that the fire had been set.[12] At the end of March a horrible school fire burned ten elementary school pupils to death at Cleveland Hills School near Buffalo, New York.

The ten children died when a fire trapped them in a one-story frame annex to a suburban school. Nineteen children and two adults were burned or injured and taken to hospitals in ambulances. The elementary school had an enrollment of 1,200 and was located next to a high school, which was evacuated. The fire followed a blast that a spectator likened to the noise from a jet plane. The fire chief said the fire was caused by a "heat blast." The Cheektowaga, New York, fire took place on April 1, 1954. The next day another child died; on April 3 two more children died; and when two more children died, the death toll from the fire reached 15.[13] There were other school fires that year, but none was as devastating as this one that killed 15 sixth graders. The incident provoked an inquiry into fire laws in New York state.[14]

1958

During 1958, several important symbolic acts signaled the fact that the United States had entered a new era of possibilities, some of them promising, some threatening.

Sputnik had been launched into orbit in 1957, but it was not until January 31, 1958, that America entered the space race with the Soviets by placing its first satellite, *Explorer*, into orbit. In that same year, however, the air force dropped a nuclear bomb on Florence, South Carolina, by accident.[15] On April 2, the United States imposed an arms embargo on Cuba. On August 4, the submarine *Nautilus* completed passage under the North Pole. On December 18, the largest satellite in history was launched by the United States.[16]

And on December 1, one of the worst school fires in history claimed the lives of 92 children and three nuns in Chicago. *Newsweek* reported that no fire in history had been reported with "such sickening immediacy" as the fire at Our Lady of the Angels School:

> Less than an hour after the first fire alarm was sounded the bulky impediments of radio and television—vidicom cameras, sound trucks, cables, and recorders—were on the scene and moving in close along with the usual small army of newspaper reporters and still photographers. Cameras immediately began focusing on the smoldering school building. A helicopter from WGN hovered overhead. Reporters talking into chest microphones recorded on tape the horrifying testimony of witnesses and survivors.[17]

The school was housed in two buildings. It was the older two-story brick building that burned. Firemen fighting their way into one classroom reported that they found 24 children dead at their desks. They were certain that confusion and panic had added to the death toll. Some of the children jumped from windows while others were pushed; still others were trampled as they tried to find exits. Smaller children huddled in corridors, totally confused.

Fire officials at the scene did not agree about the origin of the fire. Chicago's fire commissioner said at the time that the fire might have been caused by oil, but he said he was mystified about how the fire had spread so quickly. The head of the police arson squad remarked that the fire appeared to have started in a corridor below the first floor in a corner where rubbish might have been. The city's building commissioner said that there were six exits from the second floor and that they were of adequate width for escape.

Adding to the mystery of the fire's origin was the fact that a woman who owned a store about a block from the school reported that a strange man had entered the store just before the fire alarms went off and asked for a public telephone. When she told him none was available, he said, "I was going to report that the school's on fire."

The police reported that they found a thirty-gallon metal can, sealed at both ends, at the bottom of the basement stairway where the fire was believed to have started. Pupils said that they had heard strange sounds coming from the school's radiators just before flames raced through the building. Flames spread so rapidly that many children were killed at their desks before firemen arrived. It was believed that nuns, priests, lay teachers, and janitors rescued more than a thousand of the children in the school.[18]

Indeed, quick thinking by teachers saved many lives, as students were directed to place textbooks and desks by the doors, which kept the smoke back and held it off until they were rescued. The first two teachers to discover the smoke quickly evacuated their students from the building and tried to ring the alarm, which they discovered was broken.

A priest and a custodian swung children from the window ledge in order to save their lives. Parents ran though the first floor looking for any stray children, while neighbors took many of the injured and dying children into their homes and administered care until they could be taken to the hospital.

Some of the children who had jumped lay dying on the sidewalks when firemen arrived. The streets were clogged with traffic because many parents had abandoned their cars, leaving them to run down the city blocks for signs of their children. All kinds of conveyances—milk trucks, private cars, and newspaper trucks—all were used to take the children to the hospital.

There were many reasons why Our Lady of the Angels' fire was so devastating. The fire occurred just 18 minutes before the end of the school day. Later analysis pointed to human errors as the chief causes. Fire officials determined that a student who had been smoking and tossed the burning cigarette into a trashcan set the fire. The investigation proved that there were several contributors to the spread of the fire. The raging flame sweeping through the building could not be controlled. Its force broke a window that allowed the flames to spread upward into the second floor where the most damage was done to the building and to lives. The first major contributor to the fire was the inadequacy of fire exits. The National Fire Protection Association found that the exits did not adhere to the 1949 Municipal Code of Chicago, which called for enclosures of all stairways in schools. (The school was built before 1949 so the code did not apply.) The stairways were open; substandard doors present on the second floor were blocked during the fire.

The interior finish in the school was a second contributing factor to the fire's ferocity. The ceilings of the classrooms on the second floor were finished with combustible cellulose fiber acoustical tile. Stairwells, wooden floors, and doors were coated with heavy, combustible materials. The third contributor was the absence of detection—there was no automatic sprinkler system. The manual fire alarm system was in substandard condition. The alarm-sending switches were not accessible to most of the students in the building and, even worse, the two alarm switches were not distinguishable from the ordinary light switches. A final factor was the sloppy housekeeping. Bundled newspapers and test papers were bound among other debris at the base of the stairwell. A wooden storage closet containing wooden chairs, screen panels, and combustible materials was also located at the base of the stairwell.

Students at Our Lady of the Angels School were used to frequent fire drills, but students had not been educated about what to do when they had safely exited the school. Some of the students who had been rescued went back into the burning school to look for siblings. The students on the second floor had been told by teachers to sit at their desks and wait for help. While a few dared to jump from the windows, the smaller children were not tall enough to reach window ledges.

When custodians brought ladders to rescue children on the second floor, they found that the ladders were too short. In front of the school, an iron fence kept many parents and neighbors from rescuing the children as they dangled from the burning windows. Perhaps worst of all, the fire department was given the wrong address.[19]

THE IMPACT OF THE CHICAGO FIRE

Cities all across the country were alarmed by the fire. The December 15 edition of *Newsweek* reported that schools in all parts of the country were having fire drills, many of them at times when the children were not used to having them, such as when they were in the cafeteria having lunch. Other measures being taken were special drills, sudden inspections, and rapid elimination of hazards long neglected. In Los Angeles, authorities gave one school a week to install an outside stairway. Cities began to look more closely at their school buildings. In Boston, the fire commissioner ordered immediate inspection of every school building, including public, private, and nursery institutions. Similar orders were given in many other big cities.

In New York, Mayor Robert F. Wagner demanded a complete inspection of the city's 1,500 public, private, and parochial schools. Some 1,869 schools were inspected there.[20]

The fire commissioner, who threatened to recommend that all schools be closed if they were not brought into compliance, peremptorily closed ten of the schools.

The magazine reported that conditions of schools varied from state to state. Most schools in California, it said, were modern one-story structures less than 20 years old, whereas in Michigan the 1,800 state schools—most one-room rural—were of a "combustible nature." The U.S. Office of Education estimated that there were at least six school fires each day, most of them when pupils were absent. The office also reported that a national survey had revealed that nearly one school building in five is a potential firetrap and another one in five is on the borderline.

The article concluded with a list of recommendations prepared by the National Education Association. It suggested, among other things, that heating plant and fuel rooms be separated from other portions of the building and that all doors be equipped with panic-bar locks, with all exit doors opening outward.[21]

The 1958 Chicago fire brought about an awareness of the need for emergency crisis planning and had a very significant long-term impact on the enforcement of fire safety codes for schools around the nation.

Even though schools are now among the safest public buildings, largely because of the laws and safeguards that were put into place after the Chicago fire and other school fires, there are still about 8,000 school fires each year, with about half of them of incendiary or suspicious origin.

One of the oldest school buildings in New York, built about 1890, burned about a month before the tragic Chicago fire of 1958. No one was hurt in the five-alarm blaze in the elementary school known as the Stinson-McIver School.[22]

On April 6, 1959, *Newsweek* took a survey of schools in eight major cities, asking that schools be rated according to a seven-point checklist, including enclosed stairwells, proper exits, safe finish on the walls, safeguarded trash, fire drills, effective alarm plan, and sprinklers in use. The city-by-city NFPA ratings took into account whether the city was taking precautions to improve safety.

Washington, D.C. was rated good plus, with all conditions being met except sprinklers. San Francisco was rated good, with legislation pending to enclose stairwells. Los Angeles was rated good or almost good. New York was rated good minus, as was Atlanta, where only 10 percent of the schools had enclosed stairwells. Chicago was rated fair to good because it failed to meet most of the seven points. Detroit and Pittsburgh were also rated fair to good. Every city except Pittsburgh did not have sufficient sprinklers.[23]

SCHOOL FIRES AND POLITICS IN THE 1960s

The Chicago school fire continued to have an impact well into the 1960s, sometimes with political overtones. In New York, the Teachers Guild wrote to the mayor in January 1960 with a warning that New York could experience an even worse fire than Chicago if the city's school overcrowding problem was not dealt with:

> The guild charged that the Fire Department had no maximum occupancy figure for the schoolrooms such as there is in theaters and restaurants; that a maximum occupancy regulation in the Health Code was not enforced, and that children seated in the aisles and two in a seat violated the official view of the Fire Department concerning fire hazards.

The superintendent of schools condemned the guild's statements as "an irresponsible use of the basic concerns of parents for the safety of their children to feather the guild's own organizational nest." Other city agencies also defended their actions with regard to the schools, disclaiming any responsibility for code violations.[24]

Less than a month after the union complaints about the danger in schools, the wall of a century-old building collapsed, and if it had not been Lincoln's Birthday, there would have been a major tragedy. The school was closed when tons of brick and mortar plunged from the attic wall on the fourth floor into two classrooms in a school annex, crushing desks and chairs. A whole section of the school had collapsed, leaving a triangular hole about 40 feet wide and 10 feet high. Other debris fell into an enclosed passageway. "This would have been tragic if it had happened on a regular school day," a school board spokesman said. The classrooms housed second grade students in one and mentally retarded children in another.[25]

The New York fire department, like those in other American cities, continued to be diligent about school safety inspections. In May 1961, the department closed two schools that did not meet code for fire safety. Nine classrooms in one public school opened on a dead-end corridor with only one exit. Also, the school had failed to install a sprinkler system. The five-story fireproof building had been constructed in 1900. A parochial school was also closed because it had failed to install a sprinkler system.[26]

In March 1963, a serious fire in a 38-year-old Long Island high school injured 50 students, many of whom jumped from windows of the wooden structure. A nearby hospital reported that it had admitted 42 pupils and a teacher, most of them suffering from smoke poisoning, shock, and cuts. Many others were treated at the scene. A group of teachers held a blanket to break the fall of students leaping from the second floor of the building.

The first was called "a near disaster" because it was believed a boiler had blown up in the school. All 900 students in the school might have been killed. Flames were first reported in the ceiling over the stage of the auditorium at about 1:55 P.M., and by 3:30 P.M. the structure was burned out. In New York, 75 miles away, Mayor Wagner ordered the city hospital to supply anything needed.[27]

FIRES RELATED TO RACIAL TURMOIL

During the 1960s, many school fires were attributed to troubles resulting from the Civil Rights Movement.[28] For instance, in July 1964, a black school was destroyed by fire in Tazewell, Tennessee. The school, 38 miles north of Knoxville, served about 50 students. No one was hurt in the blaze. In 1965, an all-black school burned in Mount Sterling, Kentucky. The DuBois School there had been the center of a controversy. Policemen who arrived first at the fire saw a large kerosene can burning under the steps of the school. The one-story brick school served grades one through twelve.[29]

The New York City Superintendent of Schools was called upon in 1966 to defend the safety of some of his schools. The City buildings commissioner said that 30 schools had "hazardous" violations. The superintendent had to admit that the school system had a backlog of $70 million in needed school repairs because of insufficient funds in the budget.[30]

Sometimes during the Civil Rights era it was clear that arson was the cause of certain fires. For instance, when the school administration building burned in Plainfield, New Jersey in March, 1969, during the time of turbulent relations between blacks and whites, it was fairly clear that one side or another had something to do with it. A racial free for all had transpired just days before.[31] Still, fires of suspicious origin have continued from the 1960s to the present. In 1966, a 63-year-old school burned in a suspicious fire. The school building was erected on the site of the oldest school in New Jersey, having served children from first through eighth grade. No one was hurt in the fire.[32]

One New York school had three fires in one week. On two of the days, all of the children in the school had to be evacuated.[33] In the next month, a Hebrew school was set afire.[34] In April 1967, 700 pupils were evacuated from a burning school in Queens.[35]

During a time of intense racial turmoil, when the rate of violence was rising rapidly, bombs, firebombs, and threats of bombs closed many American schools. In March 1970 for instance, George Washington High School in New York was closed because of firebombs and bomb threats. All over the city, powerful bombs exploding in the early morning within 29 minutes of each other closed many buildings. Bombings were on the increase all across the nation.[36]

In Reading, Massachusetts, a new high school (one and a half years old) in a 17-million-dollar wing was damaged in 1973 when a firebomb went off and damaged a classroom.[37] In Howell, New Jersey an arsonist set fire to the Land O'Pine School, causing $500,000 worth of damages.[38] Yet all of this deliberate damage seemed small in comparison with the number of fires being set in the South Bronx, where more than 12,300 fires raged in 1974. Officials estimated that at least arsonists started 30 percent of the fires.[39] One Bronx boy even admitted that he set fires for money during this time.

The rash of arson cases continued around the country during this period. In Washington, D.C., in January 1979, arson by two teenagers caused $4.5 million in damages to Fort Hunt High School. The early morning fire gutted a portion of the school that forced relocation of all of its 1,745 students. Students told a reporter that persons who broke a window outside the principal's office, poured in gasoline, and threw a gasoline bottle in on it started the fire.[40] The two teenaged arsonists, who were later caught, received a year in prison, a fine of $10,000 and 3,000 hours of volunteer community work. The two were caught in March and held in jail until July.[41]

Police held two other teenage boys in April 1979 for bombing a high school's chemistry laboratory in Stafford, Connecticut. Damage from the blast and fire was confined to the laboratory but smoke damaged the entire school. No one was hurt.[42]

In 1980, in Washington, D.C. again, four fires, including one in an elementary school, were set by the same arsonist. The investigator who had not yet caught the suspect said, "School fires are usually set by young males, possibly a dropout, someone who didn't like school." The school fire damaged four classrooms and left four others with smoke damage. While students were moved to other schools, workmen backed a garbage truck up to the school and shoveled mounds of burned school materials into the truck.[43]

Another case of arson in nearby Alexandria was more dangerous. At the MacArthur Elementary School, 598 students and 41 staff members were evacuated in the late morning as fire destroyed four classrooms and damaged four others. The fire marshal said that the blaze was deliberately set and he knew one or two students set it. The fire melted sections of the roof, weakened the brick walls, and sent acrid smoke throughout the building. A secretary said that they heard an explosion in the back of the school and then saw smoke pouring from the back classrooms.[44]

A few days earlier, Roosevelt High School in Washington was the locale for yet another suspicious fire. A new wing with new furniture was badly damaged. At the junior high school next to Roosevelt, six fires—all of them deliberately set—were reported in days just prior to the Roosevelt fire. At the junior high, the cafeteria was badly damaged by fire. At another Washington high school, two fires were reported in the same week.[45]

Fire officials in Newark, New Jersey, had another problem. As one fireman said, "Fire alarms go off so often in Newark that no one pays attention to them anymore." In 1980 there were 520 false alarms in Newark schools and nearly 400 malfunctions in the system, in all calling Newark firemen to schools 1,183 times. By October 1981, the department had responded to 919 false alarms. As a result, only one fire truck was sent to schools during the daytime. On November 8, 1980, a fire at the Oliver Street school was answered by one engine, and, had the fire not been on the roof of the school, many children could have been hurt or killed. It took the fire department seven hours to contain the blaze. Another problem in the Newark schools at the time was the principals were chaining doors shut to keep out intruders. Any kind of obstruction to a potential exit from a school was a violation of the state's code for planning and construction.[46]

OKLAHOMA NIGHTMARE, 1982

Six were killed in an Oklahoma school explosion in January 1982. When an explosion tore through the kitchen of an elementary school in the Oklahoma City school district, children eating lunch in the cafeteria were covered with bricks, glass, and metal. Outside the school, mass confusion ensued as screaming children mingled with rescue workers, ambulance attendants, and frantic parents who had rushed to the scene.

When all of the school's 270 pupils had been accounted for, five children and one teacher were dead and 35 others were wounded. Fire officials were not certain what had caused the explosion, but a kitchen worker said she was sure that a water heater had exploded. A cook had turned on a faucet and got only steam, and then the explosion occurred, knocking everybody to the floor. Fifty to 60 children were in the cafeteria when the blast ripped through the kitchen wall.

When the explosion went off, it was reported that the roof of the cafeteria lifted straight up and the came back down. The bodies were found in the rubble of the cafeteria.[47]

Two fires in California in 1985 in elementary schools were called arson, and another arson case in an elementary school happened in Silver Spring, Maryland, in the same year. The fire in Anaheim destroyed the administrative wing of a school while the other fire gutted the school's media center. The Silver Spring school was extensively damaged. No one was injured in any of the fires.[48]

DANGEROUS BUILDINGS

In the late 1980s, several elementary schools around the country were found to have either faulty building materials or materials so minimal as not to be safe. In 1987, the Anderson Elementary School in San Jose, California, burned to the ground in a devastating five-alarm fire. Built in the late 1960s, the school was constructed primarily of wood and only minimally met fire codes.[49] Another school in the San Diego district apparently had been abandoned in 1987, because the system was told by the city that the empty building was hazardous and had to be either cleaned up or torn down. Fire investigators said that the building represented a hazard. Yet the city attorney said that a city ordinance regarding unsafe buildings could not be used to force the school system to tear it down.[50]

Disaster was averted at Los Amigos High School in Fountain Valley, California, in 1989 when an explosion in an electrical vault at the rear of the school caused the school to be evacuated. The explosion sparked a small fire, and two employees received minor burns.[51]

History teaches some lessons for those who would learn. As far as school fires are concerned, there has never been a stopping point, as there is no time when one can say that there are no more fires in schools. But death and destruction were lessened because officials had learned from the past. Therefore, schools in the 1990s were less prone to mass death and destruction than school buildings had been in the past. It was the lessons those who died had left—the Chicago fire and others—that taught schools ways to avoid pupils' deaths, and being diligent about safety has helped them remain safer places.

NOTES

1. "School Tragedy in 'Village' a Century Ago," *New York Times,* March 10, 1958, pg. 31.

2. "New London Explosion," 2000. http://www.westruskccid.org/wr_newlondon_explosion.html.

3. "Fire Destroys School," *New York Times,* April 9, 1946, pg. 29.

4. "School Blast Injures 3," *New York Times,* November 26, 1946, pg. 31.

5. "1 Killed, 18 Injured in Blast at School," *New York Times,* November 14, 1946, pg. 35.

6. Amy Porter, "Death in the Classroom," *Collier's,* Vol. 122, No. 14, October 2, 1948, pgs. 13–25.

7. Ibid.

8. "Blast Wrecks School," *New York Times,* August 2, 1950, pg. 26.

9. "Fire Routs 500 Pupils," *New York Times,* May 13, 1950, pg. 19.

10. "Maine School Building Burns," *New York Times,* August 5, 1951, pg. 55.

11. "School Blast, Fire Trap Boy Vandals," *New York Times,* September 21, 1953, pg. 26.

12. "School Fire Routs 550," *New York Times,* February 6, 1954, pg. 14.

13. "10 Pupils Burned to Death Near Buffalo," *New York Times,* April 1, 1954, pg. 1. Follow-up stories were in the *Times* on April 2, 3, and 4. Paul Carroll, "Survivors Recall Ordeal of Deadly School Fire 40 Years Ago," *Buffalo News,* March 27, 1994, pg. 1.

14. "Fire Law Inquiry Set," *New York Times,* June 16, 1954, pg. 7.

15. The trigger charge exploded, but the warhead did not detonate on March 11, 1958.

16. Robert Pavey, "1958: The United States Officially Entered the Space Race, Racial Integration Issues Heated Up," *Augusta Chronicle.* http:// celebrate2000.jacksonville.com/stories/090699/his_1958.shtml.

17. "Nightmare in the News," *Newsweek* (December 15, 1958), pg. 98.

18. "Disasters: The Chicago School Fire," *Time* (December 15, 1958), pg. 10.

19. "90 Perish in Chicago School Fire," *New York Times,* December 2, 1958, pg. 1. "Nightmare in the News," *Newsweek* (December 15, 1958), pg. 98. David Cowan and John Kuenster, *To Sleep With the Angels: The Story of a Fire* (Elephant Paperbacks, Ivan R. Dee, Publisher, Chicago), 1996 is an excellent work.

20. "Two More Schools Closed in Fire Drive," *New York Times,* December 17, 1958, pg. 2.

21. "Urgent Mission: Safe Schools," *Newsweek* (December 15, 1958), pgs. 31–34.

22. "Five Alarm Fire Sweeps Old West Side School," *New York Times,* October 28, 1958, pg. 37.

23. "Good and Not-So-Good," *Newsweek* (April 6, 1959), pg. 106.

24. "Fire Hazard Seen in City's Schools," *New York Times,* January 11, 1960, pg. 21.

25. "Wall Collapses at Empty School," *New York Times,* February 13, 1960, pg. 42.

26. "Parts of 2 Schools Shut in Fire Drive," *New York Times,* May 2, 1961, pg. 10.

27. "Fire in School Injures Scores," *New York Times,* March 9, 1963, pg. 4.

28. Most of the important racially motivated fires and violence are covered in Chapter 5 of this book.

29. "2 Negro Buildings Burn in Kentucky," *New York Times,* August 31, 1965, pg. 37. "Negro School Destroyed in Tazewell, TN," *New York Times,* July 24, 1964, pg. 9.

30. "School Buildings Safety Is Defending by Donovan," September 12, 1966, *New York Times,* pg. 37.

31. "School Building Burned in Jersey," *New York Times,* March 9, 1969, pg. 72.

32. "63-Year-Old Jersey School Ruined in Suspicious Fire," *New York Times,* October 4, 1966, pg. 13.

33. "School Has 3rd Fire in Week," *New York Times,* January 10, 1967, pg. 26.

34. "Hebrew School Set Afire," *New York Times,* February 9, 1967, pg. 36.

35. "700 Pupils Flee Burning Queens School in 3 Minutes," *New York Times,* April 13, 1967, pg. 1.

36. "Bombings on Rise Over the Nation," *New York Times,* March 13, 1970, pg. 1.

37. "Fire Bomb Damages School," *New York Times,* March 24, 1973, pg. 18.

38. "Man Held for Arson in School Fire," *New York Times,* May 13, 1974, pg. 66.

39. "20% Rise in Fires Is Adding to Decline of South Bronx," *New York Times,* May 18, 1975, pgs. 1, 50.

40. "Second Teenager Arrested in Fort Hunt School Fire," *Washington Post,* January 7, 1979, pg. B1.

41. "2 Teen Arsonists Get Prison Term, Fine, Work Order," *Washington Post,* July 14, 1979, pg. A1.

42. "Two Students Held in School Bombing," *New York Times,* April 7, 1979, pg. 26.

43. "Same Person Suspected of Setting 3 Fires in SE," *Washington Post,* February 12, 1980, pg. C5.

44. "Pupils Flee Alexandria Fire Believed Set by a Student," *Washington Post,* February 18, 1981, pg. C1.

45. "Roosevelt High School Fires Damage Wing," *Washington Post,* February 13, 1981, pg. B4.

46. "Firemen Fear For Schools," *New York Times,* December 13, 1981, pg. 26.

47. "6 Killed in Oklahoma School Explosion," *New York Times,* January 20, 1982, pg. 14.

48. "Arson is Suspected in Elementary School Fire," *Los Angeles Times,* February 13, 1985, pg. 2-2. "2 Children Blamed in $23,000 School Fire," *San Diego Union Tribune,* April 28, 1985, pg. B9. "Silver Spring Fire Called 'Result of Arson,'" *Washington Post,* June 16, 1985, pg. B7.

49. "6 Alarm School Fire in San Jose," San Jose Fire Department, August 19, 2000. http://www.sjfd.com/santaearsa.html.

50. "Safety Ordinance Can't Be Used for Dana School," *San Diego Union Tribune,* October 16, 1987, pg. B1.

51. "Los Amigos High Evacuated After Explosion in Vault," *Los Angeles Times,* September 22, 1989, pgs. 2–14.

Chapter 5

The Encroachment of an Old Catastrophe (1945–1992)

Catastrophic events affecting the safety and well-being of schools have included school bus crashes, hurricanes and tornadoes, poisonings, gym accidents, contagious illnesses, asbestos in older buildings and other environmental dangers, the involvement of students in traffic accidents, human folly, and quite a few phenomena that could only be called "freak" accidents. Like the gods of ancient mythology, catastrophes large and small encroach themselves upon man's life at will, respecting neither person nor institution nor age nor imperfection of character. Children have often been—even in American schoolhouses—victims of these gods, who have taught that life is a series of attachments and separations, as one psychologist, who perhaps overlooked how much they also destroyed and damaged, once put it.

This chapter recounts and is concerned primarily with the ramifications such devastating events have caused. As a prelude to the postwar era, we shall first look at some earlier catastrophes that profoundly affected the conduct of schools after the war and then examine later events that also had a deleterious impact upon the schools.

PRE-WAR BUS ACCIDENTS

During the 1930s, the nation experienced two of its worst school bus crashes. An accident in Williamsport, Maryland, on April 11, 1935, in which the bus drove onto a railroad crossing in front of an approaching train, killed fourteen children, with another eleven injured.

Twenty-five students, a chaperone, and a driver were riding on the bus, returning from an all-day field trip to the University of Maryland in College Park. The driver stopped the bus at the Baltimore Road grade crossing; he looked both ways and proceeded across three sets of tracks. Coming toward him was a Washington-bound *St. Louis Flyer*, which was traveling at approximately 56 miles per hour. When the driver heard the warning bells of the approaching locomotive, he stepped on the gas, but it was too late, as the train sliced through the rear section of the bus, dragging it more than 1,700 feet down the tracks. Occupants were tossed out of the bus and bodies lay scattered along the side.

A grand jury eventually cleared the driver of manslaughter charges, even though the Interstate Commerce Commission blamed him for the crash. Several surviving students testified that they had not heard the train whistle or bells either.

The nation was shocked by the accident. President Franklin D. Roosevelt ordered $200 million from the Public Works Fund to be used to eliminate the "deathtrap grade crossings."[1]

Three years later an even more devastating accident occurred in another part of the country. There was a fine snow falling on December 1, 1938 in Riverton, Utah, when a witness saw a school bus stop at a railroad crossing at 8:43 A.M. The bus then proceeded on to the track. There was a westbound *Denver and Rio Grande Western Railroad* freight train traveling at 52 miles per hour that struck the school bus operated by the Jordan school district at a country road crossing approximately 2.7 miles west of Riverton.

Twenty-three children and the driver were killed in the accident, and 15 others were injured. The train's engineman said the locomotive's whistle was sounding, and when the school bus was noticed, the train's air brakes were applied. Surviving children said that the windows of the bus were foggy and steamed at the time and it was impossible to see through them. None of the pupils said that they heard the approaching train. Later, an investigation showed that there was nothing to obstruct the eastward view of the driver other than foggy windows. Visibility was determined to be about one-half mile that morning.

Partly because of these two accidents, in 1939 representatives of the then 48 states gathered to develop standards and recommendations for safety guidelines for school buses. In all, a total of twelve national conferences on school transportation were held, attended by representatives from each state who gathered to revise existing and to establish new safety standards for operating procedures for school buses.[2]

POST-WAR SCHOOL BUS ACCIDENTS

Since the advent of consolidated schools and school busing, school officials across the country have had a major safety concern, especially with the growth in the number of schools after the war and the increasing number of suburbs. During the 1950s and 1960s, there were several devastating bus accidents at various locations around the nation.[3]

One of the most poignant tragedies occurred in Spring City, Tennessee, on August 22, 1955, when a 110-car freight train slammed into a school bus loaded with school children. School had been in session for only a week when the bus driver picked up 43 students, then drove to the Highway 68 train crossing that was two blocks from the school. Children were standing up in the aisles because the bus was so crowded. At 3:58 P.M., there were freight cars parked on a sidetrack, hindering the driver's view. The children began to yell, "Train, train, train!" and the driver had begun to cross, when the train smashed into the rear of the bus, tearing it open and flipping it on its side. Eleven children were killed and 30 others were injured in the accident.

One of the survivors of the accident later recounted details of the gruesome scene, remembering waking and then walking over bodies because he was dazed. A reporter at the scene said that "Parents picked up parts of clothing, odd shoes, and carried them about, trying to locate their child or other children." Ten of the children died there at the scene and another one died two days later. Ambulances were called from towns as far away as Crossville and Athens. Many of the injured were driven to area hospitals in private vehicles.[4]

Another train-school bus accident occurred in North Harvey, Illinois, on December 4, 1958. In that accident, a freight train hit a nursery school bus carrying eleven children. Apparently the driver ignored warning lights and drove in front of the train. One child was killed and the other ten children and the driver were injured.[5]

The nation's worst bus accident happened in rural eastern Kentucky in 1958 and killed 27 people. February 28, 1958, was a cold, cloudy day. A bus driver began his route from Cow Creek to the consolidated schools in Prestonsburg. The bus carried both elementary and secondary school children, ranging in age from 8 to 17.

Two hundred yards ahead of the bus a pickup truck was mired in the mud. A wrecker was maneuvering across the road to pull it out. The bus struck the wrecker's left rear bumper and fender, then turned a hard left and lunged toward the Big Sandy River. After hitting a parked car, the bus careened down the riverbank, plunging into the flooded river. Once in the water, it bobbed on the muddy surface for a few minutes. Then water came in through the broken windshield. Some children sat stunned while others leapt into the aisle. One boy kicked the back door open, and other boys began jumping out.

The bus was about 30 feet from the riverbank. Some of the children who got out were able to swim to the shore. Other children managed to escape through windows. Many of the small children were frozen with fear, and others could not swim once they were in the water. Three men helped save several children.

Some of the children looked back from the bank to see the bus sinking, with little arms sticking out the windows. The strong currents in the river swept many of the children away while the bus itself was swept about 250 yards downstream. It later took army engineers 53 hours to find the vehicle. Volunteers discovered only 15 bodies on the bus. The bodies of the other children were found much later, many miles downstream. Three families lost all of their children.[6]

On September 10, 1959, seven passengers died and twelve more were injured when a school bus stalled on a rail crossing in western Maryland. A 36-passenger Garrett County school bus was proceeding across the track when it stalled; the driver saw a train coming and instructed the 27 children to exit the bus. Investigation revealed that there were faulty crossing signals and that the driver had not made an effort to evacuate the children.

In 1960, there were two terrible bus accidents. On June 26, in an accident in Pekin, Illinois, 22 passengers were injured. In Greeley, Colorado, on December 14th, twenty children were killed when a school bus drove onto a rail-highway grade crossing in front of an approaching train. Sixteen other children were injured in that accident. The train was traveling 79 miles per hour when it slammed into the side of the 60-passenger bus, tearing it in half. Parts of the bus were carried 455 feet down the track. The crossing did not have flashing lights or a warning signal, only a cross buck sign. The school bus windows were frosted because of the extreme cold that morning. The driver of the bus was tried and found innocent of wrongdoing in the crash.[7]

A crash in Somerdale, New Jersey, in 1967 killed two passengers and injured three others. There were other vehicles stopped at a crossing when the school bus driver tried to proceed across the tracks at an unreduced speed. An investigation showed that the bus driver's ability to see the train might have been restricted.[8]

FREAK INCIDENTS AND BLEAK CONDITIONS IN SCHOOLS

Freak incidents and occurrences plagued schools in the post-war era. But once in a while a freak incident had a happy conclusion, as in the 1972 New Jersey case in which the driver of a speeding school bus died and slumped over the wheel. Two boys aged 12 and 13 saved the other 26 children on the bus when they ran to the front, where one boy slipped into the driver's seat as the dead driver fell away. The two boys then drove the bus to the side of the road and stopped it.[9]

In another incident, a "crazed man" entered a girls' school in New York and frightened girls in a gym class. As the man stepped outside into the street, he was confronted by a policeman who chased him and shot him dead. The shooting caused controversy in the days following.[10] In Oklahoma City, 435 teenagers were sitting on bleachers having their photograph taken when the bleachers collapsed, injuring fifty students, six of them seriously. The victims were all girls, and many of them suffered broken bones.[11] In a tragic incident in New Jersey, a ten-year-old girl was killed when an upright piano fell on her during a gym class.[12]

In New Jersey in 1973, a 12 year-old-boy in a middle school died when he was trapped between a wall and a moving motor-driven partition used to divide a gymnasium. What baffled school officials was that the wall moved very slowly and they did not know who could have been operating the 60-foot-long, 25-foot-high wall, which was controlled by a key. Other teachers and students were in the gymnasium when the accident happened.[13]

Vandals at a grammar school in a fourth-floor laboratory triggered one school blast in 1953. When the boys, who were students at the school, caused the explosion, they were spattered with burning rubber cement. They became hysterical, climbing out on a window ledge, then back into the burning room, where police and firemen rescued them. The boys were carried out of the building after their Sunday morning escapade.[14]

In 1961, in one New York school, a rat running across the room surprised Mayor Wagner, who was taking an inspection trip in response to complaints of unsanitary conditions. The infestation of rats in the 61-year-old building was real, as the mayor learned. In the weeks preceding his visit, rats had been seen in increasing numbers. School officials reported to the mayor that none of the students was bitten but that the appearance of the rodents disrupted class work. The 1,300 students in the school came from the most depressed area of Harlem, and school officials said that many of them were used to seeing rats.[15]

A similar experience awaited six members of Congress in 1963 when they toured two public schools in Washington. When they came out, they said one of the schools was "shocking," "terrible," and "a blight." One congressman said "My God!" when he saw that wrapping paper was being used as window shades. One of the schools was 69 years old and the other was 76 years old. All agreed that the condition of the schools was a "disgrace."[16]

PUPILS POISONED BY FOOD AND AIR

An incident at a Jewish school in New York in 1967 was every school administrator's nightmare. One day, 241 students became ill. Six of them were taken to the hospital, and 235 others had fever, vomiting, and diarrhea. Fourteen teachers also became ill. Department of Health experts said that the children had been poisoned in the school cafeteria, probably by ingesting salmonella bacteria that they got through tuna fish salad. The Department of Health insisted that the school stop serving food while they checked all eating utensils. While salmonella poisoning is rarely fatal, and none of the affected seemed to be seriously ill, some of the children ran fevers of 103 degrees.[17]

A bizarre incident occurred in Newark in June 1974 when workmen demolishing an old brewery accidentally ripped into an ammonia line, sending acrid fumes into a nearby parochial school. More than 80 children were taken to the hospital for eye irritation, nausea, and dizziness. The fumes were detected about 9:20 A.M. and thought to be smoke until workmen ran into the building saying that ammonia had been released. To add to the confusion, the first report put out said that an explosion had occurred at the school. Dozens of terrified parents, some still in their nightclothes, came to the school when they heard the reports. One fireman said, "I thank God for the wind. If that stuff had lingered, we could have been in real trouble." The two-story building was evacuated rapidly, with most of the 265 pupils being led to a lot along the river about two blocks away. The principal, who had remained in the building until all children were out, had to be hospitalized. The fire director said that the pipes had been purged of ammonia a couple of years before but that some residue remained in them. That area of Newark had experienced several gas main breaks and serious fires in addition to the ammonia leak.[18]

Thirty-two students and teachers in a Roman Catholic grammar school in Chicago in 1979 became ill when they breathed what were thought to be natural gas fumes, which apparently were escaping from pipes in the building. Because the school was in danger of being blown up, all of the students were evacuated, and 12 were rushed to the hospital.

Gas department officials seemed unsure as to how much gas had actually escaped. School officials opened all the windows in the building to air it out.[19]

In Cleveland in 1979, a public elementary school had a very similar occurrence. Though gas company tests showed no natural gas leaks, by about mid-morning 100 pupils were sick. One teacher reported that he had thought he smelled something strange when he arrived at work that morning, but children did not begin to get sick until later in the morning.[20]

SHOP AND PLAYGROUND DANGERS[21]

In Gainesville, Florida, a principal and some teachers learned what it is like to be helpless when a child is hurt. A five-year-old girl caught her finger in a playground ride in 1972 while a doctor, a school principal, and a fireman said that they "could only stand and watch" for 70 minutes while the girl screamed in agony. The adults claimed they were helpless to do anything without the permission of the parents. "I would have left myself liable for any consequences," the principal said.

The principal added that if attempts were made to free the child's hand and some greater damage was done to her hand, he could have been sued. He said that he had people calling the state attorney general's office while the ordeal was taking place, and that fear was confirmed.

After the parents were found, the child was taken to the university hospital where doctors were unable to save the tip of her index finger, which was severed to the bone at about the base of the fingernail.

The girl had been playing on a jungle gym and stuck her finger into a hole on a shaft that turned the ride. The finger was sliced when it slipped into another shaft. The principal did hold the child during her ordeal. He said the girl was in shock.[22]

At Morris Hills High School in Rockaway Township, New Jersey, a 15-year-old boy was electrocuted by a welding machine he was using in an electronics shop class. Some malfunction caused the machine to electrocute the boy when it was switched on.[23]

BEYOND THE PRINCIPAL'S CONTROL

Many other things, it seemed, were beyond the principal's control in the modern age of litigation. The average principal probably didn't know this: in February 1974, a state crime expert charged that there were student-run "brokerages" in the New York City schools, where teenaged boys were buying and selling guns, narcotics, and prostitutes. These brokerages, he said, functioned like miniature stock exchanges. Usually, the students bought these goods and sold them at higher prices on the street.

Usually, he claimed, teachers knew about these services but were afraid to talk about them. The teachers were deathly afraid of the students, who would promise to set them on fire if they talked, he said. The school officials were usually unwilling to aid the police in investigating these matters, the official claimed. The crime expert had written an article called "Crime in the Schools," which was recently published and which stated that the crime situation in the schools was far worse than school officials would admit. The state expert claimed that up to 15 percent of the boys in some high schools were involved in criminal activities. He compared some of the schools to prisons, where younger boys learned the criminal skills from older boys.[24]

Many principals, especially in urban areas, find that they have little control over the physical facilities in which their schools are located.

In New York in 1974, the city health department conducted a survey of schools and found that there were health and safety violations in 90 percent of them. The health inspectors rated the schools on five categories: food handling, sanitation, lighting, vermin, and structural defects and safety. Almost every school had at least one violation, and some schools had many of them. Some of the violations were corrected "on the spot," but all eventually had to be corrected.[25]

A school for emotionally disturbed children in Prince Georges County in Maryland had to close in 1979 when an infestation of lice attacked the children. The school, where 40 children boarded, apparently had a long history of health problems. In this incident, bird lice, which came from pigeons that roosted in the rafters, spread rapidly to all of the children. There was little else school officials could do but send the children home and fumigate the entire building.[26]

A sad episode in Chicago in 1979 left the whole city in shock: in the middle of the night, two mentally retarded boys wandered out of the dormitory where they stayed at a special school. The boys went outside into the freezing cold of the night and were not able to get back into the building. The two eight-year-olds, clothed only in their pajamas, were found frozen to death, huddled together on the front steps of the school.[27]

Another thing beyond the grasp of the principal was a teacher who had personal or mental problems. When teachers commit suicide in school, the trauma of a damaged life is spread to all of the young people in attendance. For instance, in 1974, a substitute teacher in Brooklyn jumped to his death from the school's fourth-floor ledge during lunch hour when many students were watching. The school's principal had tried to persuade the man to come back into the building from the ledge, and as he turned to enter, he lost his footing and fell to his death. Other teachers said that the substitute teacher, the father of three, was distraught.[28]

One principal must have been very grateful for lunchtime in 1976. When all of the children were in the cafeteria having lunch in a separate wing of the school building, a propane gas blast ripped through the rest of the school. Four men were injured in the explosion, but none of the school's 1,000 students was hurt.[29]

One New York high school principal wrote to the newspaper about things that had gone out of his control. He said that his power as a principal was being gradually eroded: "I am constantly running an obstacle course in my attempt to provide safety and security for my pupils and my staff," he said. Budget cuts had reduced his security force by 40 percent, reduced his school aides by 30 percent, and cut his teaching personnel by 25 percent. Furthermore, administrative regulations were handicapping him, he stated.[30]

In another city, principals were asked to find out if there was any asbestos in their school buildings. In the 104 public schools in Tulsa, school principals had to find any remaining asbestos that was used in schools in the 1950s and 1960s to fireproof buildings and improve acoustics in classrooms.[31]

Another hazard faced by principals was the danger that a chemical would blow up in a laboratory as students worked there. In Kingston, Pennsylvania, in 1977, an explosion occurred in the chemistry lab of Wyoming Valley West High School when phosphorus ignited, causing a fire that burned the teacher and 15 students.[32]

Perhaps the most bizarre incident a principal had to deal with took place in a private school in Miami in 1979. Mass hysteria broke out among the students, who ran through the school kicking holes in the walls, breaking windows, and smashing things. What may have started the incident was a demonstration of hypnosis in a science class. But the owner of the school thought that his political opponents had engineered the hysteria. Reporters talking with children as they filed out of the school following the incident said that some said demonic possession had caused the children to go wild.[33]

NATURAL DISASTERS, 1970s

One of nature's deadliest storms is a tornado, and when a tornado hits a school, children are placed in danger. Even though it is rare for a tornado to hit a school, there have been several disasters in schools because gyms and auditoriums are particularly vulnerable, although sometimes it is the classroom, which is most dangerous. The worst ten tornado-related disasters in schools included two in Illinois on the same day. On March 18, 1925, two schools were struck by tornados—in one, in Desoto, 33 children were killed, and in another, in Murphysboro, Illinois, 25 children were killed. In 1955, a tornado struck a school in Commerce Landing, Mississippi, and killed 17 children. In 1967, 13 children were killed in a school in Belvidere, Illinois. In 1989, nine students were killed when a tornado blew down a freestanding cafeteria wall at an elementary school near Newburg, New York.[34]

In at least one case, classrooms were the most dangerous spot in the school. In May 1978, a tornado dipped out of a darkened sky and crashed into an elementary school, knocking off part of the roof, uprooting trees, and picking up portable classrooms and tossing them into the air. The tornado, which was part of a storm system crossing Florida that morning, hit the school at 11:48 A.M. while many of the children were eating lunch in the cafeteria instead of sitting in the classrooms, which sustained the greatest amount of damage.

And the children in the classrooms were most vulnerable. Two were killed and 96 others were injured. It was the darkest day for Belcher Elementary School in Clearwater. One little boy said, "The roof just blew off and it didn't come down. If it came down, I'd still be there. I'm glad I ain't dead."[35]

In June, the school system realized that the children in Belcher Elementary School still needed help to get over the trauma the tornado had caused. A little girl whose five-year-old brother was killed by the twister said she was still afraid when it rained. A psychologist brought in by the school said that one in every two children was still frightened. Teachers were told to watch for signs of stress among the children, including crying, violence, and daydreaming. Psychological help was offered to parents and teachers, too. One consultant to the school system said, "Children will learn they can survive tragedy, that life is a series of attachments and separations. To go back to the classroom and ignore this would be a real disservice."[36]

SCHOOL BUS ACCIDENTS IN THE 1970s AND 1980s

Railroad and school bus collisions have continued to be a major problem. There were seven fatal train-bus crashes during the 1970s and two in the 1980s. In March 1972, five children were killed and 44 injured in Congers, New York. In Littlefield, Texas, the 68-year-old driver of a school bus that was struck by a train in a crash that killed seven children was not licensed to operate the vehicle.[37] In October 1974, a crash in Aragon, Georgia, killed seven and injured 71 persons. In November 1975, a bus driver was killed when a train hit the bus in Madison County, Indiana. In August 1976, nine were killed and eight injured when a bus and train collided. In 1979, there were accidents in January in Williamson, Illinois, where a bus driver was killed, and in Chicago, where two were killed and 13 injured in another accident. Both of the train-bus collisions in the 1980s happened in 1984. In April, a crash in Carrsville, Virginia, took a life and caused 26 others to be injured. In Port St. Lucie, Florida, two were killed and one was injured in a crash.

More common were highway crashes in which buses were hit by other vehicles. In May 1973, for instance, a bus carrying 32 children who had been on a field trip crashed head-on with a pickup truck. The bus burst into flames. Both drivers were killed. Ten of the children received injuries. But teachers saved the rest of the children by kicking out side windows and pulling the youngsters to safety before the bus became engulfed in flames.[38]

In Canton, Ohio, in May of the same year, a busload of preschool children collided head-on with a car, killing the car's driver. Twenty persons on the bus were injured.[39]

One of the most tragic school bus crashes in American history happened on Friday, May 21, 1976, in California. Members of a school choir at Yuba City High School in Sacramento Valley were traveling to Orinda, California, to watch a performance as a reward for the choir's yearlong work. The school bus had just crossed over the Martinez-Benecia Bridge over an arm of the San Francisco Bay, leaving the freeway to pull into a rest stop, when it smashed through 50 feet of guardrail.

A witness described the bus: "Suddenly a big cloud of dust went up, the bus leaned over, hit the rail and its wheels went up. Then it dropped over and landed directly on its top." The bus fell 30 feet and landed in a marsh. Twenty-eight students were killed in the crash, and twenty others were seriously injured.

One of the students who survived the crash said that the bus was going too fast. The National Transportation Safety Board said that the crash was the worst since 1967 when the board was established. The roof of the vehicle collapsed upon impact, with the top crushed to the level of the seats. The bus skidded on its top for 30 feet. After the crash, a crane was brought in to lift the bus so that the dead could be removed and the injured taken to hospitals. Traffic in the area was stopped for two hours. Police did not know the final number of fatalities at the time, since several children had died on the way to hospitals. The bus was 26 years old.[40]

In 1977, four handicapped students were killed when a freight train struck the back of a minibus in which they were riding. There was a heavy fog in the area, which greatly reduced visibility.[41] In 1987, five other handicapped children would die when a tractor-trailer hit their school bus broadside. The driver also was killed in the accident, which took place in Bronson, Florida.[42]

In Roby, Texas, in December 1978, a tractor-trailer rammed into a school bus at a rural intersection. Riding on the bus were the boys' and girls' junior high school basketball teams being driven to a tournament in Hermleigh, Texas. Three girls and one boy were killed in the collision. The school's principal, the bus driver, and the driver of the truck were injured, as were 19 other persons. The truck was described as going at full speed, hitting the bus so hard that the bus was "nearly disintegrated, upside down and ripped off its chassis." In the windy twenty-degree weather, the students lay on the ground as others stood near them, placing blankets over them. One observer said, "They had to be in shock. There was no crying at all. Some of them looked in real bad shape."[43]

There have been accidents in which two school buses were involved. In May 1980, a school bus swerved to avoid another school bus that was unloading children, and as it did so, it tipped over. The driver may have been distracted by a disturbance on the bus. The accident injured 27 students.[44]

In a plunge reminiscent of the terrible Prestonsburg, Kentucky, crash, a bus in Dorchester, South Carolina, in October 1980, was hit from behind by another vehicle and plunged down an embankment. One 17-year-old student was pinned in the wreck for 20 minutes before he could be pried loose. Twenty-nine students were taken to hospitals with injuries.[45]

A boy was killed when a grocery truck slammed into his school bus in Clarksdale, Mississippi, in July 1982. The boy was thrown out of the bus and up under the truck. Another 19 were injured.[46] In another accident that same year, one student was killed and 25 others injured in Galveston, Texas, as the bus returned from a football game. The bus crashed through a railing and toppled to the northbound lanes. The bus was forced off the road by a car that fell off the bridge and into water.[47]

In 1985, there was a head-on collision in North Carolina between a produce truck and a school bus that killed six persons, including five students and the bus driver.[48] Another accident in 1985—this one in St. Louis—killed an 18-year-old girl and injured 17 other students.[49]

Sometimes a school bus driver becomes a hero when he or she saves the children on the bus. This was the case with a driver whose bus stalled on a railroad crossing in Perry, Michigan, in 1986. She told the 47 passengers to get off the bus, and all of them escaped before the train hit.[50]

Two of the nation's worst school bus accidents happened in Kentucky in 1988 and in Texas in 1989. In Carrollton, Kentucky, 67 young people were riding an 11-year-old school bus on an interstate highway when a pickup truck headed the wrong way on the highway hit them head on. Of the 27 people who were killed, 19 female and eight male victims died of smoke inhalation. Nine others were in critical condition, and dozens more were treated for smoke inhalation, burns, and broken bones at four hospitals in northern Kentucky. The bus was returning from a day's outing at King's Island in Cincinnati when the crash occurred about 11:00 P.M. on Interstate 71. The bus driver was killed, and the driver of the pickup truck was in critical condition.[51]

The Texas bus accident was very much like an earlier Kentucky accident, mentioned above, in which a school bus plunged into the Big Sandy River in 1959. A fully loaded school bus was hit by a soft drink truck and plunged forty feet into an unbarricaded gravel pit, flipped upside down, and then sank. Aboard were 80 children. Children trapped in the bus struggled to get out through open windows and the bus door. At least 21 children were killed and dozens were injured.[52] These two accidents, together with the Yuba City, California, accident and the 1959 Kentucky crash, were among the nation's worst.

HAZARDS OF THE 1980s

An increasing danger to schools became apparent in the 1980s, and this was the threat posed by toxic chemicals and dangerous fumes. Several incidents in California in 1986 illustrate that new state laws sometimes bring on unexpected problems, the first of which was a catch-22 that the schools could not avoid. When the state passed two new hazardous waste laws, the Los Angeles County School District thought that it had a satisfactory way to deal with toxic wastes. The plan was to send a team to collect all old and hazardous chemicals from the schools and take them to the Van Nuys Science Materials Center from which a hazardous waste company would pick them up and haul them away. But then someone called the firemen, who, after inspecting the building and the materials, closed the building because it posed a health and safety hazard.

Similar dilemmas awaited other schools around the state of California and probably in many other schools across the country. Some schools said that they were finding it impossible to comply with all of the state laws and regulations. In Los Angeles, two state laws and a municipal ordinance had jurisdiction over scores of colleges and schools.[53]

In September 1986, parents of children at an elementary school in South Gate near Long Beach expressed their concern about a next-door company that produced steel drums for oil. Parents and school employees complained of pungent smells coming from that and other nearby companies. A few months earlier there had been a chlorine spill at another nearby plant. School staff and parents said that children in the school had complained about similar symptoms for several years: headaches, stomachaches, sore throats, swollen eyes, chest pains, and allergies.

One parent said that very strong strange odors were always in the school. When the chlorine spilled, 71 people, including 27 children, were taken to hospitals. The school principal, who was one of those taken to the hospital, said that the spill had brought about a unified community stand about relocating the school.[54]

In November 1987, fumes from a chemical that was being used to open a drain in a high school in San Diego caused dizziness and nausea and led to the evacuation of 1,800 students in the school. The fumes overcame a custodial worker using a commercial drain cleaner to unclog a sewer pipe under the snack bar in the cafeteria. In the cafeteria, located on the top floor of the school building over a downstairs snack bar, two food preparation classes and cafeteria employees were at work. Fire officials described the cleaner as containing sulfuric acid.[55]

Another environmental problem was found in 1987 in Long Island, where an elementary school had unacceptable levels of asbestos and polychlorinated biphenyls, or PCBs. Floor tile debris and dust samples inside a fire-damaged wing of the school contained elevated asbestos levels. As a consequence of this finding, schools across Long Island were examined for asbestos. The schools were trying to comply with the terms of the Asbestos Hazard Emergency Response Act of 1986 regarding inspection of schools with materials containing asbestos.[56]

SHADES OF LOVE CANAL

Ever since the 1978 articles exposing the Love Canal fiasco and the 99th Street School located on the canal, Americans had been suspicious of places where schools were built.[57]

A report called "Poisoned Schools: Invisible Threats, Visible Actions" was released by environmental groups in 2001 in an effort to get states to issue guidelines on where schools can be built. Lois Gibbs, who helped uncover the Love Canal dumpsite, was one of the leaders of the effort. Gibbs said that many schools across the country were built on contaminated ground, and she and other environmentalists are trying to get states to develop policies prohibiting building new schools on former dump sites. School architect Michael Hall says that every school built in the past seven years has had a type of environmental challenge, including underground storage tanks, toxic dumps, abandoned landfills and wetlands, or power lines or electromagnetic fields.[58]

The Long Beach section of *The Los Angeles Times* carried a story in 1988 that said an oil field equipment company had leaked a poisonous solvent into the ground water and that there was also a large pool of gasoline from another location, and the two substances had flowed under an elementary school next to the company. The article then detailed other cases where the state had uncovered dangerous toxic spills in the ground water.[59]

In 1988, a parochial school in Bay Park had to be evacuated because chemicals used to make illegal drugs had spilled onto the school's playground. Illegal drug makers dumped three five-gallon drums onto the school property on a Sunday.[60] No doubt there have been many other instances around the country where schoolchildren were placed in harm's way by the presence of contaminating chemical substances.

EARTHQUAKES, TORNADOS, SNOWSTORMS

At about the same time in 1987, on the other side of the country, students in Washington, D.C., were stranded in school classrooms because of a freak snowstorm. In one of the suburban Washington counties, workers were bringing blankets and food about 10:00 P.M. Seven of the Prince George's school buses were stranded in snow for five hours that day. The elementary school students were freed by a snowplow about 6:15 P.M. In an elementary school in Fairfax County, Virginia, 900 students were stranded until 8:30 P.M.[61]

The Field Act in California was passed to ensure that schools are built to withstand earthquakes. The *St. Louis Post-Dispatch* carried a story in 1989 that stated that schools in Missouri and Illinois had no such law and that students there were in great peril, as thousands of pupils in schools would be in great jeopardy if an earthquake should strike and it was estimated that a fourth of all casualties in such an event would be pupils. The New Madrid Fault in Missouri is about 40 miles wide and 120 miles long. Besides Missouri, it touches Illinois, Arkansas, and Tennessee. Because of community awareness brought about by this kind of publicity, planning efforts in earthquake-prone areas have been redoubled.[62]

Many schools have survived potentially catastrophic events. Two instances will suffice to illustrate these near-disasters. In 1990, a tornado ripped through Auburn, Alabama, damaging an elementary school and a middle school after the children were in classrooms. The tornado dropped a tree in the media center shortly after the room was evacuated. While both schools sustained damage, no one was hurt. The city board of education later commended city employees (firemen) for helping to evacuate the children. Most children reached home after the storm had passed later in the morning.[63] In South Carolina in 1992, flash flooding nearly took the lives of six children as a school bus barely avoided floodwater. Up to nine and one-half inches of rain fell on the town of Allendale, washing out many roads, bridges, and houses, and killing three people.[64]

NOTES

1. "Railroad-Bus Collisions: Williamsport, Maryland," 2000. http://www.stnonline.com/stn/schoolbussafety/railroadcrossings/rr_crash.html.

2. Ibid.

3. Since there are about 8,000 school bus accidents in the United States each year, this book uses selected examples.

4. "Memories Still Poignant of 1955 Train, Bus Wreck," *Times and Free Press,* April 2, 2000. http://www.timesfreepress.com/2000/APR/02APR00/NEWSOLD09.html, and "Railroad-School Bus Collisions," http://www.stnonline.com/stn/schoolbussafety/railroadcrossings/rr_crash.html.

5. Ibid.

6. "Cause of the '58 Bus Disaster Still A Mystery," *Lexington Herald-Leader,* February 28, 1988. http://www.alltel.net/-davefowler/pages/bwreck/html.

7. "Railroad-School Bus Collisions" and "20 Children Killed As School Bus Slammed by Train," http://www.greeleytrib.com/history/stories/schoolbus.html.

8. "Railroad-School Bus Collisions."

9. "2 Boys Stop Bus After Driver Dies," *New York Times,* December 22, 1972, pg. 64.

10. "Policeman's Shot Kills Crazed Man Who Invades 46th St. Girls' School," *New York Times,* June 5, 1951, pg. 1. See "Shooting of Crazed Man Criticized," *New York Times,* June 11, 1951, pg. 14.

11. "50 Teen-Agers Injured As Bleachers Collapse," *New York Times,* April 25, 1952, pg. 16.

12. "Girl Killed in School," *New York Times,* January 9, 1953, pg. 22.

13. "Boy's Death in Gym Under Study," *New York Times,* April 2, 1973, pg. 75.

14. "School Blast, Fire Trap Boy Vandals," *New York Times,* September 21, 1953, pg. 26.

15. "Mayor Sees Rat Chased At School," *New York Times,* May 27, 1961, pgs. 1, 48.

16. "2 Capital Schools Shock Legislators," *New York Times,* March 13, 1963, pg. 9.

17. "241 in School Hit by Food Poisoning," *New York Times,* May 25, 1967, pg. 30.

18. "Demolition Ammonia Fumes Send 80 Newark Pupils to Hospitals," *New York Times,* June 6, 1978, pg. New Jersey, 1.

19. "Fumes Make 32 Ill at School," *Chicago Tribune,* March 29, 1979, pg. 1–3–2.

20. "Fumes Fell 100 Pupils in Ohio," *Chicago Tribune,* February 28, 1979, pg. 2–4–1.

21. Shop and playground dangers are so common that we have provided only a few examples. However, schools have become much more aware of these dangers in recent years.

22. "4 Stand and Watch Girl Caught in Ride on School Grounds," *New York Times,* July 30, 1972, pg. 44.

23. "Welding Machine Kills Student," *New York Times,* March 26, 1975, pg. 88.

24. "Crime 'Brokerages' Reported in Some High Schools of City," *New York Times,* February 26, 1974, pg. 41.

25. "Health and Safety Survey Finds Violations in 90% of the Schools," *New York Times,* December 3, 1974, pg. 25.

26. "School Closes to Attack Its Lice Problem," *Washington Post,* June 5, 1979, pg. C1.

27. "2 Mentally Retarded Boys Die in Cold," *Chicago Tribune,* January 5, 1979, pg. 1–1–3.

28. "Teacher Dies in Fall From Ledge," *New York Times,* January 3, 1974, pg. 39.

29. "Lunchtime Break Saves Pupils," *New York Times,* September 30, 1976, pg. 44.

30. "Our Fettered Principals," *New York Times,* January 28, 1976, pg. 32.

31. "Asbestos Search in Tulsa," *New York Times,* January 8, 1977, pg. 9.

32. "16 Hurt in Fire in Class," *New York Times,* January 8, 1977, pg. 22.

33. "'Everybody Went Wild'—Panic in Miami School," *Chicago Tribune,* October 27, 1979, pg. 1–6–2.

34. "The Ten Worst Tornado Related Disasters in Schools," http://www.tornadoproject.com/toptens/topten2.html.

35. "Tornado Kills 2 and Injures 96 in Florida," *New York Times,* May 5, 1978, pg. 12.

36. "Children Counseled on Fear of Tornado," *New York Times,* June 11, 1978, pg. 43.

37. "7 Deaths Linked to Driver," *New York Times,* February 9, 1973, pg. 71. This accident is not included in "Railroad-School Bus Collisions" cited above.

38. "Drivers Die as School Bus and Truck Collide Head On," *New York Times,* May 16, 1973, pg. 26.

39. "Collision Kills 1, Injures 20," *New York Times,* May 31, 1973, pg. 18.

40. "28 in School Choir Killed in Bus Crash in California," *New York Times,* May 22, 1976, pgs. 1, 26.

41. "Four Handicapped Students Killed As Freight Train Strikes Minibus," *New York Times,* February 11, 1977, pg. 11. This incident is not included in the "Railroad-School Bus Collisions" accounts.

42. "Six Die as Truck Hits Bus of Handicapped Students," *Los Angeles Times,* August 29, 1987, part 1, pg. 18.

43. "4 Teen-Agers Killed And 22 Hurt in Texas In a School Bus Crash," *New York Times,* December 9, 1978, pg. 8.

44. "School Bus Overturns, Injuring 27 in Dallas," *St. Louis Post-Dispatch,* May 25, 1980, pg. 11A.

45. "School Bus Plunge Injures 30," *New York Times,* October 24, 1980, pg. B5.

46. "Bus-Truck Crash Kills Youth," *New York Times,* July 23, 1982, pg. A24.

47. "Bus Rider Killed, 25 Hurt," *New York Times,* October 10, 1982, section 1, pg. 24.

48. "Carolina Crash Kills Six," *Los Angeles Times,* June 1, 1985, part 1, pg. 10.

49. "Student Killed, 17 Hurt in St. Louis Bus Crash," *New York Times,* November 12, 1985, pg. A16.

50. "Driver Saves Children as Train Hits Bus," *New York Times,* February 7, 1986, pg. D16.

51. "Fiery Crash Kills 27 in Kentucky as Truck and Youths' Bus Collide," *New York Times,* May 16, 1988, pg. A1.

52. "19 Die as School Bus, Hit by Truck, Sinks in Watery Pit," *Los Angeles Times,* September 22, 1989, part 1, pg. 1.

53. "School Effort to Obey Laws on Chemicals Goes Awry," *Los Angeles Times,* June 9, 1986, part 2, pg. 6.

54. "Parents Fear Foul Fumes at School," *Los Angeles Times,* September 7, 1986, part 9, pg. 1.

55. "School Back to Normal After Mishap," *San Diego Union-Tribune,* November 12, 1987, B-11.

56. "School Allays Asbestos Fear," *New York Times,* August 30, 1987, section 11, pg. 12.

57. On August 7, 1978, President Jimmy Carter declared a federal emergency at Love Canal, a former chemical landfill that became a 15-acre neighborhood of the city of Niagara Falls, New York. Beneath the 99th Street School, near the middle of the settlement, and the rest of the neighborhood were contaminated chemicals. See "Background on the Love Canal," http://ublib.buffalo.edu/libraries/projects/lovecanal/background lovecanal.html.

58. "More Schools Sit on Contamination," *USA Today,* March 19, 2001. http://detnews.com/2001/schools/0103/21/a04-201246.html.

59. "Trouble Spreads Underground from Leaking Tanks," *The Los Angeles Times,* August 28, 1988, part 9, pg. 1.

60. "450 Back in School; Spill Cleaned Up," *The San Diego Union-Tribune,* March 29, 1988, pg. B1.

61. "Students Stranded by Storm, Confusion," *Washington Post,* November 12, 1987, pg. C1.

62. "Schools: In Great Peril," *St. Louis Post-Dispatch,* September 19, 1989, pg. 1A.

63. "Local Officials Assess Storm Damage," *Opelika-Auburn News,* February 23, 1990, pgs. 1, 10.

64. "Flash Floods in South Carolina, Georgia Cause Washouts, Kill 3," *Los Angeles Times,* October 10, 1992, pg. A14.

Chapter 6

Civil Rights, Uncivil Schools (1954–1969)

THE CIVIL RIGHTS MOVEMENT

Very few events in American history have had such a profound, sustained effect upon the schools as did the Civil Rights Movement and the other rights movements that accompanied or followed it. As good and necessary as these egalitarian imperatives were for American democracy, there can be little doubt that their sweeping movements adversely affected the safety and well-being of nearly every public and private school in the United States for a period that was neither brief nor painless—it was, and some would argue still is, a period of adjustment that required every bit of the commitment and perseverance educational leaders could muster and sustain.[1]

Georgia's segregationist governor Herman Talmadge warned or threatened in 1954 that ending segregation in schools in the South would "create chaos not seen since Reconstruction days." Ironically, his words turned out to be an accurate prediction. His statement followed the apocalyptic prediction or admonition by Governor James F. Byrnes of South Carolina that an end to school segregation "would mark the beginning of the end of civilization in the South as we have known it." This also had a ring of ironic truth. Talmadge then warned that he would turn the state's schools over to private individuals if the Supreme Court outlawed school segregation.[2]

Two months later, on May 17, 1954, the United States Supreme Court ruled in *Brown v. Board of Education of Topeka* that racially segregated public schools were unconstitutional. The landmark Brown decision overturned the legal policies established by the *Plessy v. Ferguson* decision, coming about after a series of court decisions on specific educational challenges. However, there were few means at the time to implement these court decisions.[3]

The impact of the Brown decision on all of America would be far-reaching, affecting every aspect of life. This would, of course, include the safety of schools, as the disruptions following the decision would have long-term and sometimes devastating results for many schools, sometimes even getting in the way of racial harmony and creating violence in the years to come.

The shock of the Supreme Court's decision gradually helped cause the Civil Rights Movement, promoted a new militancy among disadvantaged peoples about schools, and inaugurated a whole new era in which diverse groups of Americans would seek equality under the law, including the right to better schools. While it would be a decade later before the most drastic disruptions would occur in the schools, there were immediate repercussions, especially in the South.

The Brown decision prompted many confrontations to come in the future between the federal government and the states and between white and black citizens—sometimes but not always in the South. In some places, notably Baltimore, Washington, Kansas, and Arizona, there were rapid steps taken toward desegregation of the schools, followed sometimes rapidly by demonstrations that opposed it. Concomitant violence often placed school safety in jeopardy.

THE 1950s

On October 1, 1954, an angry crowd of 800 white adults and students attacked four black pupils in front of a south Baltimore high school. Violence flared in protest against desegregation ordered by the local school board. The school board planned to keep the schools open despite the violence at the school and picketing at five other schools.[4]

In 1954 and succeeding years, hundreds of school systems abandoned racially segregated schools. The reaction many times was similar to that in Baltimore. Clinton, Tennessee, for instance, had a typical struggle in ensuing years: the school board and other white citizens faced down a mob in 1956; the high school was bombed in 1958. In Prince Edward County, Virginia, the public schools were closed down for five years, from 1959 to 1964, leaving 1,700 black children without schooling during that period.[5]

What happened in Sturgis, Kentucky, in September 1956, could be seen as a foreshadowing of a more famous event to take place in Little Rock, Arkansas, in the following year. On the eighth of September, black students did not go to Sturgis High School—formerly an all-white school—as planned, because their parents apparently received threats that they would lose their jobs. Even though Kentucky national guardsmen with bayoneted rifles, sidearms, and three tanks were ready to escort the nine students, fear of violence and fear of fathers' job loss kept the students at home. In Sturgis, a small town 170 miles west of Louisville, a crowd of about 200 gathered but quieted down when word spread that the nine students were not coming. Less than half of the student body of 300 attended school that day.[6]

In New York in the same year, black citizens demanded the desegregation of public schools. "Feeder schools, busing, and pairing were just a few of the many schemes that were attempted in an effort to integrate Public Education. But housing segregation and matters of class and race prejudice constantly blocked efforts to desegregate public education." Yet civil rights leaders persisted in their efforts to integrate the schools all during the "Decade of Turmoil," as one writer called it.[7]

Little Rock, Arkansas, in 1957, was the site of a confrontation known around the world. On September 2, 1957, Governor Orval Faubus ordered the National Guard to surround Central High to prevent nine black students from enrolling. The Guard did this on September 4th. After a federal judge intervened, the nine students entered the school on September 23rd but were removed because the city police were unable to control a large mob of whites outside the school. President Eisenhower federalized the National Guard and sent the 101st Airborne Division of the U.S. Army to assure that the integration of Central High School would proceed.

At the end of the first year, with Dr. Martin Luther King present, Ernest Green, one of the nine black students, became the first African-American to graduate from Central High School. This, however, was not the end of Governor Faubus' resistance to integration, and only after two years of strife and a long period in which the public schools were closed, did high schools in Little Rock open in the fall of 1959.[8]

By 1957, there had been at least seven bombings of public schools and threats of bombings in dozens of others. Two black schools, three schools with racially mixed classes, and two all-white schools were hit by actual explosions, with damage ranging from shattered windows in a Champaign, Illinois, grade school to virtually complete destruction of a new junior-senior high school in Osage, West Virginia.

The first big bombing was at the Hattie Cotton School in Nashville. Three carefully timed explosions went off between 5:17 and 5:31 A.M. on Tuesday, September 10, 1957. The explosions were regarded by police as the work of an expert, which could not be said of the next three explosions.

The second bombing took place at a black grade school[9] in Chattanooga in January 1958. The school was the largest black school in Hamilton County and one of the largest in the state. The third was in Charlotte, North Carolina, where bomb planners got caught. An explosion at a black high school in Jacksonville, Florida, did minor damage.

A blast in a Clinton, Tennessee, school was timed for Sunday morning when no children would be in class. The explosion wrecked 16 of the 22 classrooms in the high school. That explosion wrecked the entire building and was timed to go off six hours before school opened. Two bombs hit schools in Illinois during this time. They were at Champaign on October 21, 1958, and Chicago on November 12th. Both bombs were pipes filled with black powder, and they did but minor damage.[10]

In September 1959, three bomb explosions destroyed a city-owned station wagon, a construction company partially owned by the mayor, and the office of the Little Rock school board. A guard was called for all of the city's schools in the aftermath of the bombings as all police were called out. Two weeks before that, two tear gas bombs had been thrown into the board of education building. The three bomb explosions came within 38 minutes of each other.[11]

THE 1960s

In July 1960, three white men in Little Rock intended to bomb both a public school facility and a black college dormitory. F.B.I. agents caught two of the three just as they touched a lighted match to 40 sticks of dynamite under the college building. Two hours later the public school warehouse blew up and federal agents arrested the third man. The college building was in the vicinity of Central High School, which had operated peacefully in the previous year. This was the third bombing in Little Rock in less than a year.[12]

But clashes and confrontations were by no means restricted to the South. In New Rochelle, New York, in September 1960, when 23 blacks began a sit-down strike in front of an all-white facility because the children had been refused enrollment, the police promptly evicted the group. The parents of the children, who threatened to take their case to the courts, were accused of violating the State Compulsory Education Law. The local school board had a rule that required that all children attend school in their own neighborhoods.[13]

The various confrontations continued unceasingly throughout parts of the country. In Alabama, Governor George Wallace delayed integration of the Tuskegee schools by sealing off the high school and declaring that he made the move to "preserve the peace." Wallace took the same measure in Huntsville and was expected to do the same in Birmingham and Mobile. Wallace confronted the Kennedy administration in an attempt to force President Kennedy to use federal troops. But Wallace did not "stand in the schoolhouse door" as he did in June when he blocked entry to the University of Alabama.[14] Wallace was later placed under federal court injunctions.

Racial issues such as the integration of suburban schools in the North continued to occupy school officials. Local pressures and state education officials, together with federal Office of Education personnel, ordered local schools to decrease "de facto" segregation. With schools shut down all over the country in protest—either for or against integration—one of the largest boycotts took place in New York City, where 275,638 pupils stayed home from school.[15]

While bombings and bomb scares continued through the 1960s, racial violence closed other schools. In Enterprise, Mississippi, in 1965, a white man brandishing a shotgun went to registration at an integrated high school and announced he would "clean out" the black people. An F.B.I. agent arrested him.[16] At about the same time, a savage bomb exploded in a black school in rural North Carolina. The blast went off before school opened and demolished one classroom. No one was injured.[17] In Cleveland, the huge high school named for the school that had once burned, Collinwood High, was closed for a day in March 1965 when racial violence broke out. Fights developed in the racially mixed neighborhood in Cleveland before classes started for the day.[18] After a one-day shutdown, Collinwood High School reopened for classes, and 36 persons were arrested. Only 955 of Collinwood's 3,320 students had reported for classes.[19]

Police remained busy all during this era in response to "racial unrest"—boycotts, and demonstrations mostly. For instance, in Jonesboro, Louisiana, police barricaded the black area of town because the high school was being boycotted and better facilities demanded.[20] In Crawfordville, Georgia, ten black persons were dragged from the highway when they tried to stop buses carrying white students to a segregated school. Later they tried again and some were jailed.[21] In Harlem, the principal of a junior high school complained that gangs of black boys roamed the halls shouting racial epithets, interrupting classes, and beating students.[22]

Whites instigated at least as many trouble spots in the schools. In Grenada, Mississippi, a gang of angry whites carrying ax handles surrounded the two public schools that were integrated and attacked black persons who attempted to leave after classes. One 12-year-old black boy was made to run a gauntlet of whites for a full block, which he left limping. One boy was beaten, cursed, thrown to the ground; a local policeman refused to help him. The crowd also turned on newsmen and photographers and began beating them. State highway patrolmen entered the town in force to break up the mob.[23]

Many futile gestures were less demonstrations of hatred or meanness than they were expressions of remorse about a changing way of life. For instance, when white mothers in Malverine, Long Island, protested the integration of their neighborhood school in February 1966, it seemed that they objected more passionately to the end of the neighborhood schools system than they did to integration. As they expressed friendship toward the black community, they tried to block the transfer of school equipment from another school. They climbed on a furniture van to denounce the integration order of State Education Commissioner James E. Allen, Jr. Police then arrested nine of the women. The new integration plan abandoned the neighborhood school system by implementing a plan whereby attendance at three schools would be based on grade level. The women were charged with disorderly conduct.[24]

In another Long Island town, a white school board member suggested that African-American children who were being brought from the city to live in Amityville were becoming a burden on his school system. While black leaders and school officials criticized the man's remarks, they did concede that an influx of children from the city had increased the school rolls of the community.[25]

The changing American social order was often acknowledged by black leaders and resisted by white leaders. Robert C. Weaver, first black cabinet member in the United States, said in Philadelphia, "Many nonwhites, who have been repeatedly denied meaningful participation in the dominant society now look to a substitute social order which will afford them a significant role and provide a sense of full participation." This point of view accepting more radical blacks represented a break from the traditional rejection of radicalism.[26] In contrast, when black demonstrators who ripped down the American flag demonstrated black radicalism in Cordele, Georgia, the state's governor denounced the incident. A few days later, 71 black persons were arrested for marching against segregation and the state of school facilities. Most of the 71 were school children, and their march followed a day of demonstrations by the Ku Klux Klan.[27]

THE LATE 1960s

Race relations grew more strident in the last three years of the 1960s, with an increasing amount of violence and disorder affecting the schools. Early in 1967 at the annual meeting of the N.A.A.C.P., where traditionalists were returned to the board over more radical insurgents, Roy Wilkins, the executive director, said the following about rioting:

> "Young Negroes will riot," he said, "because the world of education has failed to reach and teach the language of democracy, opportunity, and dignity. We cannot talk to these people. The language of the white community and of white municipal officials is not their language. Bluntly stated," Mr. Wilkins concluded, "the alternative to the dilly-dallying of the day is riots."

Wilkens decried the failure of Congress to pass a Civil Rights Bill in 1966.[28]

It certainly appeared that Wilkens was correct about riots, because rioting characterized every section of the country for the remainder of 1967 and on into later years. In a Houston riot in May, a policeman was killed and two other policemen and a student were wounded. The police arrested 488 college students and charged five of them with inciting a riot, a felony that carries a penalty of up to 40 years.[29] In just the last three months of the year, there were other riots:

- Hundreds of students in a junior high school in Detroit went on a rampage on October 9th, causing such destruction that the school had to close at noon.[30]

- On October 11th, racial violence broke out at Hughes High in Cincinnati, and blacks in the predominantly black school beat 14 whites.[31]

- October 12th, nine students were hurt in Newark as clashes closed the high school. This was the second day of fighting at Barringer High, the largest in the city.[32]

- On October 20th, a disturbance at a high school in Los Angeles turned into street clashes. Four persons were injured and 31 were arrested.[33] Trouble began again the next day at Maual High School, and 15 more persons were arrested.[34]

- October 24th, racial disturbances broke out at two suburban high schools in Chicago.[35]

- Sixty students were suspended from Joliet Township West High on November 2nd when a fistfight broke out in the school cafeteria.[36]

- In Philadelphia on November 18th, a demonstration by 3,500 pupils from the city's 10 predominantly black high schools became a riot in which the demonstrators threw rocks, upset barricades, ran on the tops of automobiles, assaulted passersby and battled about 400 policemen.[37]

- On November 21st, Chicago jailed 80 after racial fights broke out in a high school and spread through the entire Near North Side.[38]

- On December 13th, a school racial clash in Trenton, New Jersey, turned into bands of youths who harassed the entire city after the high school was closed because of fights.[39]

- On December 16th, a racial incident in New Haven disrupted into an outburst in which bands of youths roamed the high school causing destruction and forcing the closing of the school.[40]

These were a few of the racial riots of 1967.

TWO VIOLENT YEARS

If the late 1960s could be called the age of militant extremism from both whites and blacks, the two years 1968 and 1969 stand as two of the most violent in the history of the American school—and the American community, for that matter—because 1968 was the year in which Martin Luther King was assassinated. And perhaps it was at this time that black radicals really came into their own and openly into the public eye, even using the public school as a forum, having had the violence of the early sixties as a backdrop for their renewed militancy. The incendiary speech of a radical leader in a public school in Harlem in early 1968, Herman B. Ferguson, is a good example: Ferguson, who had been suspended as assistant principal at a Queens public school after being accused of conspiring to murder moderate black leaders, said to 600 people at a memorial program for Malcolm X that they should obtain weapons for self-defense against whites and practice using them so that they would be ready when "hunting season" began. Ferguson served as a paid advisor to the governing board of Intermediate School 201 in East Harlem.

Ferguson said that the United States was stockpiling weapons in preparation for urban riots just as it had prepared for war against "our brothers the North Vietnamese and the Vietcong."

Other speakers on the program denounced "the white man and his bitch," described the United States as "the fourth Reich," and urged black youth not to serve in the armed forces against "their colored brothers" in Vietnam. The audience for the program was made up of community members, celebrity speakers, and some school-age youth—although the organizers of the program had agreed not to admit school children as a prerequisite to using a public school for the program.[41]

It was not long before fights between black and white youths began again with a renewed fervor at many high schools, but it was the King assassination that set off the most explosive violence across the country. The date was April 4, 1968.

A good deal of in-school fighting took place in two racial clashes within two months in New Haven. Around 20 policemen were sent to Hill House High School to restore order. Sixty-eight percent of the 1,761 students in the school were black.[42] Fistfights between black and white students closed the high school in Trenton during the same month. Like the New Haven school, this was the second outbreak in as many months in Trenton. When the fighting got out of hand in the cafeteria, officials closed the school for the day.[43]

A school in Hartsdale, New York, that had been cited as a model of quality-integrated education became the scene of a vicious fight between white and black students in March. Police arrested four white students who were using chains. Two white students were sent to the hospital. Fighting began in the corridors of the high school shortly after students began arriving at 8:00 A.M. School officials had to close the sprawling campus grounds—on which both the junior and senior high schools sit—for everyone except students and their parents. The superintendent of schools said that whites had instigated the fighting by painting epithets on the school walls.[44]

On the same day, black students at White Plains High School boycotted classes to protest the lack of studies in black history. Once again, epithets scrawled on school walls provided the impetus for the dispute.[45] Not far away in Bridgeport, fighting broke out at a school dance. Three policemen were injured. They had to fire shots in the air to stop the fighting among the contestants.[46]

One of the most dangerous aspects of the racial fighting involved arson and firebombing. In Cincinnati, four fires were started at public schools, bringing the number of arson-caused blazes to 14 in three days. In Elizabeth, New Jersey, firebombs were thrown at a junior high school, setting off fires. The mayor called the fire bombings "a wanton, criminal act." It was about 5:45 A.M. when two bombs were thrown into two different parts of the school.[47]

MARTIN LUTHER KING, JR. MURDERED

When Martin Luther King, Jr. was murdered in Memphis on April 4th, violent outbreaks took place all over the country. Rioting, looting, and violence characterized most of the big cities in the United States for the next few nights. Washington, D.C., Nashville, Raleigh, and New York were among the cities where the disorders were particularly out of hand on the first night. The next night Chicago, Detroit, and Boston had perhaps the worst rioting.[48]

On April 8th, most of the 1,300 students in Rahway High School in New Jersey walked out of an assembly and began rampaging through the halls for 30 minutes or so. The students, 80 percent of whom were white, were enraged that the school had not closed to honor Dr. Martin Luther King, Jr.[49]

In May 1968, racial confrontations continued. On May 10th, white youths left an assembly meeting and marched outside the school in Newark, New Jersey, shouting white power slogans and demanding the reinstatement of five white students who had been suspended for fighting.

Only about 20 percent of the student population was black. The origin of the trouble seemed to have been when a black girl danced with a white boy the previous Friday night at a school dance. A free-for-all started by white and black girls on the playground on Monday involved nearly the whole school. The mayor of Newark tried to resolve the dispute.[50]

But Mayor Addonizio was not alone—other cities in New Jersey had similar problems. The schools in Camden were equally full of racial troubles. Black students there demanded that a black person replace the principal; they also insisted that black history be included in the curriculum. The principal said that he intended to retire that year.[51]

In what seemed like a faddish thing, students in New Haven went on a rampage on May 24th in a junior high school, scuffling and breaking windows until the school was closed at 10:00 A.M. The students overturned furniture, broke windows, and then stood in the playground throwing stones at passing cars.[52]

As far away as Iowa, racial disturbances upset American high schools. In Waterloo, Iowa, sporadic shooting, fires, and clashes between police and students, which led to the closing of East High School, spread and left seven policemen injured and 13 youths arrested. Fires wiped out at least three blocks of business buildings and the high school. In Denver, violence characterized the Northeast Five Points area.

In Grand Rapids, Michigan, Grand Rapids Union High School was set to open again on Monday after racial brawling on Friday, September 15th. In Decatur, Illinois, a football game was cancelled after police had to break up a disturbance by blacks and whites. Fighting began there after another stabbed one youth in the stomach.[53]

In suburban Chicago, in September 1968, 15 students were injured and nine were suspended when fights between blacks and whites broke out in the hallways of Maywood's Proviso East High School. Another five students were arrested for throwing bottles and bricks at police cars.[54]

Often fighting between blacks and whites would take place at school sporting events. In Titusville, Florida, and in Orlando in September 1968, fighting injured at least 13 persons, including three policemen. The disruption began at the Titusville game after the band began playing "Dixie," the school's theme song. Black youths rushed the band members and began beating them. Five whites and five blacks were arrested. In Orlando, fighting started when a predominantly white school beat a predominantly black school in football. The disturbances took place 40 miles apart.[55]

In an incident in Brooklyn, two policemen were hurt when firebombs were thrown at a police communications truck parked at a junior high school. In York, Pennsylvania, the mayor imposed a curfew after classes at the junior high school were suspended when a demonstration threatened to become violent.[56]

It was not always black students who started demonstrations and boycotts. In Trenton in September 1968, 250 white students wearing "white power" and "Wallace for President" signs boycotted classes, pledging not to return until black students stopped "taking potshots" at them. The high school had about 3,500 students of which about half were black. The whites said that the blacks had attacked them shortly after about 50 black students walked out of classes in protest against alleged police brutality.[57]

As schools opened in Boston in September 1968, they were rife with contention. Violence that began in the schools spilled over into the streets and became major confrontations. The dispute started when black students wanted to wear African dress to Boston English High School and to organize black student unions. The principal approved the request, which was then turned down by the superintendent. Roving bands of black youths smashed store windows, stoned passing cars driven by whites, and tangled with reinforced police patrols.

Boston's school system, run by five elected board members called the School Committee, had been at odds with the black community for several years, at first over alleged *de facto* segregation and then over community control of the schools. One black lawyer said that one of the school system's defects was that it in no way reflected black culture. Mayor White announced the formation of a bi-racial committee under his leadership to study school reform in Boston.[58]

Toward the end of 1968, as confrontations and disputes continued in schools around the country—in such places as Syracuse, New York, and Chicago—Christopher Jencks, a well-known Harvard expert on education, suggested that since the public school system in New York was on the brink of collapse, black nationalists should create their own schools for black children. Jencks said that the origin of the crisis was simple: public schools had not been able to teach black children to read and write and this had left the rest of the curriculum unworkable. He pointed out that most liberals had abandoned integration as the solution to the problem because bringing black children into predominantly white schools had not improved their academic performance. The programs then preoccupying educators, called "compensatory" or "remedial," were not working either.[59]

In November 1968, a three-judge federal panel upheld the plan for "freedom of choice" that the Supreme Court had earlier rejected for southern schools. The Louisiana judges said that the freedom of choice plans were working fine in 31 northern parishes. The judges had been asked by the National Association for the Advancement of Colored People and the Justice Department to order geographic zoning in the 31 parishes. "Freedom of choice is a permissible means for a constitutionally required end—the complete abolition of segregation and its effects," the judges ruled.[60]

Some of the most violent disruptions of the year took place in New York[61] in December, where the state closed a junior high school after bands of youths disrupted at least 12 city schools. As the band went from school to school, they beat up teachers and threw missiles at policemen, injuring three of them. Twenty-two persons were arrested outside the schools. The youths also broke windows on the Franklin Avenue BMT shuttle in Brooklyn and ran out on the tracks, forcing the line out of service for some time.[62]

The fall of 1968 had seen a rising number of racial disorders and general student protests around the country, said *School Management,* a journal for educators. An educational psychologist said in another journal that "Massive nonviolent protests and more active demonstrations sparked by increasingly sophisticated, yet disillusioned and frustrated teen-agers take place now." Some educators thought that most of the rebellion was being instigated by mature activists like Eldridge Cleaver and Tom Hayden.[63]

1969

The next year after King's assassination, brawling, fighting, and firebombing continued in the nation's schools as black and white youngsters continued a high level of racial animosity. Early in 1969, six were hurt and four arrested as racial fighting forced officials to close Canarsie High School in New York. Black and white youths fought on every corridor of the school and in the cafeteria before police came into the school to restore order.[64]

By March, when it seemed that violence in the New York schools had reached crisis proportions, Mayor Lindsay named 13 persons to a committee to stem the violence and calm the schools. Meanwhile, explosive devices went off in several high schools. Speaking of the violence, Lindsay said, "It's a very real problem. I do have a sense of urgency about it." Lindsay promised that unruly students in the schools would be arrested.[65]

In Hamden, Connecticut, the high school suspended 40 students who were involved in a racial brawl. Police came into the school to help quell the violence and arrested seven students. In Miami in early February, boycotting white students at Miami Central High School went to the beaches after demanding the expulsion of 25 black students for beating up two white boys. Sixty percent of the students in the Miami school stayed away. The black students were suspended for 10 days. The black students had stormed the school cafeteria in the previous week, demanding more blacks in the school administration and a greater emphasis on black culture. In New Haven, black and white students fought after a Brotherhood Week assembly.[66]

It was a rather significant trend in urban schools to begin to hire their own guards. In March 1969, Newark, New Jersey, initiated a security force to patrol and be available in its eight high schools. The city had experienced much racial violence over the previous two years. Teachers said, "They don't want a police state, but they want some way of keeping students and teachers from getting hurt in tense situations when some students start flinging chairs in the lunchroom and sometimes start slashing with knives." The superintendent of schools said that he hoped the guards could help bring about a permanent peace in the schools.[67]

Another significant milestone was passed in April 1969 when Senator Robert C. Byrd introduced legislation that would make it a federal crime to disrupt a school receiving government aid. The senator called school administrators "weak-kneed and spineless" for "mollycoddling" student radicals. He said a law was needed to "counter a wave of anarchy and revolution engulfing high schools and colleges throughout the land." The bill would subject anyone who interfered with the normal operations of a school to a year in prison. Almost every school in the country receives some kind of federal aid. Liberals were expected to oppose the bill.[68]

Unrest in the schools was evident in every section of the country. A survey conducted by the National Association of Secondary School Principals said that three out of every five principals had some form of protests in their schools with unrest just as likely to occur in junior high schools as in high schools. "The high school principal is replacing the college president as the most embattled American," one official of the NEA said. Secretary of Health, Education, and Welfare Robert H. Finch told an audience that "we must be prepared for much greater disorders in the secondary field" than have been seen in the colleges.[69]

Racial disharmony is not jeopardizing the safety of most schools on a daily basis in the same way that it did in the 20-year period covered by this chapter. But in some places, racial disturbances are still prevalent and do affect the schools. Schools are obviously affected by the kind of neighborhood in which they are located. Huge high schools like Reading High School in Reading, Pennsylvania, where there is a very high percentage of recent immigrants and poor people, as well as a high crime rate, are obviously deeply affected by the locale and its economic condition. This is not to say that schools like Reading are not doing their job well—that is a particularly well-run school that, compared to the setting in which it is located, is very safe indeed.

NOTES

1. The literature on this subject is so extensive that the authors try to demonstrate the movement's impact by selecting relevant and representative instances in which schools presented a target or when students, parents, or supporters were placed in harm's way by actions and events that transpired during this time. The time period we have assigned the Civil Rights era is decidedly arbitrary; it could be argued that it continues until the present day.

2. "Talmadge Defends School Segregation," *New York Times*, March 27, 1954, pg. 19.

3. Karen Wolff, "From Plessey v. Ferguson to Brown v. Board of Education: The Supreme Court Rules on School Desegregation," http://www.yale.edu/ynhti/pubs/A5/wolff.html.

4. "Baltimore Crowd Attacks Four Pupils," *New York Times*, October 1, 1954, pg. 18.

5. Wolff, "From Plessey v. Ferguson."

6. "Sturgis Negroes Get Job Threats, Keep Pupils Home," *New York Times,* September 8, 1956, pg. 1.

7. Jitu K. Weusi, "Decade of Turmoil: An Analysis of Struggle Over Public School Governance in New City in the 1960s," http://www.nbufront.org/html/FRONTalView/ArticlesPapers/jitu2.html.

8. "Essential History," June 26, 2000. http://www.ualr.edu/-CHAP2.html.

9. The authors are occasionally using the term "Negro" and "Negro School" because they were used in journalism produced at the time. Otherwise, Afro-Americans will be called "black" or "Afro-American."

10. "Rise in School Bombings: What's Being Done About It," *U.S. News & World Report,* November 21, 1958, pg. 57.

11. "Little Rock Blast Rips School Office," *New York Times,* September 8, 1959, pgs. 1, 33.

12. "3 Whites Seized in Bomb Attempt," *New York Times,* July 13, 1960, pg. 28.

13. "New Rochelle Quashes School Sitdown by Negroes," *New York Times,* September 11, 1960, pg. 1.

14. "Alabama Police Prevent Opening of Tuskegee High," *New York Times,* September 3, 1960, pg. 1. "Wallace Closes 4 More Schools Due to Integrate," *New York Times,* September 7, 1963, pg. 1.

15. "Chester, PA., Sets School Reopening," *New York Times,* April 24, 1964, pg. 23, and "275,639 Pupils Stay Home in Integration Boycott; Total 175,000 Over Normal," *New York Times,* September 15, 1964, pg. 1.

16. "White Man Held in Threat," *New York Times,* August 20, 1965, pg. 33.

17. "Blast Rocks Negro School in Rural North Carolina," *New York Times,* October 26, 1965, pg. 22.

18. "Cleveland School Is Closed for a Day By Racial Violence," *New York Times,* March 19, 1965, pg. 19.

19. "36 Seized in Ohio in Racial Dispute," *New York Times,* March 20, 1965, pg. 11.

20. "Louisiana Police Block Negro Area," *New York Times,* March 12, 1965, pg. 19.

21. "Negroes Block White Bus," *New York Times,* October 2, 1965, pg. 3. "Georgia Negroes Jailed," *New York Times,* October 7, 1965, pg. 3.

22. "Harlem Principal Tells of Violence," *New York Times,* November 8, 1965, pg. 23.

23. "Grenada Negroes Beaten At School," *New York Times,* September 13, 1966, pgs. 1, 28.

24. "Malverne Women in School Protest," *New York Times,* February 22, 1966, pg. 25.

25. "L.I. Town Divided on Negro Influx," *New York Times,* March 16, 1966, pg. 47.

26. "Weaver Cites Rise of Negro Radical," *New York Times,* August 2, 1966, pg. 67.

27. "Georgia Governor Orders Protection of Flag at Cordele," *New York Times,* April 12, 1966, pg. 13. "71 Arrested in Georgia," *New York Times,* April 5, 1966, pg. 23.

28. "5 of 6 Insurgents Lost In N.A.A.C.P.," *New York Times,* January 4, 1967, pg. 21.

29. "Shot Kills Texas Policeman in Riot at a Negro College," *New York Times,* May 18, 1967, pgs. 1, 42.

30. "Hundreds of Students Riot at a Junior High in Detroit," *New York Times,* October 10, 1967, pg. 96.

31. "14 Whites Beaten by Negroes in Ohio," *New York Times,* October 12, 1967, pg. 48.

32. "9 Students Are Hurt in Newark As Clashes Close High School," October 12, 1967, pg. 39.

33. "31 Held in Outbreak in Coast Negro Area," *New York Times,* October 20, 1967, pg. 56.

34. "Negroes Dispersed in Los Angeles Area," *New York Times,* October 21, 1967, pg. 18.

35. "2 Schools in Chicago Area Guarded After Race Strife," *New York Times,* October 25, 1967, pg. 30.

36. "Illinois School Suspends 60," *New York Times,* November 3, 1967, pg. 21.

37. "Philadelphia Seizes 57 in Negro Rioting," *New York Times,* November 18, 1967, pg. 1.

38. "Chicago Jails 80 in Racial Fights," *New York Times,* November 22, 1967, pg. 60.

39. "Bands of Youths Harass Trenton," *New York Times,* December 14, 1967, pg. 39.

40. "Negro Students Disrupt School," *New York Times,* December 16, 1967, pg. 37.

41. "Negroes Urged at I.S.201 To Arm for 'Self-Defense,'" *New York Times,* February 22, 1968, pgs. 1, 28.

42. "2D Clash Disrupts New Haven School," *New York Times,* February 6, 1968, pg. 32.

43. "Racial Fights Close Trenton High School," *New York Times,* February 29, 1968, pg. 45.

44. "Racial Disorders Erupt at School," *New York Times,* March 26, 1968, pg. 48.

45. "Negroes Boycott Suburban School," *New York Times,* March 27, 1968, pg. 35.

46. "3 Policemen are Injured at Bridgeport School Dance," *New York Times,* March 25, 1968, pg. 37.

47. "More Cincinnati School Fires," *New York Times,* April 4, 1968,

pg. 43. "A Jersey School is Fire Bombed," *New York Times*, April 4, 1968, pg. 50.

48. "Martin Luther King is Slain in Memphis," *New York Times*, April 5, 1968, pg. 1. "Army Troops in Capital as Negroes Riot," *New York Times*, April 6, 1968, pg. 1.

49. "1,300 Students in Rahway in Outbreak Over Dr. King," *New York Times*, April 9, 1968, pg. 30.

50. "Addonizio Seeks End of Racial Fighting at School in Newark," *New York Times*, May 10, 1968, pg. 26.

51. "Classes Resume in Camden School," *New York Times*, May 11, 1968, pg. 2.

52. "New Haven School Closed in Rampage," *New York Times*, May 29, 1968, pg. 20.

53. "Guard Summoned in Iowa Outbreak," *New York Times*, September 15, 1968, pg. 64.

54. "15 Injured, 9 Suspended in High School Racial Strife," *New York Times*, September 19, 1968, pg. 41.

55. "Florida Students in Racial Melees," *New York Times*, September 21, 1968, pg. 14.

56. "Curfew Imposed in York, Pa.," *New York Times*, September 24, 1968, pg. 93. "Firebombs Hurled in Ocean Hill Area; Two Policemen Hurt," *New York Times*, September 20, 1968, pg. 37.

57. "250 White Pupils Picket in Trenton," *New York Times*, September 26, 1968, pg. 34.

58. "Troubled Boston Grapples With Negro Unrest in Schools," *New York Times*, September 29, 1968, pg. 45.

59. "Private Schools for Black Children," *New York Times*, November 3, 1968, pg. 30. "Negroes Invade Syracuse School," *New York Times*, October 29, 1968, pg. 39. "24% Out of School in Chicago Boycott," *New York Times*, October 22, 1968, pg. 35.

60. "U.S. Court Upholds Freedom of Choice in South's Schools," *New York Times*, November 15, 1968, pg. 29.

61. The authors want to acknowledge that part of New York's "school crisis" in 1968 involved the teacher strike and student strikes, which seem to be related to the teacher strikes.

62. "State Closes J.H.S.271; Student Bands Disrupt at Least 12 City Schools," *New York Times*, December 3, 1968, pg. 1. "Youths Clash with Police and Teachers Are Beaten," *New York Times*, December 3, 1968, pg. 1.

63. "Disorders Increase in High Schools," *New York Times*, December 16, 1968, pg. 43.

64. "Six Hurt and Four Arrested as Racial Battles Shut Canarsie High School," *New York Times*, February 26, 1969, pg. 27.

65. "Mayor Names 13 to Calm Schools," *New York Times,* March 13, 1969, pgs. 1, 41.

66. "School Suspends 40 After Racial Brawl," *New York Times,* January 29, 1969, pg. 20. "School Boycotted by Whites in Miami," *New York Times,* February 4, 1969, pg. 28. "A Brotherhood Assembly Ends in Fight at High School," *New York Times,* February 21, 1969, pg. 48.

67. "Newark Schools Get Guard Corps," *New York Times,* March 9, 1969, pg. 14.

68. "Byrd Bill Curbs School Disruptor," *New York Times,* April 23, 1969, pg. 23.

69. "High School Unrest Rises, Alarming U.S. Educators," *New York Times,* May 9, 1969, pgs. 1, 30.

Chapter 7

The Demise of Discipline (1959–1969)

THE CONTROL OF THE SCHOOLS

"What has happened to teaching?" is a question—sometimes expressed as "Why can't teachers teach?" or "Why are our schools so mediocre?"—posed by critics and supporters alike these days about the seeming differences in grade and high school teaching now as opposed to the profession's difficulties around forty years ago, when many of today's retiring teachers were starting out. In an informal forum of teacher-friends, the authors asked a group of retiring teachers to reflect on the differences between the two times. After a couple of hours of discussion, we requested that the participants rank the difficulties they face now, especially if these obstacles to good teaching were not present when they first started.

The group decided that the most troublesome problem for modern teachers was the same one that had always bothered teachers the most. Not surprisingly, it is the perennial concern in most polls: discipline.[1] One articulate teacher expressed it this way: "The loss of discipline in its broadest sense has greatly altered the teacher's ability to provide instruction of the highest sort. By discipline, we mean order. We are talking about the teacher's control of behavior, teachers' control of the classroom, the children and parents' lack of respect for the teacher, order in our daily schedule which is so often interfered with by numerous outside activities, the teacher's control of time so that sufficient time can be spent in the most crucial areas of learning, and so forth. In other words, the methods of control at our disposal 35 years ago have all dissipated—we can't spank, we can't belittle egos, we can't use any kind of fear (even the deprivation of entertainment), we can't require a dress code, etc. We are constantly battling to keep order in the school."

Echoes of the sounds of the battle over control of the school that began in the era of the 1960s and '70s still resonate through American education. That struggle, which had an impact upon the well being of virtually every school in the country, was related to the rights movements of the time, and although it exhibited some of the same contentious disputation and mean-spiritedness as they, it also had no clear winner. The struggle resulted in what we are calling "the demise of discipline," a phenomenon that threatens the traditional order and safety of virtually every school in America. The struggle coincided with a documented rise in crime on school campuses.

The competing parties in the conflict included students, parents, teachers, unions, administrators, politicians, and taxpayers, variously opposing each other on different occasions. Fostering, encouraging, and promoting the dispute was no one single force, but a myriad of social factors, including an increasingly militant spirit among teachers, more litigious and control-hungry parents, an avaricious mass media, a further politicizing of the schools by politicians for the purpose of spoils, the spirit of protest that characterized the age, a baby boom generation that had been raised with a minimum of parental discipline, the attempt to mainstream away every malady, the pressure on schools to "produce" a predetermined number of "educated" graduates—even during periods when the birth rate declined—and a new "entitlement" attitude that carried with it a spirit of indolence and a conviction that everyone is entitled to succeed, and the pressure on teachers to be popular, all in no particular order of priority.

At the same time, there was a pronounced inflation in the traditional meaning of grades, so that in the new scheme virtually everyone passed, some more gloriously than ever would have been imagined in erstwhile estimations of effort. The destruction of the integrity of grades closely paralleled and was directly related to the demise of discipline in the schools.

To find the cause of the decline in discipline and the related inflation of grades, one looks first at the teachers, who backed in earnest away from the erstwhile rigor of traditional school discipline. Discipline eroded and standards fell, not because teachers had lost the courage of their conviction or their passion for their profession, but because teachers, in their new isolation, found it impossible to stand against five very powerful societal forces that worked against them. These were the threats, particularly from students, which faced teachers—a new belligerence that often resulted in physical attacks upon their persons. Second and third new factors were the heightened aggressiveness of parents against teachers, a partial consequence of which, in turn, was the new militancy among teachers, which came about because teachers believed that taking the offensive was the only way to save the authority of their profession. At the same time, administrations and school boards that were under duress from politicians, government agencies, and voters were beginning to pressure teachers—and even to set themselves up against teachers—at the same time that they were piling on additional bureaucratic burdens. A fifth factor was a portion of the mass media that helped teach young people to rebel against the establishment while simultaneously seeking out teachers' weaknesses, exploiting every opportunity to portray the worst aspects of the teaching dilemma. All of these factors tended to obfuscate, confuse, and belittle the role of the teacher in the American school. The net effect of this was to make schools less safe, more vulnerable to new threats, and less able to govern themselves.

There is a saying among teachers that teachers are afraid of principals, principals are afraid of superintendents, superintendents are afraid of school boards, school boards are afraid of parents (voters), and parents are afraid of their children, which leaves children running the schools. To what degree this is an exaggeration seems to depend upon the aggressiveness and affluence of the parents, the place in which they live and how political it is, the courage of the school board and the superintendent, and the power of the teachers union(s). It does seem clear to most older educators that somewhere—most likely beginning in the turmoil of the 1960s—teachers began to lose a grip on the discipline of children in their classrooms.

SPARE THE ROD

Perhaps it began before the 1960s and just came out into the open more fully during that era. For instance, on December 30, 1959, a group of scientists urged teachers to "spare the rod" in dealing with problem children. Instead of spanking, they were told to segregate pupils from their peers as a more effective measure of punishment. Dr. Lawrence E. Vredevoe of the University of California, who had conducted a massive study, presented his findings at the annual meeting of the American Association for the Advancement of Science in Chicago. Dr. Vredevoe and his associates had visited 874 schools over a period of eleven years and had interviewed 1,000 teachers and administrators and 4,000 students. They had found that segregating an offender from friends was the most effective punishment. As proof of the efficacy of this plan, the scientists suggested that many students expressed a preference for corporal punishment over separation.[2]

Furthermore, the study indicated that the three major trends outside the schools contributing to "the current discipline problems" were 1) a breakdown in the general agreement on what constituted right and wrong in student conduct; 2) a growing tendency for the enforcing agency to be on trial rather than the perpetrator; 3) the result of the population explosion and the subsequent uprooting of families, now more often concentrated in industrial and commercial centers.[3]

Not everyone agreed with this. In Valdosta, Georgia, a group of teachers who could no longer paddle students resigned to protest an edict by the school board there. Then the school board reversed itself and backed the teachers, who returned to work after closing the high school. The dispute was sparked when a principal, a teacher, and an assistant football coach had criminal charges brought against them by parents of a boy who was spanked in school, having been found out of class at an unauthorized time.[4]

THE LITIGATION FACTOR

Teachers were bothered by the growing tendency for the enforcing agency (the school and the teacher) to be on trial, increasingly placing the burden of responsibility on them rather than on the students and parents. At the annual convention of the National Education Association in 1960, the central question was whether or not a teacher could hit a student who had attacked him or her. A lawyer told teachers on the association's defense commission that they had a legal right to strike back when a student had struck them but that they were losing most of the court battles that followed such a striking. If a parent brings suit against a teacher, the attorney said, courts are increasingly deciding against teachers. The lawyer also stated that in almost every state teachers stand in place of the parent and therefore have the same right to administer corporal punishment, unless such action is forbidden by law. However, the teacher's action must always be considered reasonable, he added.[5]

It is difficult to ascertain just how profoundly legal suits against the schools brought by students and parents undermined traditional school discipline, but it is certain that a new fear of litigation crept into the traditional authoritarian attitude held by school officials. In July 1964, a New Jersey jury awarded $1.2 million to a boy who had been paralyzed in a gymnasium fall. The award was believed to have been the highest of its kind ever made. The injury, which paralyzed the boy from the neck down, was sustained when the student fell during a gymnastic stunt in Chatham Borough High School. He suffered a broken vertebra and a sheared nerve. The plaintiffs contended that the boy was not properly supervised while performing the stunt, which consisted of leaping from a springboard over an obstacle and ending with a forward tumble. The gymnasium instructor was out of the gym at the time.[6]

In his book, *America Goes to School: Law, Reform, and Crisis in Public Education,* Robert M. Hardaway argues that there are several reasons schools have failed to provide a safe and disciplined learning environment. He says the adoption of what he calls "The Prussian System" placed greater emphasis on administration and hierarchical control and took authority away from the teachers. Then courts applied constitutional principles in ways that resulted in the denial of equal educational opportunity. He cites several cases to prove his point. In *Goss v. Lopez,* the Supreme Court considered a case in which students had committed violent acts in the presence of a principal, who had suspended one of the students. The Court ruled that the suspension was unconstitutional because the student accused of the assault on a policeman had not been provided with due process by being given a hearing. He then cites other court decisions that have required even more formal due process requirements. He says a New Jersey court reversed a suspension of a student accused of assault on female students because he was not given a hearing at which he was accorded the right to cross-examination. In the Supreme Court case of *Wood v. Strickland,* a school principal suspended a student who poured alcohol into punch at a student affair. The Supreme Court ruled that administrations were not immune from suit and monetary damages if he knew that the action he took would violate the student's constitutional rights.

Other court decisions allowed students to sue teachers and administrators for using excessive punishment or failing to allow them the right of counsel at expulsion hearings. In 1992, the Supreme Court ruled that schools could be liable for monetary damages in cases alleging gender discrimination. Even more damaging to discipline has been the way in which courts have dealt with the time-honored concept of *in loco parentis*. In the 1985 case of *New Jersey v. T.L.O.*, the Supreme Court said that the concept was not consonant with public education laws and therefore school officials cannot claim parents' immunity from the strictures of the Fifth Amendment, meaning that searches made by educators were unreasonable. About this, the Dean of the University of Colorado Law School opined that, "The suppression of evidence and inability to provide students with a safe and drug-free environment is not the only consequence of such decisions. Teachers themselves become targets of civil lawsuits by students claiming that such searches are unconstitutional." In the case of *Tinker v. Des Moines,* the Supreme Court decided that students should be allowed to violate school regulations by wearing protest armbands, a First Amendment right.[7]

STUDENT DRESS AND BEHAVIOR

On the surface, the opening salvos in what was to become a sustained war to determine who really would control the schools were probably made by school authorities who moved to reverse the deteriorating state of student dress and decorum in the early and mid-sixties.

Many of these episodes seem in retrospect to have been trifling matters in themselves—as for instance an incident in Livingston, New Jersey, in 1962. There eight high school students were suspended because they had not adhered to the letter of the new code for student dress, which stated that students must either button shirts all the way to the neck if a tie were worn or leave the shirt open at the neck if no tie were worn. The suspended boys were wearing shirts buttoned up to the neck, but without a tie. The vice principal in charge of discipline proclaimed that "we have a well disciplined school here and we aim to keep it that way." About 200 students demonstrated in the high school parking lot. Later some of the students drove through the town with car horns blaring. This simple "token of rebellion against authority" masked a struggle that would become more blatant at a later time.[8]

Many more such incidents in the burgeoning struggle for power would become apparent about 1965. When the Edwin O. Smith High School in Storrs, Connecticut, decided to bar an 18-year-old senior from classes until he shaved his beard in March 1965, for instance, a student demonstration followed. The student began to picket the school immediately after his suspension. He was joined by classmates and students from other schools, many wearing beards, in protest; signs bore such slogans as "Beards Cannot Preclude Brains," and the youths chanted, "Rhyme and reason, beards are in season."[9]

Attempts to legislate student behavior, even from the highest levels of state government, were not uncommon during a period when hippies were just being recognized as part of a counterculture movement in the colleges. In May 1965, in the state of Illinois, the House of Representatives passed an atavistic bill to allow teachers to spank schoolchildren.[10]

More common were frenzied attempts by school systems to promulgate rules for student dress and behavior. In Provincetown, Massachusetts, school officials put a ban on extremes of dress and hairstyles: the hemlines of girls' skirts had to fall below the knees, and boys had to have shirts tucked in; in addition, no tobacco products were allowed on school property. The principal's diatribe to the gathered students that day may have provoked a smile or two: "If a teacher spots a package of cigarettes in your pocket he is going to ask you for one, er—the whole package," he exhorted. Turning to another subject—males who wear earrings and girls in beehive hairdos—the principal warned, "Let no one fight this, let no one fight this, because you're going to fight a losing battle." The code prohibited jeans, dungarees, garrison belts, engineer boots, steel clips on shoes, or "unusual footwear of any kind." Tight clothing of any kind was prohibited.

Also, students were to be required to show "a proper attitude and respect" to teachers at all times. Precluded were displays of affection, gum chewing, and smoking. The response to the code came primarily from angry parents. In the face of that power, the valiant principal did not give up, however. When he told the assembled students, "Now, we are going to fight the battle for that hemline," some chuckles were heard in the crowd. He continued, offering a further explanation: "Often when you sit down, the dress creeps up—not a very good teaching situation."[11]

It seemed that the more adamant principals became, the more protest was evoked from students. When New York City principals all across the city denounced long hair on male students, they blamed the fad on the Beatles. While private schools could be more dictatorial about hairstyles, some public schools expelled students who wore their hair too long. In spite of some rebellion, most of the disciplined students eventually did as they were told.[12]

The schools in Toms River, New Jersey, rebuked girl students for another kind of infraction, the wearing of "granny dresses." At a regional high school dance, a vice principal asked two girls who were wearing dresses which covered them from neck to ankles to leave. It was angry parents who protested this ridiculous action. The superintendent, who had to look into the matter, said that the junior class had decided that the dance should be in school clothes, and the girls had been asked to leave because their clothes did not fit that description. After one of the girls' mothers pointed out that there were boys present in jeans and sweatshirts and girls in slacks, the vice principal admitted that he doubted that he would kick the girls out again if he had it to do over.[13]

The struggle over grooming continued, reaching a kind of crescendo in January 1968 when the Brien McMahon High School in Norwalk, Connecticut, suspended 53 boys in a dispute over the length of their hair. William Borders of the *New York Times* wrote, "The suspensions came amid a continuing controversy between parents and their children, teachers and their pupils, and among youngsters themselves over the propriety of the teen-age fad of long hair and long sideburns." Dr. Luther A. Howard, the school's principal, expelled the boys as he inspected, room to room, through the school. He was acting to enforce a dress code adopted by the school board in 1964.

Subsequently, a Norwalk school official said that the administration was "backing him all the way," even though the mass suspensions surprised and upset the community. Some parents were ready to take the matter to court.[14] The American Civil Liberties Union considered taking the case, and then did take the case of four of the students to the Court of Common Pleas in Bridgeport, where Dr. Howard had to defend his actions before a judge, saying that long hair could be a distraction in the classroom.[15]

Another case that the American Civil Liberties Union took at that time involved a defense of girls wearing slacks to school. Girls who were barred from school for wearing slacks during a cold spell got the sympathy of the A.C.L.U., which prepared a five-page memorandum to school officials about the matter, which was seen as a part of "general harassment." Spokespersons for the city superintendent and the state commissioner of education had to admit that state guidelines only prohibited clothing that was unsafe or so distractive that it upset the educational program.[16]

At a Catholic school in New Hampshire on the same day, the principal took more immediate action: he had 18 boys taken from classes to the barber to have their hair shorn. Apparently, there was little rebellion, at least outwardly, among these boys.[17]

VIOLENT ATTACKS UPON TEACHERS

Two things seemed to be becoming apparent at this point: parents were often resisting decisions by school officials, and the struggle over long hair and inappropriate dress would eventually—as it evolved into more and more serious concerns over misbehavior—cause disruption in the schools and even jeopardize the safety of students. A pattern of resistance, especially on the parts of students and their parents, was now obvious.

In the incipient period of rebellion leading up to the anti-war strife of the late sixties and early seventies, the teacher as authority figure was often the victim of violent student outrage. Because of this, the voices of teachers' associations were becoming more strident. An incident in New York in 1964 is illustrative. A 14-year-old girl whom the teacher had refused to admit to class beat a 59-year-old female teacher. The girl struck the teacher in the face, breaking her eyeglasses and then began punching her repeatedly. A male teacher then came to subdue the girl and, assisted by other teachers, took her to the principal's office. The teacher later told a reporter that she attributed the attack to the school's overcrowding and the discontinuance of separating problem children from others. In the previous week, a 15-year-old boy had stabbed a 23-year-old teacher in the back with a knife. Following the attack upon the teacher, the president of the United Federation of Teachers telegraphed the superintendent of schools asking for protection for teachers.[18]

Later in the same month, students, making a total of 23 attacks in one week in the city, attacked six more teachers. In one incident, a girl bit a teacher on the arm when the teacher tried to take razor blades away from her. Several of the attacks involved knife-wielding boys; another involved a fourth grader who twisted his teacher's arm when she attempted to break up a fight.[19] While it was unusual for primary students to attack teachers, junior high schoolers seemed to be involved more and more frequently in attacks upon teachers.

Two fifteen-year-old boys, in separate incidents, proved this asser-
tion. In one attack, a boy was arrested and charged with assault after he hit his male teacher in the chest.[20] In another incident, a
15-year-old pulled a loaded .28-caliber revolver and threatened three
classmates and his teacher, who confiscated the weapon.[21] In another
junior high school, three boys stabbed another child in a washroom
and then went on a rampage, stabbing two people in subway stations.[22]

In March 1966, a teacher was shot in the abdomen as he tried to
intercept a boy running toward him in the hall carrying a loaded
shotgun in a Long Island high school. The boy, apparently on the way
to shoot other students, ran outside after he shot the language teacher.
Prior to that encounter, the assistant principal, a former professional
basketball player, had stopped the boy and tried to talk the boy into
giving up the gun, but the boy ran past him and darted away. Then
other students reported seeing him on all three floors of the school
as he looked into classrooms; the teacher whom he shot then accosted
him. The police caught the gun-toting student as he tried to escape.
The teacher died on June 14th.[23]

In the same year, a past president of the Philadelphia Federation
of Teachers claimed that the city had lost 415 new teachers because
they feared attacks by pupils.[24] Celia Pinkus spoke in county court
after a judge committed a boy who had punched his teacher on the
arm. Ms. Pinkus told the judge that new teachers refuse jobs when
they are assigned to schools with reputations for violence.[25] The year
1968 would be a difficult one for teachers because of student defi-
ance. In the Bronx, New York, a 16-year-old student slashed his
physical education teacher with a knife after the teacher had reprimanded him. Teachers would be slashed in several other encounters
with students that year and every subsequent year.[26]

In spite of schools' attempts to protect teachers, it is still more
likely that a student will attack a teacher than a fellow student.[27]

LAWSUITS AGAINST TEACHERS

Three legal actions taken against teachers in 1967 provide evidence
that the disciplinary ability of teachers was changing in the face of
increased litigation by parents. In Chicago, the school board received
a suit of $50,000 from a boy whose parents charged that he suffered
brain damage when books were thrown in an elementary school in
the previous year.[28] In New Jersey, a 26-year-old female English

teacher cut the shoulder-length hair on a 15-year-old boy because the boy jokingly told her to go ahead and cut his hair. The boy's parents then filed assault and battery charges against the teacher. Although the judge dropped the charges, the teacher was "properly reprimanded" by the school superintendent. In San Diego, a 16-year-old and his parents won an out-of-court settlement against a male teacher who had cut the boy's hair with sheep shears. The teacher said he had permission of the school administration to do so.[29]

Justice Lewis Powell gave an opinion on how the law should regard attacks on teachers:

> Without first establishing discipline and maintaining order, teachers cannot begin to educate their students. And apart from education, the school has an obligation to protect pupils from mistreatment by other children, and also to protect teachers themselves from violence by the few students whose conduct in recent years has prompted national concern.[30]

In some states, teacher's unions have tried to provide protection for teachers against monetary damages assessed in lawsuits.

PARENTS AGAINST TEACHERS

In loco parentis notwithstanding, there were signs that a rift was developing between teachers and parents as early as 1960, with insinuations that teachers were growing increasingly afraid of parents. Ironically, as the concept of *in loco parentis* was losing legal force, teachers were taking on more and more of the roles formerly assumed to be parental duties. At the same time, teachers' increasing fear of possessive and militant parents may have been intimated in the article "Pressure From Ambitious Parents Blamed for High School Cheating." The feature based its conclusions upon answers received in a survey of student leaders who told the writer that parents' ambitions for their children were placing an increasing burden upon young people so that they were tense and anxious and could not concentrate on their studies.

The students reported that cheating was widespread among high school students; this fact was collaborated by school administrators and teachers. In one school, children were changing the grades on their report cards: "The principal of the school in the middle-class neighborhood disclosed that a certain group of parents tries to pressure the school as well as the children. He constantly had been

badgered by a band of mothers who want their children's marks up-
graded to ease admission to college."[31]

In February 1968, parents made a new kind of charge against
teachers. Officers of a parent-teacher organization accused teachers
at a junior high school of "the deliberate incitement of our children
to demonstrate." The parents association claimed that the teachers
were in "an insidious power struggle" with the principal of the
school. Further, they charged that the teachers had "organized the
children's demonstration. They supplied them with school materials
and put slogans in their mouths. Then, they left their posts to encourage unrestrained disorders."

Eighth graders at the school had picketed the school in the previous week and then run through the building fighting, disrupting
classes, and turning off lights.

The United Federation of Teachers headquarters in Manhattan
responded that the parents' charges were "nonsense." One sixth
grade teacher explained that teachers were discontented over the lack
of discipline in the school: the teacher cited a "decline in the sense
of authority" as the school's major problem. However, he said further that while the principal seemed to be cooperative with parent
groups, "there is a mixed relationship with the teachers," which he
explained further by saying, "Certain dedicated teachers are hampered by others who have other ideologies; there are a handful of
teachers causing this disruption and confusion." For her part, the
principal blamed the troubles on the teacher shortage, which was
"aggravated by absenteeism."

The parents groups had given the superintendent a list of "teacher
troublemakers" and suggested that if he took no suitable action, they
would seek help from the New York State Commissioner of Education.[32]

In April 1968, an even more militant group of parents took the
stage in Brooklyn. A massive boycott by parents in Brooklyn kept
6,000 students out of eight schools. The parents wanted community
control of the schools in their neighborhoods. Two upper-grade
schools were chosen as targets of the parents' demonstration, and
nearly 100 percent of the students stayed home. Though there was
no organized boycott of the elementary schools, many of the students
stayed home anyway.

Parents in Brooklyn demanded control over school budgets, the
hiring and dismissal of teachers, the construction and renovation of

school buildings, and the establishment of curriculum, all powers normally controlled by school boards and their designated administrations. Signs in front of the affected schools said, "We want to control our schools," "We want our children educated," and "Closed by the PTA."

By the time of this incident, New York schools had been decentralized to the point at which local governing boards had been established to operate the districts. Conflict arose when "actual authority" was not turned over to the local boards. But the PTA made it clear that it was they and not the local boards that were conducting the boycott. The superintendent attributed the boycott to the governing board, which he claimed was attempting to usurp powers from the board of education that could not legally be taken. "It is unfortunate that the children should be denied education over a matter that should be discussed around the table by adults," he said.[33]

INCREASED ADMINISTRATIVE RESPONSIBILITIES FOR TEACHERS

As pressure increased for national and state governments to provide safe school environments and as teachers were expected to be more and more accountable, they had to bear greater administrative responsibilities. This, of course, took time away from actual teaching. At the same time, under the Individuals with Disabilities Education Act, teachers were being forced to teach a more heterogeneous group of students as children with physical, behavioral, and emotional problems were "mainstreamed" into their classrooms. Burdensome individual educational plans (IEPs) had to be created and maintained for each of these students, thus further increasing the administrative burden on teachers, who seldom have the benefit of secretarial help.[34] Teachers were thus deprived of time to devote to classroom discipline.

THE PORTRAYAL OF TEACHERS IN THE MEDIA

In the introductory remarks in this chapter, we averred that the media has sometimes presented teachers and the teaching profession in an unfavorable light. Sometimes portrayals of teachers, especially in some of the print media and in the television talk and shock shows, have been deleterious to education. Sometimes teachers themselves have not presented their profession well, as some of the incidents we have cited show. Recently, however, at least one good TV drama show, *Boston Public*, has given promise that the difficulty high school teachers have is being fairly presented. Reflecting the complexity of contemporary culture for both student and adult, the program gives a convincing picture of the many difficulties that contemporary teachers face.

In 1999, the United States began to experience a severe teacher shortage. Swelling enrollments and a push to reduce class sizes were coming about at the same time that many teachers were retiring. However, the problem was not necessarily one of overall supply; the problem seemed to be more closely related to geography and expertise, as teachers in certain states where there is an oversupply refuse to move to the states with shortages. Also, there are insufficient numbers of teachers in certain fields, particularly math and science.[35]

Another problem surfacing is that urban areas such as New York are losing teachers to suburban areas. Nearly 1,700 teachers left New York City to teach elsewhere in 2000.[36]

Some years before, concern was raised about the inadequate number of minority teachers, as their numbers actually seemed to be dwindling at a time when the percentage of black and Hispanic students in public schools was growing.[37]

Therefore, the inadequate pay of teachers, combined with the qualifications required of them, makes the dilemma of the teaching profession even more difficult. "We are being asked to do more for less," one teacher said. "We just can't continue to be all things to all people."

The demise of discipline is a complicated and contradictory problem in many respects. But it is for the reasons we have cited and possibly for others that the discipline maintained in American schools in the early 1950s seems to have been eroded, and when it was relaxed, schools became less safe than they were in previous times.

NOTES

1. The Gallup Poll on the Public's Attitudes Toward the Public Schools identifies discipline as the number one public concern in all but one year since 1969. National School Boards Association, *Toward Better and Safer Schools: A School Leader's Guide to Delinquency Prevention*, 1984, cited in James A. Rapp, Frank Carrington, and George Nicholson, *School Crime & Violence Victims' Rights* (Malibu, CA: Pepperdine University Press, 1986), pg. 2.

2. "Teachers Urged to Spare the Rod," *New York Times*, January 3, 1960, pg. 50.

3. Ibid.

4. "Paddling Backed; School Crisis Ends," *New York Times*, April 30, 1960, pg. 23.

5. "Teachers' Topic is Self Defense," *New York Times*, June 29, 1960, pg. 72.

6. "Jersey Jury Awards $1.2 Million to Youth Paralyzed in Gym Fall," *New York Times*, July 4, 1964, pgs. 1, 7.

7. Robert M. Hardaway, *America Goes to School: Law, Reform, and Crisis in Public Education* (Westport, CT: Praeger Publishers, 1995), pgs. 151–158.

8. "8 Students Suspended for Improper Dress," *New York Times*, April 13, 1962, pg. 26.

9. "Youths March at School Barring Bearded Student," *New York Times*, April 1, 1965, pg. 33.

10. "Spanking Bill Passed," *New York Times*, May 5, 1965, pg. 42.

11. "Provincetown Puts Ban on Extremes," *New York Times*, September 13, 1965, pg. 37.

12. "Schools in the Area Give Notice That Long Hair is For Girls Only," *New York Times*, September 13, 1965, pg. 37.

13. "Grannies Are Out, Two Girls Learn," *New York Times*, November 13, 1965, pg. 31.

14. "Norwalk School Suspends 53 in Hairline Dispute," *New York Times*, January 30, 1968, pg. 43.

15. "Long Hair Battles End At Barber and Court," *New York Times*, February 6, 1968, pg. 47.

16. "Liberties Union Goes to Defense of Girls Wearing Slacks to School," *New York Times*, January 30, 1968, pg. 43.

17. "18 New Hampshire Boys Taken From Class and Shorn," *New York Times*, February 6, 1968, pg. 47.

18. "Girl, 14, Beats Woman Teacher; Union Asks Protection in Bronx," *New York Times*, March 4, 1964, pg. 1.

19. "6 More Teachers Attacked in Day," *New York Times*, March 12, 1964, pg. 37.

20. "Brooklyn Boy, 15, Arrested in Assault on A Teacher," *New York Times*, March 18, 1964, pg. 33.

21. "Boy, 15, Seized in School In Gun Threat to Pupils," *New York Times*, May 1, 1964, pg. 9.

22. "3 Stab Fellow Student in School, Then Knife 2 in Subway Stations," *New York Times*, November 7, 1964, pg. 1.

23. "L.I. Teacher Shot by Boy in School," *New York Times*, March 28, 1966, pg. 34. "Teacher Shot by Youth Dies in Bay Shore Hospital," *New York Times*, June 14, 1966, pg. 94.

24. By 1978, approximately 5,200 teachers were being physically attacked each month, and they were five times more likely than students to be seriously injured in those attacks. NIE, U.S. Department of Health, Education and Welfare, *Violent Schools—Safe Schools: The Safe School Study Report to the Congress,* 1978.

25. "Teacher Says Fear Causes Many to Shun Philadelphia," *New York Times,* February 25, 1966, pg. 15.

26. "Teacher Slashed in Bronx," *New York Times,* January 3, 1968, pg. 39.

27. In Boston, there were 171 assaults on school staff and 118 student-on-student incidents in 1999. The scholar who made this study reported that this comparison was true in every year studied (since 1993). He said the reason students attack teachers reflects a growing loss of respect for authority figures. Jeff Jurmain, "Attacks on Teachers More Likely Than on Students," *The Boston Channel,* January 26, 2001. http://www.thebostonchannel.com/bos/news/stories/news-20010126-161445.html.

28. "Boy Sues School for $500,000," *New York Times,* February 7, 1967, pg. 22.

29. "School Reprimands Teacher Who Cut Student's Hair," *New York Times,* November 19, 1967, pg. 43. "Suit Over Haircut Settled," *New York Times,* May 31, 1967, pg. 14.

30. Cited in James A. Rapp, Frank Carrington, and George Nicholson, *School Crime and Violence Victim's Rights* (Malibu, CA: Pepperdine University Press, 1986), pg. 10.

31. "Pressure From Ambitious Parents Blamed For High School Cheating," *New York Times,* May 31, 1960, pg. 25.

32. "Parents Say Teachers Incited Pupils," *New York Times,* February 6, 1968, pg. 32.

33. "8 Brooklyn Schools Boycotted by 6,000; Control Demanded," *New York Times,* April 11, 1968, pgs. 1, 36.

34. We are certainly not arguing against the justice of this important act; we are only making the point that it does place additional burdens on the classroom teacher, dividing her (his) time up among more students.

35. "As Students Return, Schools Cope with Severe Shortage of Teachers," *New York Times,* August 31, 1999, pg. A1.

36. "Survey Shows More Teachers Are Leaving for Jobs in Suburban Schools," *New York Times,* April 13, 2001, pg. B4.

37. "Ranks of Minority Teachers are Dwindling, Experts Fear," *New York Times,* February 9, 1986, section 1, pg. 1.

Chapter 8

A Decadent Counterculture (1970–2001)

Bruce Schulman puts forth an interesting thesis in his book *The Seventies: The Great Shift in American Society and Politics.*[1] He says that the America that produced the New Deal and the Civil Rights Movement shifted in the 1970s toward the sovereignty of the free market and private life. Traditionalists had looked at the decade and observed the decline of traditional moral values. But Schulman saw in the 1970s a shift of the nation's center of gravity away from the northeast to the southward and westward suburbs, whose residents harbored a deep suspicion of government, elitism, and racial resentment and were committed to a highly personal religiosity. A new conservative age emerged in which middle-class Americans opposed student protestors and black militants and espoused older values of patriotism, duty, and self-restraint. The old liberalism of the 1960s was diminished to the point of being just another life-style choice for a minority.[2]

Another culture—what was in essence a counterculture—becoming more visible in the 1970s seemed to have a great impact upon the safety and well-being of America's high schools. It involved alternate and often unsanctioned life-style choices made by young Americans about the issues of sex, drugs, and gangs. It was not, by any means, all good or healthy in traditional terms; in fact, from a conservative point of view, it was decadent, wasteful, and repugnant. Schools had to find remedies for these growing threats.[3]

Intrusions of social problems such as sexual issues, gangs, and the widespread use of drugs—which now infected most schools—were the great problems for schools during the seventies and beyond. Implicit in all three problems increasingly was the unruly behavior of suburban youth, as these were no longer exclusively urban problems. This chapter is concerned with these three threats to the school: sexual wrongdoing, drugs, and the connection between drugs and gangs.[4]

OLD AND NEW SEXUAL ISSUES IN THE 1970s

The impact of the new sexual freedom being enjoyed by women and homosexuals, the spread of AIDS, and the more open interchanges between the school and outside community were new currents schools had to deal with in the decade of the 1970s. Some of the older issues more directly confronting schools with a heightened urgency included sexual attacks on teachers and students by intruders, rape, sexual assaults by teachers on students and vice versa, and sexual harassment. This discussion will begin with these latter dilemmas, because they had the most direct impact upon the safety of schools.

The federal legislation in which Title IX was included passed in 1972. Title IX said that "No person in the United States shall, on the basis of sex, be excluded from participation in, be denied the benefits of, or be subjected to discrimination under any education program or activity receiving Federal financial assistance." This landmark law ultimately would change many policies and reporting procedures in schools. One important result of Title IX would be that so many more violations would be reported that the ancient problem would receive greatly enhanced visibility. Students being assaulted or harassed by other students and by teachers was no doubt an old problem.

Sexual assault on a teacher by a student had been, at least before the classic film *Blackboard Jungle,* another hidden, if not forbidden, topic. If and when it happened, it was not a welcome subject in any quarter. But by March 1971, large school districts were forced to attack some of these problems head on, as New York City did when the chancellor of the school system called a meeting to announce new action to curb violent assaults on teachers. The meeting was called in direct response to the rapes of two teachers in the previous week on the same day. At that meeting Chancellor Scribner said there had been 287 attacks on school personnel in 1970. One of the attackers, a 15-year-old boy, was caught a few days later.[5]

The assaulted teacher was a 23-year-old who was in the school at 4:00 P.M. The attacker, who took her by surprise, carried a knife and raped her after pushing her into a closet and holding a butcher knife to her throat.[6]

Another intruder entered an elementary school and raped a Paterson, New Jersey, teacher in January 1973. The intruder, who was 17 years old, raped the 21-year-old woman at knifepoint. He forced the woman out of the classroom while terrified fourth graders looked on, taking her into the cloakroom. The young woman, who planned to be married in May, noted that during the rape "[the students] were very, very quiet. . . . They just sat there and stared."[7] In February, a would-be rapist was frightened away by other teachers when his victim screamed from her classroom. The first-grade teacher was alone when the intruder struck her in the mouth, knocked her to the floor, and attempted to rip off her clothes.[8]

In March, police charged a 17-year-old in Harlem with the rape of a teacher's assistant. He had tied the young woman up and then raped her.[9] In September, police in East Brunswick, New Jersey, found the nude body of a 28-year-old teacher floating in South River.[10]

While sexual attacks on teachers continued through the 1970s, the rape of schoolgirls was also a problem school boards often had to face. For instance, in Washington, D.C., in June 1976, a court ordered the district to pay $640,000 to a ten-year-old girl who was raped on three different occasions by a janitor in her elementary school. The girl's family said the school system was required to protect the girl from attacks by employees.[11]

Elementary schools in the District of Columbia had sexual assaults on two ten-year-old girls in 1979. Teenaged males who roamed the schools were the problem. The principal ordered teachers to escort students to the restrooms. In one of the cases, two teenaged boys cornered a 10-year-old girl, stripped her, and attempted to rape her but ran when a teacher entered.[12]

Four high school boys raped a 15-year-old girl in a classroom while the teacher was out of the room in Montgomery County, Maryland, in December 1979.[13]

In October 1971, the city health commissioner in New York announced that venereal disease was increasing among high school students. The bureau planned a training program for teachers, saying that teenagers did not know about a state law under which minors can be examined and treated for venereal disease without their parents' knowledge or consent. In 1970, there were 36,783 reported cases of gonorrhea and 3,798 cases of syphilis. Reported cases were only the tip of the iceberg, according to officials. New York ranked eighth among major cities in reported cases of infectious syphilis. The city was not among the nation's top ten for cases of gonorrhea.[14]

Another element, which sometimes had a sordid twist, entered the arena in a more prominent way in the 1970s. This involved teachers having sexual relations with students. Some of the incidents appeared to be mere romances, as when a 40-year-old teacher married his former student, 18, after a two-year romance in a New Jersey high school. Their romance had scandalized the community and led to the teacher's suspension. When the girl reached the legal age, however, and the couple was married, the teacher may have gotten his job back. The mother said, "We will always hold the school to blame."[15]

In Salem, Massachusetts, in 1978, the Salem School Committee asked town residents to disclose information about alleged partying which involved sex between teachers and high school students. There was an allegation that at least five teachers had provided liquor, marijuana, and a trip to Bermuda for favored female students. A local newspaper had reported that the teachers maintained an apartment for parties with students. The allegations arose when a mother found her daughter's diary listing dates, guests, and activities of parties at the apartment.[16]

In a Long Island school, an administrative aide was charged with sexually abusing five girls who had been sent to his office for disciplinary purposes. The suspect, a married man, was charged with six counts of sexual abuse and one of attempted sodomy. The girls were all 15 or 16 years old. The abuse had taken place in the man's office, or he had taken them to lunch and then to a remote construction site.[17]

In January 1979, a 24-year-old teacher's aide was charged with 14 counts of sodomy and one rape with handicapped and mentally retarded students in Fairfax County, Virginia. The charges involved three male students and a girl, 18. Parents complained that school and police were too slow in taking action against the suspect. The incidents had occurred over several months.[18]

In the same month, another suburban Washington county had a similar problem. The Montgomery County, Maryland, superintendent recommended the dismissal of a 29-year-old teacher who was alleged to have had sex with a 14-year-old girl at his home. The teacher disputed the charges against him.[19] In June, another Maryland teacher was found innocent of charges that he molested a 12-year-old student on an overnight trip.[20]

A feature article in *The Washington Post* in November 1977 highlighted what seemed to be a growing problem in the schools. Eighteen Maryland suburban schoolteachers had recently been cleared of sexual charges students had made against them. "In the last five years 18 teachers in Maryland have been accused—and cleared—of sexual assault on their students," the author stated. She pointed out that Prince George's County was advising all teachers not to touch students. An attorney for the Maryland Teachers' Association said, "The pressure of going through such an ordeal shakes a teacher's faith in education and the community. It's far worse than most charges, it touches on morals, on taboos."[21]

Nevertheless, accusations by students continued. In December 1978, another Maryland teacher was charged with having sex with a student who was in her early teens.[22] Another accusation came against a 44-year-old teacher that year, again from Montgomery County, the following May by a male special education student, age 12.[23]

SEXUAL PROBLEMS IN THE SCHOOLS, 1980s

As the 1980s opened, awareness of sexual harassment, and in particular the harassment of students, was gaining increased attention. The National Advisory Council on Women's Education issued a report in October 1980 saying that the sexual harassment of students, which violated federal law prohibiting discrimination in federally financed education programs, was on the rise, according to the latest survey. The Council recommended that the U.S. Department of Education "establish sexual harassment as a sex-based discrimination" and pointed out that only a few institutions had adequate mechanisms "for dealing with this increasingly visible problem." The Council defined five categories of sexual harassment:

1. general sexist remarks or behavior including crude jokes;
2. inappropriate and offensive sexual advances;

3. solicitation of sexual activity by promise of rewards;
4. coercion of sex by threat of punishment;
5. sexual crimes and misdemeanors.[24]

Just how complicated sexual harassment charges could be became apparent in 1981 when a Burlington, North Carolina, elementary school principal was charged by five women with sexual harassment. The 40-year-old principal was suspended for three days and transferred to the system's central office. A five-member peer review panel made a decision on the allegations. The decision was to be kept secret under state law, but a local newspaper found out the results and would have published them had not a judge issued a temporary restraining order. A justice of the state supreme court said that the ban was the first court order of "prior restraint" of a publication.[25]

Another result of the increased visibility of sexual harassment was the outcome of court cases in which victims of sexual assaults sued and won punitive damages. For instance, in a case in New York, the board of education was ordered in 1983 to pay an 18-year-old girl $3 million in damages because she was raped in the stairwell of a Bronx junior high school five years previously. Lawyers had argued on behalf of the girl that the board of education was negligent in not supervising the rapist and failing to protect the girl, who was 13 at the time. The boy who attacked the girl was 16 when the incident occurred. The board planned to appeal the ruling.[26]

Parents, as well as the courts, would put pressure on teachers who sexually assaulted students. In 1984, a sixth-grade teacher in California who pleaded no contest to a sexual advance on a teenage boy, did not return to school after parents called a meeting with the superintendent. The group of parents planned to present a petition to the school board.[27]

More and more often, teachers were required to learn about and teach about sexual abuses. In New Jersey in 1983, teachers would be required to introduce such topics as "child abuse," "sexual assault," and "incest" into their classrooms. "Sexual abuse is the most under-reported crime in the country, but to report it is the most important factor in stopping it," reported an official who pointed out that even in a very rural county there had been 23 sexual assaults on children.[28]

Court cases by students against teachers who had assaulted them continued throughout the decade. So did state prosecutions of offenders through the courts. In 1982, a Superior Court jury in Hackensack, New Jersey, convicted a Leonia schoolteacher in the sexual assault on a fourth-grade pupil. During the Christmas vacation, a 39-year-old teacher had a nine-year-old boy in his home, where he was alleged to have committed the assault. The elementary school teacher of 14 years had a good deal of support from community residents, who had held a benefit dinner at a local church to help raise funds for his defense.[29] The police and the courts prosecuted an increasing number of male educators who molested boys during the 1980s.[30]

Among the school personnel accused by children of rape or sexual molestation around the country during the remainder of the 1980s were teachers, a school bus driver, a janitor, a principal, a social worker, and several coaches. A coach in Missouri was charged with sodomizing one of the football team's former players. A coach in Anaheim was arrested for having sexual relations with two girls. A St. Louis coach was charged with the abuse of a girl, age six. A coach in Rockville, Maryland, was charged with sexual assault on two girls.[31]

Rapes and other sexual assaults occurred with such frequency in some parts of the country in the late 1980s that schools began implementing sterner security measures on bathrooms, which were usually patrolled by teachers. Often sexual assaults on school property would take place in bathrooms, gymnasiums, deserted stairwells, or on school buses. Older boys committed many of the assaults but sometimes an intruder from the outside would come into the school bathrooms. After an attack upon two eight-year-old girls in the bathroom by a 15-year-old, the school system tightened security in 1985.[32] In 1989, Fairfax County schools in Virginia were locking all exterior doors to the school during school hours and allowing students to go to the bathroom only in pairs. The superintendent's decision to tighten security came after the attack on a nine-year-old girl by a knife-wielding man in a bathroom at an elementary school in McLean.[33]

MORE OF THE SAME IN THE 1990s

By 1990, with the papers reporting stories of rapes in school, sexual assaults in bathrooms, teachers assaulting students, and so forth, the media began to speak out against sexual harassment and assault. An editorial in *The St. Louis Post Dispatch* in May 1990 took issue with a police detective who had said, "There is nothing out of control at the high school." The editorial pointed out that the male students who had assaulted a female student should be charged and tried. The teacher who left them unsupervised was also wrong. The editorial concluded: "So there is something wrong here. These male students should be prosecuted to fullest extent of the law, as adults, because they knew what they were doing every time they did it!"[34]

A case came to the Supreme Court in December 1991 concerning the matter of whether a child who had been sexually harassed by a teacher could seek monetary damages from the school system. A former Georgia high school student brought the suit. In 1986, a coach began showing favoritism to a tenth-grade girl, and then he brought her to his office and had sexual intercourse with her. The girl told other teachers and the guidance counselor about the affair. The case prompted much interest because it was the first since Clarence Thomas had been confirmed as a justice.[35]

In *Franklin v. Gwinette County Pub. Sch., 503 U.S. 60*, 1992, the U.S. Supreme Court ruled that sexual harassment violates the federal law against discrimination in education (Title IX). Students may sue for damages for sexual harassment under that law. Until that ruling, monetary relief for the victims of sexual harassment was not an option.

The most comprehensive look at gender discrimination against girls came in a study released by the American Association of University Women in 1992. The study noted a disturbing rise in sexual harassment of girls by boys. The increase was attributed, at least in part, to the inclination of school officials to dismiss harassment, as "boys will be boys."

The study showed that until they start school, girls perform at about the same confidence level as boys, but girls, unlike boys, do not emerge from school with the same degree of confidence. Some of the factors causing this, the study indicated, were that some teachers pay more attention to boys than girls; the gender gap was declining in math but increasing in science; curricula and textbooks ignore female perspectives and reinforce stereotypes. The report provided 40 recommendations aimed at equalizing treatment, including changing teaching methods to meet the needs of girls, encouraging girls in math and science, toughening school policies against sexual harassment and placing girls' problems on the agenda of education reformers.[36]

The study said that four out of every five teenagers in a survey said that either students or teachers had sexually harassed them. After harassment, another big problem was the number of (presumably false) accusations leveled at teachers. Media stories began to emphasize the kind of hurt that sexual harassment can cause.[37]

As police and the courts handled more and more sexual harassment cases, incidents such as one that happened in July 1993 became more common. A Norfolk high school teacher was the second Virginia teacher to commit suicide after he was informed that police were investigating a report that he had a sexual relationship with a student. The 51-year-old teacher jumped off the Monitor-Merrimac Memorial Bridge-Tunnel into the James River and drowned when he learned that he had been charged in five felony warrants. Another Virginia teacher had committed suicide two months earlier, after he was charged with sexual harassment.[38]

The alleged rape victim of a former Atlanta school principal sued the Atlanta superintendent of schools and the Atlanta school board in federal court complaining that they knew about sexual harassment charges made by teachers against him and had done nothing. The suit alleged that the former principal had used his position to harass female teachers and other female staff members.[39]

A different kind of scandal shocked Birmingham, Alabama, in January 1998 when two middle school students crawled under a table in the back of a computer lab classroom and had sexual intercourse with other students watching and with the teacher still in the room. Parents of the two said that a 15-year-old gang member who threatened to kill them if they did not do it coerced them into the act. One of the girl's friends said, "She didn't have no choice but to . . . (have sex with) that boy. They told her they'd kill her if she didn't. I know those . . . (expletive). If they tell you they're going to hurt you, they will."

The two students were suspended from school, and the teacher was put on administrative leave pending an investigation. The witness said that the boy and girl crawled under a table while several other students used coats and jackets to shield them from view, and at the same time other students surrounded the teacher to divert his attention. The Birmingham police chief said that his department was pursuing the idea of charging the female gang member with rape because her threats compelled the victim against her will. The girl's mother said that she had learned that the older girl, a member of the Bloods gang, was planning to force every girl in the class to have sex. The 15-year-old gang member was not suspended.[40]

The 15-year-old was charged a few days later with harassment by threatening and intimidating the two seventh graders. The member of the Bloods was also suspended from school. Members of the state legislature called the police chief and school superintendent up to explain to them what had happened. In the meantime, the girl who had engaged in the sex retained an attorney, who immediately chided the school for suspending the girl.[41]

The Los Angeles Times reported in May 1999 that there was a large increase in lawsuits by gay and lesbian students who claimed that they had been harassed in high schools. These lawsuits came about after the U.S. Supreme Court ruled that school districts could be held liable for cases involving extensive sexual harassment of students by one another. Gay harassment suits had emerged over the previous five years. Some states, like California, had attempted to legislate against such harassment. The *Times* article suggested that gay harassment was "the last frontier in school harassment issues."[42]

But criminal activities such as rape and molestation were still the most serious problems facing educators and the society of which they are a part. Many times, educators have seen heart-rending cruelties. In 1990, a principal was haunted by something he had seen that morning—a person he thought was a young man walking along with a man who had his arm over the boy's shoulders. Later the principal found out that the "boy" was actually an 11-year-old girl who was raped by the man shortly after the principal saw them walking. The sixth grader was one of the principal's own students; she was grabbed as she walked and then dragged into the bushes, where she was beaten and raped. The principal spoke remorsefully: "Now I wish I'd gone back down there as soon as I saw them. But I only got a glimpse of them. . . . Now I know that all the while he was threatening her to keep walking."[43]

And sometimes educators were the criminals, as in the case of the teacher in Kentucky who received a two-year prison sentence for raping a 15-year-old student. The 33-year-old teacher was convicted of third-degree rape near Louisville. Another teacher was charged with child molestation after four girls testified that he had performed sexual acts with them at school in the early 1980s. The young women, 18 to 20 years old, testified that the teacher had molested them when they were 10 or 11 years old.[44] In still another case, a

30-year teacher was tried for sexually molesting four elementary school boys. Cases reaching as far back as 1956 were among those brought forward by 45 victims. The teacher was from a powerful family, and perhaps this was the reason the cases had not come to light previously.[45]

Needless to say, sex crimes continued through the 1990s and right up to the present. Sometimes they involved teachers and other school personnel.

SCHOOLS AND THE DRUG PROBLEM, 1970s

Drugs are a societal plague that are every bit as disruptive to schools as sex-related intrusions. The beginnings of the drug problem among students probably coincided with the reform and counterculture movements of the 1960s, but by the 1970s and 1980s drugs in schools had created a counterculture all their own. Soon the problem involved many more people than just high school students. Elementary and junior high students, parents, and even school personnel were affected by the drug problem.

In December 1973, an official of the New York City Board of Education announced that 374 drug arrests over the previous six and a half years had been made—not to students, but to employees of the board. The total of 374 arrested included 103 teachers.

The teachers were arrested either for selling or possessing drugs. The procedure followed by the board was that a conviction would result in the loss of a teaching post. In the overwhelming majority of the cases, the official testified, there had not been a conviction.[46]

As cases in point: in August 1973, a junior high school biology teacher was arrested and accused of selling heroin to teenagers in Harlem. The police did not accuse him of selling drugs in the school where he taught but said he was part of a drug gang in Harlem. The teacher had two ounces of heroin in his pocket and a loaded revolver on his person when police arrested him.[47] In another incident in Harlem, police found heroin and marijuana in a car two teachers were driving as they transported five children to a basketball game in East Harlem. The car was stopped after it had gone through a red light. Then police searched the car and found the narcotics.[48]

In February 1977, a House panel found that there had been a huge rise in drug use by schoolchildren from the seventh grade on up in New York City. The report said that New York's drug problem had reached crisis proportions. One statement in the report noted that "[t]he magnitude of the drug problem in the schools—as well as a 'marked increase' in alcohol use among pupils—is not being reported to the public by school authorities." One of the representatives who had helped put the report together said that four committee members had conducted hundreds of interviews in the school system and that their findings "were very startling."[49]

Realization of the extent of the drug problem worried suburban areas, too, and some towns were trying to come up with innovative ways to deal with the drug problem in the schools. In Wyckoff, New Jersey, for example, the approach to the problem involved letting pupils and teachers spend a day in a relaxed setting talking about what they could do for themselves and each other. In one school program, where seventh- and eighth-grade pupils were encouraged to make friends with one another, a counselor explained that "This sort of program gives us a positive approach for youngsters of this age because we think that those who don't have good feeling for themselves and others are likely to take drugs." The schools hoped that friendship and understanding would help reduce drug use.[50]

Meanwhile the governor of New Jersey announced that he would propose tougher penalties for use of "hard drugs" but would not tamper with a 1970 law that relaxed penalties for marijuana offenses.[51] Shortly thereafter, a New Jersey teacher was seized on a drug charge. The teacher was charged with encouraging about 20 high school students to smoke marijuana by locking the door, pulling the shades down while opening the windows, and instructing the students on cigarette rolling. The teacher denied all of the charges. He was arrested on the basis of affidavits signed by several students who said they had been a part of the party in their homeroom study class. A number of students who participated were scheduled for juvenile court appearances.[52]

THE SCHOOL DRUG "BATTLEGROUND" IN THE 1980s

Politicians began using the drug problem in schools as platforms for their campaigns in the early 1980s. In 1980, a candidate for the Montgomery County, Maryland, school board said, "The drug abuse problem is appalling. If the law is being broken in the schools and school officials are unable to restrain them, then the community at large has a responsibility. We just can't have schools that are battle-grounds." Another candidate had made drug education programs his major campaign platform.[53]

An eight-year-old heroin addict who was the subject of a story on juvenile drug abuse in a Sunday issue of *The Washington Post* became the object of an extensive police search. The story told that the boy had been addicted since age five, when his mother's boyfriend had allowed him to sniff heroin. The boy, a third-generation heroin addict, receives daily injections, sometimes administered by the same man, a drug dealer. One of the responses to the story was that an elementary school teacher called police and told them that a corner store near the school was selling dope.[54]

Some five days later, police in Washington, D.C., arrested 24 persons at 14 schools who were allegedly involved in drug trafficking in the schools. It was reported that between 1978 and 1979 the number of juveniles arrested on drug charges increased by 26 percent. One hundred fifty-eight arrests had been made from January to July 1980 in the district.[55]

In October 1981, it was announced that cocaine had become "America's 'Drug of Choice.'" The report from the Drug Enforcement Administration said that use of the drug was increasing rapidly among high school students: "When we took our first survey of high school seniors in 1975, 6 percent said they used cocaine. When we took our next survey in 1979, 12 percent said they had used it," an official said.[56]

Small towns were also affected by the drug epidemic in schools. Reports of drug dealing among students at both the high school and the elementary school in Millville, New Jersey, set off outrage in the community. The high school paper had published an anonymous interview with a drug dealer who sold to the school children. He reported that the school parking lots and bathrooms were the most popular spots for drug use. The drug dealer said that he sold marijuana to elementary school children, some of whom were heavy users. One junior student said that drugs were sold and used right in one teacher's classroom and that at lunchtime 50 or more students would be in the bathroom using drugs.[57]

In February 1983, it was reported that drug use among young people was on the decrease. But the number of heroine- and cocaine-related deaths was increasing because addicts were using stronger forms of drugs. The National Institute on Drug Abuse survey showed that one out of 16 high school seniors used marijuana daily, whereas the number had been one in nine in 1978.[58] This apparently was true in Washington, D.C., where city officials announced that the city's drug addiction rate was at an all time high and that the city had the second-highest rate of alcoholism in the country. The school system designated substance-abuse teams in each school in the city.[59]

In 1986, police and schools working together made numerous drug arrests and expulsions. In Los Angeles, Washington, D.C., and many other places, students were expelled. At Grossmont Union High School near San Diego, 66 students were expelled at the same time.[60]

The kind of damage done to schools by drugs and other forms of substance abuse was not always immediately apparent. But the disruptions to the lives of students, the academic programs of the school, and the criminal activity—often directed at pupils, teachers, and the school environment itself—generated by drug use took a heavy toll.

As the decade of the 1990s began, the American school faced one of its most difficult problems.

THE DRUG PROBLEM IN THE 1980s

The infestation of schools by drug sellers resulted, in 1990, in mass arrests in Los Angeles, where 113 high school students were among the 162 suspected drug dealers taken by police. An investigation at nine high schools brought about the arrests.[61] Drug raids continued through the 1990s, and usually undercover officers were involved.

In a raid in Clearwater, Florida, in 1995, detectives descended on Countryside High School and began pulling students from classes. For six weeks undercover police had attended the school. During the mass arrests, confusion ran high; two students even turned themselves in when they were not on the detectives' lists. The high profile raid—students were read their rights in front of other students—was intended to send a message to all students. The officers arrested 17 students in all. The sheriff made it clear that he did not think Countryside was worse than any other school in the country. Undercover sting operations had been conducted in about seven county high schools.[62]

Perhaps it had to happen. In 1997, a high school teacher was accused of using cocaine in his classroom. After an administrator saw the teacher snorting cocaine, the teacher was placed on administrative leave. The teacher was alleged to have used the drugs during lunchtime in his classroom.[63]

GANGS, DRUGS, AND SCHOOLS[64]

Much of the illegal drug activity often taking place in or near schools around the country involved gangs. The fact that there were some sweeping arrests of gang members selling drugs to school children may have brought about a kind of truce between gangs and the schools in which gangs did not intrude into the workings of schools and schools left gangs to their own business away from the campuses of educational institutions.

One such arrest took place in Orange County, California, in 1994. A special task force of law enforcement officers came into a Santa Ana neighborhood gripped by rampant crime and began arresting 130 people. The youngest gang member arrested was a 12-year-old boy. The charges involved selling drugs near five of the city's public schools. The massive "Operation Roundup" permitted the officers from eight different agencies to take most of the gang's members in one sweep. Undercover agents who had gained the confidence of drug dealers, making videotaped purchases of heroin and cocaine, made the arrests possible. A police spokesman said that often gangs intimidate witnesses, so few gang members are convicted, but this time he believed the charges would stick.[65]

There was a discernible and usually traceable relationship between gangs, drugs, and violence. Many of the fatal shootings during the 1990s were gang-related. Many of the other school disruptions were related to drug-use and disputes about the territoriality of gangs. For instance, it became apparent in California in 1991 that gang activity was beginning to disrupt school sporting events on a fairly large scale.[66]

A popular cheerleader was shot in the head and killed at a California school in 1992 when she got caught up in the gunfire between two gangs. She was the second student from Paramount High School to be killed by gangs within a few months.[67] Another student was stabbed to death as gang violence erupted near a San Diego high school. It was the second student death as a result of a gang fight within a week—a few days previously a student was stabbed at Mission Bay High School. Gang feuding had been responsible for nine gang killings in San Diego in the month of January 1993.[68]

Gang violence became such a problem in Los Angeles in 1993 that the papers said that in spite of zero tolerance policies, gang truces, and law enforcement sweeps, the killing continued. The paper reported that more than 50 gang-related homicides in 1993 were triple

the number of gang killings in 1989. Most school systems had insti-
tuted zero tolerance policies in which offenders would be expelled.
There were some signs that the community was fighting back to stop
the violence.[69]

But the epidemic of gang violence was not restricted to large urban areas. In a town 600 miles from Houston, drive-by shootings
were occurring in 1993 where people used to say the sidewalks would
be rolled up at 9:00 P.M. In a nearby town, 12 drive-by shootings
happened in one year. The police chief said that there were between
six and 12 gangs in the town. The school districts in the towns
adopted a ban on violence, meaning that any fight would result in
an arrest. Parents were fined for each arrest. In some of the towns
the numbers in gangs dwindled.[70]

Concerted efforts by police and school officials, with help from the
U.S. Department of Education and state education divisions gradually helped change the situation of gangs versus schools. In some
places, a kind of truce sometimes developed so that gang activity was
less and less apparent in schools. Even the number of gang-related
deaths in schools declined as the decade neared a conclusion.

GANGS AT THE TURN OF THE CENTURY

But perhaps all of that was illusory, for problems with the gangs
continued well into the late 1990s. Illegal drugs sold by gang members near schools became the target of a massive sweep in a crime-
and drug-infested neighborhood in Los Angeles in 1994. The police
crackdown ended a reign of terror by the 6th Street Gang. The massive "Operation Roundup" indicted 130 gang members.[71]

In Hartford, police reported in October 2000 that gangs that had
been dormant for several years were on the resurgence in public
schools, once again openly recruiting members in the schools. One
official said that 4-5-6, an off-shoot of the 20 Love gang, probably
had been created in the previous few months. Its membership is primarily black and it is not well organized, but it could revive the 20
Love gang. The greatest gang presence was in Bulkeley High School
and Quirk Middle School. Police were also concerned about future
recruitment efforts at an elementary school in a troubled corridor.
They said they had noticed an increased gang presence in about 1998
as second-string crime leaders completed prison terms given out during the gang-busting federal and state prosecution efforts of the early
1990s.[72]

At the turn of the century, there was evidence that gangs were making a comeback. They had already proven the harm they could do by bringing drugs, sex, and violence into schools. They had also mastered the art of intimidation—other kids were afraid to tell authorities about the gang presence in schools.

NOTES

1. Bruce J. Schulman, *The Seventies: The Great Shift in American Culture, Society, and Politics* (New York: Free Press, 2001).

2. George Packer, "The Decade Nobody Knows," *New York Times,* June 14, 2000. http://www.nytimes.com/books/01/06/10/reviews/010610.10packert.html.

3. The authors are very much indebted to Jennifer M. Watson, school safety consultant and trainer, for her helpful advice and assistance in developing ideas and materials about remedies for this chapter.

4. As in all the other chapters of this book, we have had to select incidents from among hundreds—if not thousands—of available stories about criminal and procedural violations of rules against sexual contact with students in schools across the United States. We believe, after seeing the evidence, that this is the tip of the iceberg, as we said in Chapter 1. There is very little documentation on sexual harassment cases, and even less on bullying incidents. How schools meet these challenges is of paramount interest.

5. "Scribner Promises Action to Curb School Violence," *New York Times,* March 24, 1971, pg. 6. "Boy, 15, Seized in Bronx Attack," *New York Times,* March 26, 1971, pg. 79.

6. "School Officials Seek Safeguards After Attacks on 2 Teachers," *New York Times,* March 21, 1971, pg. 53.

7. "Teacher, 20, Raped in School," *New York Times,* January 27, 1973, pg. 64. Also, "Paterson Youth is Seized After a Classroom Rape," *New York Times,* January 28, 1973, pg. 43. "Teacher, 21, Tells of Rape in School," *New York Times,* April 10, 1973, pg. 90.

8. "Queens School Robbed of $1,000; 2 Teachers Accosted in Brooklyn," *New York Times,* February 10, 1973, pg. 17.

9. "Police Team Seizes a Suspect in Rape," *New York Times,* March 21, 1973, pg. 29.

10. "Nude Body Found in River Identified by Jersey Police," *New York Times,* September 7, 1973, pg. 39.

11. "D.C. Jury Sets $640,000 As Damages in Rape Case," *New York Times,* June 25, 1976, pg. 13.

12. "Schools Assailed After Sex Attacks on 10-Year-Olds," *Washington Post,* September 22, 1979, pg. C1.

13. "Students Accused of High School Classroom Rape," *Washington Post*, December 14, 1979, pg. D1.

14. "Venereal Disease Increasing Among High School Students Here," *New York Times*, October 10, 1971, pg. 50.

15. "Teacher, 40, and Ex-Student, 18, Wed After Two-Year Romance," *New York Times*, August 12, 1973, pg. 44.

16. "An Inquiry on Teacher-Student Sex," *New York Times*, June 7, 1978, pg. 16.

17. "L.I. School Aide Accused of Sex Abuse of Girls," *New York Times*, April 11, 1978, pg. 26.

18. "Teacher Aide Charged in Acts with Children," *Washington Post*, January 10, 1979, pg. B5.

19. "Bernardo: Fire Teacher in Sex Case," *Washington Post*, January 24, 1979, pg. C2.

20. "Maryland Teacher is Acquitted on Sex Offense Charges," *Washington Post*, June 5, 1979, pg. C1.

21. "A Student's Accusation, A Teacher's Nightmare," *Washington Post*, November 3, 1977, pg. B1.

22. "Md. Teacher Charged in Sex Case with Pupil," *Washington Post*, December 15, 1978, pg. A17.

23. "Md. Student, 12, Testifies Teacher Molested Him," *Washington Post*, May 29, 1979, pg. C2.

24. "National Survey Finds the Sexual Harassing of Students is Rising," *New York Times*, October 12, 1982, pg. 47.

25. "Judge Bars Paper from Printing Data on School Aide in Sex Case," *New York Times*, May 16, 1981, pg. 16.

26. "Jury Awards $3 Million to Girl Raped in Stairwell of School," *New York Times*, April 24, 1983, pg. 1-2–46.

27. "Parent Pressure Keeps Teacher Charged With Assault Out of Classroom," *San Diego Union-Tribune*, September 5, 1984, pg. A-7.

28. "Teachers Learn About Abuse," *New York Times*, November 13, 1983, pg. 11–8.

29. "Teacher Convicted in Sex Case," *New York Times*, April 28, 1982, pg. B7.

30. See "Montgomery County Schoolteacher Arrested," *Washington Post*, July 17, 1982, pg. A9; "8 Indicted in Baltimore Child Sex Case," *Washington Post*, November 30, 1982, pg. B11; "Aide Accused of Child Abuse at State School," *Washington Post*, May 12, 1983, pg. B7; "Bethesda Man Jailed on Sex, Drug Charges Involving Juveniles," *Washington Post*, June 16, 1983, pg. B4.

31. To find some of the instances, please check "Coach in Rockville Charged in Sexual Assault on 2 Girls," *Washington Post*, March 11, 1988, pg. B3, "Coach Is Charged with Abuse of Girl, 6", *St. Louis Post Dispatch*, March 23, 1989, NP; "Coach Arrested for Alleged Sex Acts with 2 Girls,"

Los Angeles Times, January 14, 1988, pgs. 2–3; "Wentzville School Coach Charged with Sex Crime," *St. Louis Post Dispatch,* July 11, 1989, pg. 6A; "Jury in Newark Finds a Teacher Guilty of Abuse," April 16, 1988, pg. 34; "Social Worker Charged With Sexual Assault," *St. Louis Post Dispatch,* November 3, 1989, pg. 3A.

32. "Student, 15, Seized in Sexual Assaults on 8 Year Old Girls," *New York Times,* October 4, 1985, pg. B3.

33. "Fairfax to Lock Doors at All Grade Schools," *Washington Post,* February 27, 1989, pg. E5.

34. "What's Wrong at Sullivan High?" *St. Louis Post Dispatch,* May 12, 1990, pg. 3B.

35. "Court Hears Harassment Case," *St. Louis Post-Dispatch,* December 12, 1991, pg. 18A.

36. "Powerful Impact of Bias Against Girls," *Los Angeles Times,* February 22, 1992, pg. B6.

37. "The Pain of Harassment—Teenager Says She Still Lives in Fear of High School," *Seattle Times,* November 2, 1993, pg. E8.

38. "2nd Teacher Suicide is Reported: Va. Death Also Tied to Sex Charges," *Washington Post,* July 10, 1993, pg. B4.

39. "Alleged Rape Victim Sues Atlanta School Officials," *Atlanta Constitution,* October 6, 1992, pg. C2.

40. "7th Graders Say Student Forced Sex During Class," *Birmingham News,* January 17, 1998, pg. 01-A.

41. "Teen Faces Charges of Forcing Classmates Into Sex," *Birmingham News,* January 21, 1998, pg. 01-A.

42. "Abuse of Gay Students Brings Increase in Lawsuits," *Los Angeles Times,* May 28, 1999, pg. A1.

43. "Rape of La Mesa Girl, 11, Shocks Students, Teachers," *Los Angeles Times,* September 29, 1990, pg. B1.

44. "Ex-Fern Creek High Teacher Gets 2 Years for Raping Student, 15," *Courier-Journal,* October 23, 1990, pg. 5B. "Ex-Teacher to Stand Trial on 21 Counts of Child Molestation," *Los Angeles Times,* October 31, 1990, pg. B3.

45. "Teacher for 30 Years Faces Sex Abuse Sentence," *USA Today,* November 14, 1990, pg. 3A.

46. "374 Drug Arrests in 6 and ½ Years Made Among School Personnel," *New York Times,* February 10, 1973, pgs. 1, 64.

47. "Teacher is Seized on Heroin Charge," *New York Times,* August 23, 1973, pg. 41.

48. "2 Teachers Seized As Police Report Finding Heroin in Car," *New York Times,* March 25, 1971, pg. 35.

49. "House Panel Finds Big Rise in Drug Use By New York's Schoolchildren," *New York Times,* February 8, 1977, pg. 54.

50. "Wyckoff Combats Drugs With Talk and Friendship," *New York Times,* February 17, 1974, pg. 78.

51. "Marijuana Penalties To Remain Relaxed," *New York Times,* February 17, 1974, pg. 78.

52. "Teacher Seized on Drug Charge," *New York Times,* March 3, 1974, pg. 24.

53. "School Board Election Issues," *Washington Post,* April 24, 1980, pg. Md.1.

54. "Young 'Fagin' is Nabbed; Search for Boy Addict Grows," *Washington Post,* October 2, 1980, pg. C1.

55. "Drug Sales Probed at District Schools During Past Year," *Washington Post,* October 7, 1980, pg. C1.

56. "Cocaine: America's 'Drug of Choice,'" *Washington Post,* October 27, 1981, pg. A1.

57. "Story of Drugs at School Disturbs Jersey Mill City," *New York Times,* March 30, 1981, pg. B2.

58. "Heroine, Cocaine Overdoses Rise Young Americans Cut Use of Marijuana," *Washington Post,* February 4, 1983, pg. A1.

59. "D.C. Drug Addiction at Record High," *Washington Post,* April 22, 1983, pg. B1.

60. "66 Students Expelled After Drug Arrests," *San Diego Union-Tribune,* April 10, 1986, pg. B1. "Baby Faced Rookies Pull Off Drug Busts in D.C. Schools," *Washington Post,* May 10, 1986, pg. A1. "Undercover Work Nets Md. School Drug Arrests," *Washington Post,* December 16, 1986, pg. B1.

61. "162 Seized in Drug Arrests in Schools," *Los Angeles Times,* December 14, 1990, pg. B2.

62. "Drug Sting Puts Campus in Shock," *Tampa Tribune,* March 17, 1995, pg. 1.

63. "Teacher Accused of Using Cocaine in Classroom," *Los Angeles Times,* October 23, 1997, pg. B1.

64. This chapter focuses solely on gang activity in relation to drugs in the 1990s. The story of gangs is discussed in Chapter 3 as well, but the subject is too vast to be covered in its entirety in this book.

65. "Sweep Targets Santa Ana Gang," *Los Angeles Times,* September 8, 1994, pg. A1.

66. "Students, Officials Affected as Gang Violence Disrupts Sporting Events," *Los Angeles Times,* November 21, 1991, pg. 7.

67. "Gangs Send a School Back into Mourning," *Los Angeles Times,* October 1, 1992, pg. A1.

68. "Killing of Student is Second in 7 Days," *San Diego Union-Tribune,* January 29, 1993, pg. B1.

69. "Still No End in Sight to Ever-Rising Gang Toll," *Los Angeles Times,* October 24, 1993, pg. B1.

70. "Teen Gang Violence a Problem in Small Towns, Too," *Houston Chronicle,* September 16, 1993, pg. 1.

71. "Sweep Targets Santa Ana Gang," *Los Angeles Times,* September 8, 1994, pg. A1.

72. "The Gangs are Back in Hartford's Schools," *Hartford Courant,* October 18, 2000, pg. A1.

Chapter 9

Terror Comes to School (1945–1992)

THE STORY OF THE VIOLENT INTRUDER

Why have intruders in educational settings killed innocent people without having seemingly anything to gain or without even wanting the notoriety for it? One has to think in such an instance of Charles Whitman, the college student in the tower at the University of Texas in Austin, Texas, on August 1, 1966, when "that nice little boy" killed 16 other people and wounded 31 with a high-powered rifle before a police officer shot and killed him. That "madman in the tower's" death was the 17th that day. Each time a similar kind of violence is perpetrated, society is shocked because what has happened is not rational: it does not seem politically motivated, and seems to be the work of madmen.[1] And non-political intrusion's random nature makes it inexplicable. Why does an enraged killer walk into a public place and kill people wantonly when there is clearly no political motive present? It is the "crazy," insane behavior of this kind of intruder that is hard to understand, especially when anger is not even evident. The madness of rage is always bizarre, but the pathology of many incidents is often either clandestine or unknowable.

And madness of rage is no stranger to the American school. Unfortunately, it did not begin with Columbine High. The incident in Bath, Michigan, in 1927 (discussed in Chapter 1), which seems to have resulted from insane rage as much as from a sick man's political revenge scheme, shows how difficult, and sometimes futile, it is to provide reasons for a criminal's actions. It can be concluded that most terrorism is based in egregious deficiencies of ego or character, normally rationalized as revenge, almost always picking on an unsuspecting and helpless victim. Sometimes it is the culmination of bullying. And what more placid, less contentious, and undeserving victim is there than a school? Violent intrusion is the antithesis of everything schools stand for. But that has not kept madmen and bullies from intruding themselves, even if some of them are students in the school that is harried.

There is no right time in modern American history to begin to tell the story of violent intrusion in the schools. One can only point to a recent era in which such activity seems to have become more frequent, more flagrant, than it had ever been, and let the incidents of the time show that the school has been too often the victim of intruders—on different occasions and perhaps for different reasons, if any can be found.[2]

The signs of an impending era of random terror in the schools were beginning to be visible in the period after World War II. In some of the early cases, lethal violence was not always purposeful, as later violence would be, even though the terror it brought still upset the entire school. However, many of the early intrusions in the 1940s, and 1950s seem mild when judged by the severity and frequency of incidents in later decades. For the sake of comparison with a later time, only three incidents from the 1940s and 1950s are included here. For instance, there was an event early in 1945 in which two boys carried a knife to school—it was not unusual in that time for boys to carry knives all of the time. A 15-year-old junior high school student was in the basement leaving the school swimming pool when the two boys attempted to rob him at knifepoint. One of the would-be robbers stabbed the swimmer in the chest with a knife, so he grabbed a knife from the other robber and began slashing the would-be thieves, stabbing one of them in the chest.[3]

In March 1947, a 15-year-old student took out a gun at school in Newark, New Jersey, and approached his carpentry teacher in the classroom shop where he took two shots at the teacher from a distance of ten feet. He missed both times. The teacher ran out into the hall, pursued by the boy, who took a third shot at the man as he ran down the corridor. Seeking revenge, the boy had told classmates that he "had a Christmas present for the teacher" after the teacher had reprimanded him several times. The boy was apprehended, and his clear intention to kill the teacher went unrealized.[4]

A group of high school girls was in the gymnasium in their high school in New York in 1951 listening to a lecture by their health teacher when a man broke into the room. He had just come from the school office, where he had yelled at and then accosted a school clerk. Two pupils who had witnessed that encounter slipped out and told a policeman, who came back in seeking the man. The distraught man tapped one of the students on the head with a vase he was carrying, causing the teacher to begin yelling at him to leave the room; when she realized that he would not leave, she told the girls to rise, instructing them how to leave the room in an orderly fashion. The patrolman then began chasing the man, who threw the vase at him. The man lunged at the policeman, who pulled his revolver and shot him in the head.[5]

A different kind of violence began in the 1960s (see Chapter 6) and continued at what seems to be a more insane pace in the 1970s. Studies of this era are now beginning to yield an understanding of the motivation of some of the intruders.

The U.S. Secret Service in collaboration with the U.S. Department of Education with support from the National Institute of Justice conducted a "Safe Schools Initiative" which studied 37 school shootings involving 41 attackers who were current or recent students in school beginning with a shooting in 1974.[6] In over half the incidents studied, the attacker shot at least one faculty, administrator, or staff member, and in more than two-thirds of the incidents the attacker killed one or more students. The incidents took place in 26 states and were all committed by boys. In most of the incidents, the attacker planned the attack, did not just "snap," and more than half of them had revenge as a motive. Many had communicated their grievance to others prior to the attack. The student attackers came from a variety of racial backgrounds, family situations, and academic performance levels. They ranged from popular to isolated, their behavior histories varied, and few had been diagnosed with any mental disorder or substance abuse problem.[7]

The 1970s are a good period to begin the study of school shootings for several reasons. For one thing, the '70s were a period when violence in the schools was very high; authorities in the schools, leaders in government, and journalists frequently expressed their concern about schools. A report by the Carnegie Corporation issued in 1970 called public schools "oppressive, grim, and joyless."[8] This indictment of the nation's schools, which recommended a radical reordering of the classroom along more informal lines, suggested that schools are preoccupied with order, control, and routine that represses students and produces docility, passivity, and conformity.

Perhaps ironically, schools, especially those in urban areas, were concomitantly reporting rising rates of crime and violence. Interviews with school officials in twenty cities and a Senate subcommittee study showed that the growing problem of violence was calling for harsh measures such as the increased use of guards in the schools. The sub-committee study declared that the most dramatic rise in violence involved non-students who congregated in and around schools. Explosions and threats occurring at schools around the nation served to prove the findings of the report. Schools in different parts of the country experienced explosions and fires about the time of the report.

New York City's high school principals issued a report in 1972 saying that a partial count had shown that there had been more than 5,000 acts of violence and disruptive behavior in the city high schools in the previous nine months. The principals called upon the board of education to "develop policies and institute practices" to ensure that schools were safe.[9] The principals' report provided higher fig-ures than a board of education study issued two months previously. The board report said that instances of crime and violence in the city's schools had increased from 333 in 1970 to 580 in 1971. The inci-dents involved assaults on teachers and students, rapes and moles-tations, robberies, bombs and smoke bombs, and threats against staff members.[10] At least, both reports agreed that disruptive and intru-sive behavior in the schools was on the rise.

Roman Catholic schools also had their share of trouble. There were 121 children in St. Cecelia's Catholic School in Peoria, Illinois, on May 1, 1973, when three men burst into the school in mid-afternoon, holding high-powered rifles and almost a dozen pistols on one class of 24 students and two teachers. The hostage-taking ordeal lasted for two hours when 50 policemen arrived and tried to enter the build-ing but had to retreat under a volley of gunfire. One of the gunmen came out of the school holding a child in front of him. Melvin Birch, 25 years old, then fired two shots in the air, and as the child ran away, he yelled, "Kill me, kill me, kill me," and the police obliged him. The police then took the other two suspects, reputed to be members of the Black Panthers, into custody. None of the children was seriously hurt.[11]

In early 1975, the "West Virginia Textbook Case" was underway in West Virginia. A fundamentalist preacher, Reverend Martin Horan, a 36-year-old former truck driver, was carrying on a campaign against the "Godless" and "dirty" textbooks used in the local elementary schools around Charleston two years earlier. According to testimony in the trial Horan and his coal-miner protégé, Larry Elmer Stevens, had planned to place electric dynamite caps in the gasoline tanks of school buses and the cars of parents who were ignoring the anti-textbook campaign's call for a boycott by students.

Experts also said that Horan planned to place a five-gallon gasoline can on top of the Midway Elementary School's boiler and turn up the heat. Another school, the Midway School at Campbell Creek, was one of three schools actually damaged by dynamite bombs. The jury found Horan and his accomplice guilty of dynamiting those schools.[12]

HIGH SCHOOL SHOOTER, 1975

In 1975, three other incidents occurred that could have been a frightening foreshadowing of terror to come in ensuing years. In January, in Olean, New York, a 17-year-old high school senior was seen carrying canvas gun cases into the high school. Anthony Barbaro apparently set a small fire, turned in a fire alarm, and then shot at firemen as they responded. A 66-year-old custodian who went to the third floor to investigate was killed. The driver of the first fire engine to arrive was shot in the head as he stopped the fire truck. As Barbaro fired bullets and shot gun pellets from third-floor windows, the Olean police force was deployed around the school. Not all passers-by successfully ducked for cover; a meter reader was hit, and the volley of gunshots repulsed fire and policemen trying to retrieve him. One passer-by, Carmen Wright, who had her brother and four small children in the car, was killed, and her brother was injured. The children were not hurt. In the meantime, five more firemen were hit by bullets, either directly or as they ricocheted.

A personnel carrier from the National Guard armory was sent to the scene and arrived at the same time state police were surrounding the school. About that time a joint force of local and state police had entered the school through the rear and worked its way up to the top floor.

When they came to the room where the sniper had barricaded himself, police fired in and threw in a tear gas canister. When the firing stopped, the police went in to find the youth unconscious, yet wearing a gas mask. It was not until police had carried him out that his identity was known: when the gas mask was removed, Michael Barbaro, a school security officer and member of the assault party, recognized the youth as his nephew.

Afterward, teachers and friends tried to figure out why the boy had committed such atrocities. Two weeks previously, he had won a Regents scholarship. He was eighth in his class academically and had talked about becoming an engineer. His English teacher and his guidance counselor both said that Barbaro was likable and intelligent. Other teachers said that he did not seem to have a girlfriend and that he kept to himself.

However, one of Barbaro's classmates said that "guns were his life," that guns were prominently displayed in his house, and that Barbaro constantly talked about shooting and hunting. He said that Barbaro had once mentioned, "How funny it must feel to be a sniper holding off people."

That this incident did not take place in an urban area, that the boy was from a respectable small-town family of four children, certainly at least in retrospect gave it the aspect of foreshadowing similar events that would take place in the 1990s.[13]

On March 1, 1975, the quiet town of Penns Grove, New Jersey, was shocked when an intruder walked into a Catholic grammar school classroom and shot the teacher while her students looked on. The intruder to St. James Grammar School then shot and killed the school's principal, a priest, Father Thomas J. Quinlan. Motives for the shootings were unknown.[14]

Two weeks later, a Molotov cocktail was thrown against the garage door belonging to a school board member in Brooklyn. The door was badly damaged, but there were no injuries. The police posted a 24-hour guard at the brick row home, which is across the street from Junior High 68. Members of the board of education thought that the act might have been provoked by a zoning controversy that had troubled Canarsie.[15]

"SCHOOLS ARE NO LONGER SANCTUARIES," 1976

In March 1976, a retired New York teacher concluded, "The city's schools are no longer sanctuaries. They have become places of fear, invaded by vandals, muggers, rapists, gangs, disturbed and dangerous students and outsiders."[16]

His commentary was validated by two studies that came out in the same month. A report said that crime in New York City schools was up 70 percent from the first four months of the previous year. A state senator said the reason was that there had been a dismissal of more than 1,000 school safety officers because of the city's financial crisis. "Security personnel cuts have turned the schools into battlefields in which teachers and students are terrorized daily," Senator Roy M. Goodman said.[17]

A federally financed study released at the same time contended that violence was rampant in the nation's schools. The report, prepared by Better Schools, Inc. for the Law Enforcement Assistance Administration, stated, "It is fair to conclude that school violence and disruption is a serious and costly national problem."[18]

A few months later, 26 summer school students, 19 girls and seven boys ranging in age from six to 14, and their bus driver were kidnapped in Chowchilla, California, and buried alive at a rock quarry. Warrants were issued for the sons of three prominent families from a town near Palo Alto. One of the young men was the son of a businessman who owned the rock quarry where the children were discovered the following day, 100 miles from home.

The abductors had taken the children to the quarry in two vans and hidden them in a trailer, which was at least partially covered by dirt, rocks, and boards. Most of the children were from poor families, their parents unskilled workers and persons on welfare. Their hometown of Chowchilla was a farming community where there was high unemployment; most of the residents there were white southerners who had come there during the drought of the 1930s.

The bus driver picked up the children from the Dairyland Union School at 3:45 P.M. The bus made three stops to drop off children and then veered off its usual route and continued west toward the Berenda Slough, where the bus was found at about 7:00 P.M. after parents began calling the school. The driver said masked gunmen ambushed the bus and herded the children into the two vans, which were used to drive them to the quarry where they were entombed for 16 hours in the buried van. Eventually, the driver and the children were able to dig their way out of the van to safety. One of the boys then found a watchman who called the police.[19]

In Cliffside Park, New Jersey, in May 1976, a high school girl was walking down the hall when a powerful firecracker exploded in a glass-encased fire extinguisher cabinet. Glass shards hit the 14-year-old and killed her. Also hit were two other students. The hallway was filled with students when the blast went off, but Elizabeth Hennessy, a freshman honor roll student, just happened to be right next to the glass case.[20]

In Detroit, in November 1976, class was in session in an elementary school when a gunman barged in and shot the teacher five times in the head while the 29 six- and seven-year-old children watched. The 45-year-old black teacher died instantly. Police later arrested a man said to be her estranged husband.

School officials now faced a situation they had never faced before: they were very concerned about the emotional well-being of the children who had witnessed the violent death of their teacher. Parents reported that the children were afraid to go to school, wet their beds, and had nightmares. The school provided counseling for the children but feared, several months later, that the psychological damage done to the children had not been repaired.[21]

SCHOOL BUS VIOLENCE

In the immature mind, perhaps there is little difference between a prank and a serious felony, except that the meanness level is accelerated considerably. Two teenage boys in the same city, Detroit, fired shots at a moving school bus in November 1977, injuring three children who were riding the bus. Juvenile authorities held the 14-year-old who apparently did most of the shooting.[22]

Several acts of terrorism in schools and school buses grabbed the nation's attention in 1978. In March, an armed teenager in Michigan, distraught because his girlfriend had spurned him, decided to hijack her school bus. He carried an unloaded shotgun. After unsuccessfully trying to get him to give up, police shot him twice in the stomach. The girl and four other students on the bus were shaken but unhurt.[23]

A couple of months later, another school bus was struck by gunfire in Philadelphia. State police said that the bus was carrying junior high students home to Chester County after a visit to the Philadelphia zoo when gunfire on the right side of the bus shattered windows. Eight students were wounded, one girl seriously. The police were unable to capture the assailant at the time.[24] However, several days later police arrested a teenager. They uncovered a .30 06-caliber rifle, a .22-caliber rifle, ammunition for the .30 06, and spent cartridges.

The gun had been fired. The police were led to the suspect after interviewing neighborhood residents.[25]

In the same month of May, the son of Lyndon Johnson's press secretary shot and killed a teacher in Austin, Texas, who had given him a failing grade. Thirteen-year-old John Daniel Christian walked into the classroom of Wilbur Rodney Grayson, 29, who taught an accelerated English course, and shot him three times with a .22-caliber semi-automatic rifle. The boy entered the classroom 15 minutes after class had begun. Mr. Grayson was shot in the arm, chest, and forehead and was dead on arrival at the hospital. After shooting the teacher, the boy ran out of the school, tossed the rifle away, and was caught by a physical education teacher.[26]

In June 1978, a teenager chose a dramatic way to terrorize his community. He stepped to the microphone at his own high school graduation and said, "This is the American way," and shot himself. The shooting occurred after he and other members of the South Weymouth High School choral group had finished singing. As the youth lay on the ground with the revolver in his hand, he said, "There are too many issues in America today."[27]

GIRL ON A SHOOTING SPREE, 1979

A San Diego girl redefined the word "fun" when she claimed she was shooting at an elementary school in that city "for fun." On the morning of January 30, 1979, 16-year-old Brenda Spencer, who lived in a blue-collar area across from Cleveland Elementary School, began a shooting spree just after 8:50 A.M. as children were arriving at the school. The shooting lasted about 15 minutes and was followed by a six-hour siege in which she was holed up in the home from which she picked off the principal and the head custodian with a rifle, killing both men.

In addition to shooting the two men, Spencer shot two boys, six girls, and a police officer. Reporters for the San Diego Evening *Tribune* reached the girl by phone during the shooting spree. The girl told the reporter that she had received the rifle as a Christmas present. Asked why she was shooting, she said, "I just started shooting. That's it. I just did it for fun." Her father later said that she had 500 rounds of ammunition in the house.

The maintenance man was the first to be shot by the .22-caliber bullets. A mother dropping her children off at the school saw the man's body and thought he had died of a heart attack. Then she saw the body of a little girl, and she realized that bullets were still flying. At that point the principal came out to warn students to get back, and he was shot and killed. An 11-year-old boy came along and found the wounded girl lying in the street, but a teacher told him to run, and he left the girl to go inside the school.

Inside, teachers and students were lying on the floor of classrooms and restrooms. About 75 pupils were taken to the auditorium, which had brick walls. At about that time, special weapons and tactics officers surrounded the girl's home and began attempting to communicate with her by phone and by bullhorn; she quietly gave herself up several hours later.

Classmates of the child of a broken home who did not get along with her teachers described Spencer. Labeled as a tomboy who loved guns, she was skinny, sad, and loved SWAT-style television shows. Police later said that she had fantasized about being a sniper and may even have shot at the same school on a previous occasion when no one was there.[28]

Chicago, in September 1979, saw a similar occurrence by another 16-year-old with a gun. A boy with a pistol came out from behind a pile of bricks at the end of a football field and began firing the gun at the players and coaches about 60 feet from where they practiced in uniform. One of the players, a 17-year-old junior, was struck in the middle of his chest. The coach was hit in the arm by a bullet. The boy then ran off.

Hours later, police arrived at the home of a boy who said he had been beaten up earlier in the day and wanted to get revenge so he began shooting at members of the football team, even though he did not know whether his assailant was playing there or not.

The coach said that the players had just emerged from a huddle when he heard a ringing noise, then another and another. He turned to see the boy with the gun running off and the player on the ground with blood gushing from his chest. Farragut High School students were mostly black with a minority of Hispanic youths. The shooter was a Hispanic boy.[29]

At Suitland High School near Washington, D.C., in October 1979, another weapon-carrying student decided to discharge his gun on the school grounds near the stadium. A twelfth-grade boy took out a sawed-off shotgun during a lunch-hour argument and shot another student in the left hand and lower abdomen. The police charged the shooter with assault with intent to murder.[30]

TEACHERS WITH GUNS, 1979–1980

Perhaps the horror inflicted by Brenda Spencer in 1979 was one of the first acts of terrorism by a female in America's schools. But the diversification of culprits soon would broaden to include even teachers as terrorists. While previously—and perhaps still—most terrorist activity had been conducted by males, mostly young, the cast of characters in mental or psychological disarray was about to expand.

Teachers have always been the closest persons to the action in schools, and because they do work so closely with children and the adult community around the school, they are subjected to potential terrorism more than other professional persons would be. Though it is not fair to point to any one teacher as representative of a very noble group of people, teachers are human, and occasionally a teacher will act in a way that is not at all representative of the body of professional people who serve our nation's schools so well.

This was the case in 1979 when a sixth-grade teacher in Washington, D.C., was charged with kidnapping, assault, and conspiracy to murder. The teacher and his wife allegedly captured an 18-year-old neighbor, tied him up in their basement, set him on fire with lighter fluid and told him that he would be murdered.[31]

In 1980, a former high school teacher in Texas went on a shooting rampage in his local community. Alvin Lee King was to go on trial for incest charges and wanted some members of his church to serve as character witnesses for him. When they refused, he burst into a Sunday church service in the northeast Texas town of Dangerfield and began shooting people. He carried two bayoneted weapons, an AR–15 semi-automatic rifle and an M–1 carbine, and two pistols, which he began firing. King cried, "This is war," as he continued firing into the crowd. Three members of the congregation wrestled him down, but he shot and killed two of them. He then ran to a nearby fire station and shot himself in the temple. King had killed five people and injured 12 others.[32]

The following year, in 1981, another former teacher and assistant principal was charged with a shooting. The man fired a gun into a group of students after they yelled racial epithets at his daughters near their home, a few blocks from the school. He told a reporter that he was so tired of the taunting that "the wheel just fell off" on the night he fired the gun. No one was killed in the incident.[33]

An incident in a Washington, D.C., school in 1980 demonstrated that the mere act of carrying a gun into a school could be an act of terrorism. At about 10:30 A.M., about 50 people were gathered in the school's auditorium for registration. Several students were sitting in the front row, passing around a pistol when the weapon went off, killing one student.[34]

This incident at Spingarn High School was followed by three other incidents in which District of Columbia students were involved in incidents in which students carried deadly weapons into a school. Two of the incidents involved a gun and two knives.[35]

ATTACKS ON TEACHERS, 1980

Beginning in the late 1970s, attacks on teachers were frequently meant to terrorize an entire school as well as to take revenge of some sort on an authority figure. (Attacks on teachers up through the period of 1969 are discussed in Chapter 7). One teacher who gave his students failing grades in 1979 was nearly murdered by three girls and a boy, ages 12 and 13, who put poison in his coffee. The students admitted to putting mercury from a thermometer into the teacher's coffee thermos.[36]

In 1980, a teacher who was accused of sodomizing a student in Harlem was beaten to death by that student.[37]

In March 1982, Clarence Piggott, a psychology and sociology teacher in Las Vegas, was shot to death in his classroom shortly before classes began at 8:00 A.M. at Valley High School. A senior at the high school, Patrick Lizotte, 18, shot the 55-year-old teacher. As he ran from the school, the shooter fired at and hit two other students. The school's vice principal chased the assailant about five blocks before the police blocked him, ordering him to halt. When the youth pulled a .22-caliber pistol, officers opened fire, hitting him in the chest. Students who witnessed the shooting in the classroom laughed when the boy opened fire on the teacher, as they thought it was all a joke. When the teacher dropped to his knees, the students knew he had actually been shot. The two students who were shot apparently "just got in the way" as the boy was running away.[38]

In 1983, a Rockford, Illinois, teacher was shot in the neck by a student as she stood in front of the classroom. The male student, a 15-year-old, carried a .357-caliber handgun. Reportedly, he had bragged to fellow students over the previous week that he was going to shoot the teacher because she had disciplined him. Classmates thought he was joking.[39]

In Harrisburg, Pennsylvania, in October 1983, a high school English teacher was convicted of killing a fellow teacher and her two children. The teacher killed his former lover, with whom he had formerly taught at Upper Merion High School near Philadelphia, because he was the listed beneficiary of $900,000 in the female teacher's will and various life insurance policies. The defendant's attorney tried to link the former principal of the high school to the murders as well.[40]

A 24-year-old male teacher's aide who had been dismissed after fighting with a student took action that filled a school and a community with terror in 1983 on New York's Long Island. Wearing military fatigues and carrying a rifle, the aide returned to Brentwood East Junior High School, shot the boy with whom he had fought and then shot the principal of the school. Next he took 18 other students hostage and held them for nine hours. Later, he would shoot and kill himself.

In the junior high school of 980 students, the gunman took a ninth-grade class hostage around 1:00 P.M. When the gunman entered the classroom, he told the teacher to leave and made the students lie on the floor. "I'm not leaving here alive, you kids messed up my career," the students quoted him as having said. When the principal peered through the classroom door's window, he was shot in the cheek. Then the gunman approached the boy he had fought with and shot him twice. Another student carried the wounded boy out of the room.

Shortly after that, the intruder released 12 students when they became nauseated. In the meantime, police had surrounded the school. An orderly evacuation of the other classrooms in the school was effected with the use of the loudspeakers. Coats were left behind as students and teachers filed outside into the rain, where parents were eagerly awaiting their children.

The gunman released other students one at a time throughout the afternoon and evening after a radio station obliged his demand that his statement be broadcast over the radio. He also made the radio station play some of his favorite tunes. Occasionally, he would fire a gun into the corridor to keep the police at bay.

The last hostage was a 14-year-old who had served as an intermediary between the gunman and the police all day. Police negotiators, who hid in a stairwell down the hall from the gunman, were never able to negotiate with him. Finally, after 9:00 P.M., the gunman shot himself in the temple, and the final hostage ran out to waiting policemen.

The Long Island hostage-taker had a history of psychiatric problems. On his application for work as a substitute aide, the gunman had listed his 64 hours of work at the local community college but said he had no history of mental illness and had no physical or mental disabilities. Allegedly, he had made threats to members of the President's cabinet. When county officials turned this information over to the Secret Service, the shooter said that he sued them on the basis that they had betrayed a medical confidence. Neighbors said that he was a loner and that he had tried to commit suicide previously.[41]

1984 SNIPER

Chaos is the only way to describe the impact wrought by a person shooting at a school early in 1984. Like Spencer in 1979, a sniper, who lived across the street from the school, began firing at the crowded schoolyard of an elementary school in southeast Los Angeles, not far from the site of the 1965 Watts riots, where there were at least 100 children. About 2:15 P.M., as children were being dismissed for the day, a 28-year-old man with a history of "irrational behavior" and drug abuse began firing at the children who were leaving the 49th Street School in southeast Los Angeles. A man who was described as having been "wild all his life" and "with a short fuse" used a high-powered rifle to cut children down.

The sniper killed a ten-year-old girl and wounded at least 13 other people before killing himself that day. A friend said that Tyrone Mitchell was related to two persons, a sister and a cousin (others said it was his parents), who died in the 1978 mass suicide-murder of more than 900 persons at Jonestown, Guyana, in the cult led by Jim Jones.

A teacher who was there observed that many children were standing around at first as the rifle went off; later many were lying on the ground around the school hoping to avoid a bullet. Reports said that three of the injured were in critical condition that night, including an adult bystander and a boy who was hit while in his classroom.

Seven ambulances were sent to the school. Some of the injured students were taken out by police helicopter while adults evacuated others safely. One ambulance pulled onto the schoolyard so that children could be pulled into the vehicle without being shot.[42]

The insane anonymity of the sniper must have been appealing, because it was beginning to be popular as a terrorist activity. Sometime during this period, the "drive-by shooting" originated, just as did the "hate crime" that became such a frequent occurrence in the 1990s. Both were evident in an incident in June 1983 when gunmen firing automatic weapons from a passing car hit two college students and a high school student in New York near the university's campus in Washington Heights, where there is also a high school. The police called the shooting a "bias incident" and connected it to two previous shootings of the same sort on the same campus and nearby at a Jewish hospital. The police claimed to have proved that the rifle used in all three shootings was the same. The shots were fired from a moving car at a restaurant "hang out" where both high school and college students spent time. Bullets pierced the windows and went over the heads of students playing video games and eating. Witnesses said that the shots had been fired from a station wagon without a rear license plate, the same station wagon that had been used in the previous shootings, police said. None of the students was killed.[43]

STUDENT SNIPER, 1985

Another relatively new phenomenon of the 1980s was the frequency of the student sniper. Students had carried weapons to school many times in the past, and students had even shot other students in school. But a new kind of student sniper seemed to emerge about this time. Here the random shooter, no longer just as maladjusted non-student or intruder, became the student with a lethal weapon. On January 22, 1985, a 14-year-old boy in Los Angeles carried a rifle to his junior high school. At about 11:00 A.M., the principal of his school met the boy carrying an M1–A semi-automatic rifle and a .357 magnum handgun as he entered the edifice. The principal reproached him about the weapons, so the boy opened fire, killing the principal and striking a teacher who stood nearby.

The boy then walked to the classroom area of the school, where he shot another teacher and a student who were standing in the hallway. Next, the boy walked into an intermediate school wing and ducked outside, where, within minutes, he was apprehended by a police officer. About 90 minutes after the boy had entered the school, police had him in custody. The weapons belonged to his father.[44]

Another kind of terrorism against a school was revealed in an incident in the Los Angeles School District in June 1985. A school bus was carrying 45 junior high school students from Van Nuys to East Los Angeles when a pedestrian sprayed a caustic liquid through the open windows of the bus. The spray canister used by the assailant contained an ammonia-based liquid. Fourteen of the passengers suffered minor injuries to their faces and eyes when the spray came into contact with them.

The bus driver pulled the vehicle over to the side of Van Nuys Boulevard when he realized that the children were complaining of itching and burning about the eyes. The students identified a fellow 15-year-old student as the one who had sprayed them. Three ambulances, a fire engine, and a hazardous materials team arrived at the scene. While this act of terrorism turned out not to have been as dangerous as it might have been, it may have been one of the first times a chemical agent was used against fellow students.[45]

FEAR OF TERRORISM, 1986

In February 1986, a number of Long Island school districts began canceling overseas trips for students because of the fear of terrorism. School officials in those districts cited the airport bombing in Rome, the hijacking of the cruise ship *Achille Lauro*, and the crisis in relations of the United States and Libya. A bomb set off in a department store in Paris where students had visited the year previous was mentioned also.[46]

But school officials were wrestling more often with problems of domestic terrorism, such as the incident that took place on Friday, May 16, 1986, in Cokeville, Wyoming. A heavily armed couple entered the Cokeville Elementary School at about 1:00 P.M. and herded the children, teachers, and administrators into a large classroom. The man began distributing leaflets, announcing, "This is the revolution," and demanded to speak with President Reagan. They would ask for $2 million for each of the hostages in the room.

The principal said the pair behaved rationally most of the time, although the man tended to get confused sometimes. The intruder told the principal he had decided to take Cokeville hostage because it was a rural community and people there cared about their children. He also said that he expected the kidnapping to last 10 days because it would take that long for Congress to approve the ransom payment.

Teachers, substitute teachers, and at least one mother of a student sang to the students and tried to keep them calm. The couple then brought out a bomb, which was described as a crude device consisting of a detonating mechanism and two cans of gasoline. The bomb had a hair trigger that had to be held down to keep the device from exploding.

One teacher who apparently tried to escape was shot in the shoulder as he ran down the hall.

When the man went to the bathroom, he handed the device to his wife to hold while he was gone, and she accidentally set off the detonating device. The woman was killed when the bomb exploded. The husband apparently shot himself as the hostages looked on.

At least 74 people suffered second-degree burns when the bomb went off, approximately three hours after the couple had entered the building to take hostages. One witness said, "the children were all in the classroom when it went off. The classroom was demolished. I don't know how they got out alive."

Complete hysteria broke out as burned children and adults streamed out of the room after the explosion. Most had burns on their faces and arms. A local reporter said that there was a good deal of smoke pouring from the room. A secretary who was in the classroom said, "I thought we were all dead. I heard this awful noise. It was smoke and flames. Just pandemonium."

About a dozen ambulances and two school buses removed the injured. At least 32 people with burns on their faces and arms were taken to Bear Lake Memorial Hospital in Montpellier, Idaho, about 30 miles from Cokeville. The man had been the town policeman at one time, it was reported.[47]

People with extreme mental problems and high-powered weapons seemed to become more numerous as the decade of the 1980s passed. A few months later, a berserk man went on a rampage at a technical college[48] campus in Brooklyn in August 1986, shooting five people, one of them fatally. A 28-year-old student wielding two handguns killed an employee in a laboratory in one building and then ran to another building to the school's financial aid office, where he shot three more people. He fired shots at policemen behind the second building and then went to a third building, where he shot a security guard.

The shooter then exchanged fire with police as he became cornered in a stairwell in the third building. The police negotiated with him for 15 minutes, and finally he threw his guns down and came out. The arresting officer said, "He looked blank. He wasn't all there."[49]

A shooting that occurred at a large high school in Los Angeles, in September 1986, profoundly affected the school in more ways than one—actually there were two main consequences. A freshman at West Los Angeles College had been visiting a former teacher at Fairfax High School when he got into an argument with two students, one of whom pulled a gun and shot him. He died in a hospital shortly thereafter. The first impact of the shooting was a drop in enrollment, which would result in a reduced number of teachers assigned to the school. Parents decided that the school was not safe and began withdrawing their children. Within two weeks an estimated 35 students had withdrawn from the school. The second consequence was that school security was beefed up and school safety measures were much more severely enforced.[50]

Public school facilities have often been used for community social and recreational events. One such event at a school in Harlem that same September 1986 resulted in a gangland style shoot-out. Revelers at a christening celebration party, most of them Mexican immigrants, were thrown into chaos when 15 or 16 shots rang out. Two men were killed and three others were wounded in the melee—they were two sets of brothers and a by-stander. Apparently the school had been rented to the partygoers, and a spokesman for the board of education said that he did not think it was appropriate that the school had been rented to be used for a private party.[51]

Another shooting resulting from persons bringing guns onto school property occurred at Monrovia High School in California in 1986. During a football game between Monrovia and Pasadena High Schools, alleged gang members got into a fight, took out guns, and began firing. Two innocent bystanders were injured in the cross fire between two sets of bleachers. When the gunmen began shooting, police told players on the field to lie down; as the spectators were fleeing the stadium, the players crawled off the field on their hands and knees.[52]

Superintendent Donald Montgomery noted later, "What this incident did was tear down, very rapidly, public opinion about Monrovia High School and the city of Monrovia." Another official remarked, "We don't see this as a problem in any way associated with the school. . . .We see this as an isolated incident on school grounds."[53]

In December 1986, what was becoming an old story was played out in Lewistown, Montana, where a student, mad at his teacher, decided to take revenge. A 14-year-old boy went to the Fergus High School, knocked on the door of a classroom, and asked the teacher to come to the door. When she did, the boy shot her in the face, killing her. The woman who opened the door was not the teacher the boy was mad at—she was a substitute teacher.

As he walked through the corridor toward the door where he had entered, the boy shot a vice principal and then two students as others ran screaming through the halls. The boy left the school and ran about a mile to his home, where he was arrested.

The underage shooter had told an acquaintance that he was going to kill his French teacher, apparently because he was failing. When school resumed, officials called in counselors, psychologists, and clergy to help students deal with the shootings.[54]

BERSERK GUNMEN, 1987

The year 1987 saw the phenomenon of the random-killing, "berserk" gunman spread to Great Britain, where a deranged murderer killed 14 people and wounded another 16 in the quiet rural town of Thames Valley before he was captured in an empty school.[55] It was in December of the same year that a horrible massacre took place in the United States, which had a traumatic impact upon a school.

On December 23, 1987, in Dover, Arkansas, four high school students and 12 other people were killed. The gunman killed 14 of his own family members, including his children and grandchildren. Seven children were among those killed. The events of the holiday season were a shock to the high school, and needless to say were very traumatic for the young people who knew the dead students. However, the principal thought the 1,150 students in the district were adapting "just fine" on the first day back after the holidays on January 5, 1988.[56]

That dark affair seemed to be a precursor to another shooting in 1987 and four enigmatic random school shootings that would follow in 1988. On March 2, 1987, 12-year-old Nathan D. Faris from DeKalb County, Missouri, shot a thirteen-year-old classmate before killing himself. He had often been teased about being chubby and bright.[57]

1988 AND 1989—THE WORST YEARS YET

On February 11, 1988, Nicholas Elliott from Virginia Beach, Virginia, killed a teacher and wounded another person. He was prepared to open fire on the students nearby because he said that had taunted him because he was black.[58]

The second female random killer to enter a school and begin shooting emerged in a Chicago suburb on May 20th. Winnetka, Illinois, is a placid lakefront town of some 13,000 people to the north of Chicago. Laurie Wasserman Dann, 31, who lived with her parents in Glencoe, was known to federal agents for her involvement in a series of "bizarre" situations.

Dann was carrying a pistol when she walked into Hubbard Woods Elementary School, ducking into a washroom where she began firing, apparently totally at random. There she killed an eight-year-old boy. Then she entered a second grade classroom. "This is a real gun," she told the children. A child asked if that were true, so she shot him. "Yes, and I'm going to show you," she said. In all, she critically wounded five children. Then she left the school and went to a nearby house, where she shot and wounded a 20-year-old male occupant who tried to subdue her. He was later hospitalized in critical condition.

School authorities kept all children inside the Winnetka schools until the later afternoon when the siege was over. Before she killed herself, she held off police for eight hours in the house. When police stormed the house, they found her body. She had been a baby-sitter for a family that had recently notified her that they would no longer need her services. Some of the family's five children were pupils at Hubbard Woods.[59]

Another confused assailant committed what has been called "the worst possible school crisis" on September 26, 1988. A 19-year-old man parked his car in front of Oakland Elementary School in Greenwood, South Carolina, waved to the custodian who was working around the school, entered through the front door at lunch time, walked past the open door to the school's offices and into the cafeteria where first-graders were having lunch, and began shooting, wounding three students and one teacher.

The killer then left the cafeteria, went into a girls' restroom and reloaded his handgun. A teacher had followed him and tried to keep him in the restroom. They scuffled, and he shot her in the mouth and hand; then he entered a third-grade classroom, where he began emptying his gun at students. One of the third graders died in the classroom. Another died three days later.

As gunshots were heard throughout the school, some students were escaping through windows. Quickly the school emptied, with students running into nearby woods, across streets into neighbors' yards—anywhere that offered them a safe refuge.

After he had fired all of the rounds in his gun, the intruder dropped his gun and was told by the same teacher he had shot to raise his hands. He did what the unarmed teacher told him to do. The ten injured people were taken to the local hospital, and police arrested the gunman. There appeared to be no connection between the killer and the school; he had just decided to go in that day. He later admitted he had been influenced by Dann.[60]

SCHOOLYARD MASSACRE, 1989

In January 1989, another schoolyard massacre—this one with the largest number of persons struck by bullets—occurred in Stockton, California, apparently with a racist motive. A gunman in a flak jacket fired an AK47 assault rifle into the schoolyard of Cleveland Elementary School and hit 30 people. The school is located in northern Stockton in a middle-class section.

The recreation yard of the school was strewn with the bodies of dead children and the 29 children and one teacher who were wounded. The gunman later added one more fatality when he killed himself.

Patrick Edward Purdy set fire to his station wagon as a diversion and then walked into the schoolyard with the bayonet-equipped rifle and two semiautomatic pistols during recess at 11:42 A.M., entering the campus through a hole in the fence. Passing several portable classrooms about 250 yards from the L-shaped main building, he opened fire from the west side of the portables and then moved to the east side and continued spraying children with bullets. He fired 60 rounds of ammunition. As the killer sprayed the area with gunfire, children screamed and teachers frantically tried to move them into the building.

Purdy had an extensive criminal background, both in California and in Oregon.[61] He was motivated by "a festering hatred" of racial and ethnic minorities; this was an extreme example of hate crimes, the attorney general said. The 24-year-old was especially obsessed with a hatred of Asians. A report prepared for the attorney general said that Purdy was "hopelessly alienated from society by a turbulent childhood in which he was provided no love and little stability."[62]

As a child Purdy was an alcoholic. He attended the Cleveland School. Later he became a drifter, crisscrossing the nation looking for work, his grandmother said. He visited her occasionally.

All of the dead children were from refugee families from Southeast Asia. Southeast Asians made up about 60 percent of the school's enrollment. Before he committed suicide that day, he had shot 36 people and killed six of them.[63]

By their very nature, acts of terror go beyond the bounds of decency and civility. But in December 1989 a 35-year-old man performed one of the most peculiar and repugnant acts of terror in Natchez, Mississippi. Larry Bates went to the elementary school where his wife worked as a teacher's aide, ostensibly to shoot her.

The incident began when Bates, carrying a .38-caliber revolver, captured four teachers and aides—including his wife—and 19 children in a kindergarten classroom at Northside Primary School. Police responded about 1:30 P.M. when they received a report of a man on the campus. Bates lined five- and six-year-old children in front of the windows, between himself and the police. He then raped two of the teachers as the children looked on.

Bates then shot his wife—she had wounds to the scalp and back—and then allowed her and another adult to leave the room.

In the meantime, the police chief talked with Bates on the school's intercom and tried to negotiate the release of the hostages during the ordeal, which apparently distracted him for a moment. One of the teachers grabbed the gun from Bates at that point, yelling that she had the weapon, and then the police rushed him.[64]

"PROPENSITIES FOR VIOLENCE," 1990

There were other cases of deranged spouses coming to school to execute their wives not long after this one. In a sleepy southern Kentucky town a few months earlier, in May 1990, Shannon Greer, whose wife had cited his "propensities for violence," decided to go to the Waynesburg Elementary School, where she worked, to kill her. He entered the school about 9:30 A.M., shot his wife several times in the face with a shotgun, got into his car, drove from near the Pulaski County-Lincoln County border to Casey County, and shot himself in the face. The couple had been married 22 years and had grown children. The wife had been seeking a divorce. One teacher remarked afterward that "You read and see on TV about these things happening in other places, but it doesn't sink in that it could happen here."[65]

A high school sophomore, Curtis Collins, a Las Vegas student, fatally shot a junior at his school in August 1990.[66]

1991

Toward the end of 1991, when so many government and school officials were concerned with the increase in violence on school campuses around the nation, two of the most threatening types of terrorism were attacks on school buses and gang-related violence upon school children.

In June 1991, a 14-year-old San Fernando girl was wounded in a drive-by shooting near her junior high school. Her mother had placed the girl in a new school because of gang violence. She was just leaving San Fernando Junior High School when she was shot about 3:00 P.M., just after classes had ended. This was the second such shooting in a little over a month at this school.[67]

One day earlier, a Florida boy was shot and killed just after stepping off his school bus. A friend, who was charged with manslaughter, shot the boy.[68]

Gang wars were also responsible for an attack on a school bus in September 1991. Carrying 28 students, the bus was just blocks from Nogales High School near La Puente in Los Angeles in the unincorporated area north of the City of Industry. The bus was peppered with bullets. The shells struck two girls. The shooting demonstrated that, although the school was supposed to be neutral territory, gang violence was more and more often intruding into the life of the school, causing terror in the hearts of the students. The school system called in school psychologists to talk with the students who had ridden the bus and others of the 2,800 students in the school.

The shooting happened about 12:30 P.M. when male students on the bus and three males in a compact car exchanged words or hand signals. Suddenly, a gunman jumped out of the car and began firing a dozen shots from a 9-millimeter handgun as he stood in the middle of the street. The two schoolgirls who were hit by bullet fragments were not seriously hurt. Reporters who were on the school campus on Friday after the Thursday shooting said that most students did not seem to be affected by the event. One student said that she was more affected by the previous year's shooting. "I was worried last year but not this year," she said. "But I was a little freshman then."[69]

GANG VIOLENCE, 1992

Gang violence once again imposed itself on a high school in October 1992 when a second student at Paramount High School in Los Angeles was killed in a period of four months. A 16-year-old cheerleader was struck in the head by a bullet and killed as she crossed the street in front of the school, returning from a McDonald's restaurant to cheering practice. In June, gang members at the same McDonald's restaurant killed a school athlete who was to have graduated the following day with honors.

After the girl's death, the number of unarmed security guards on campus was increased, and the Los Angeles County Sheriff's Department beefed up patrols of the neighborhood. School officials no longer allowed students to leave campus at lunchtime. Students later told police that the stray bullet came from a shooter on a bicycle who fired at a passing car.[70]

Another unknown shooter at a dance at Archbishop Carroll High School in northeast Washington, D.C., shot at least three students, one of them fatally in May of 1992. The dance was being held in the third floor gymnasium of the school when a fight broke out. About 20 people went outside after the band told the crowd that it would stop playing if the fight continued. Then about 15 gunshots were heard. Authorities said that at least three other persons might have been less seriously wounded than the first three.[71]

In all, there were 16 fatal shootings at high schools in the United States in 1992, and of these at least seven were gang related. In a case that was very similar to the Kentucky case, an estranged husband in Houston went to school to kill his wife, who was chair of the special education department. After he had killed her, he turned the gun on himself, committing suicide.[72]

On May 1, 1992, Eric Houston, 20, created a siege that would never be forgotten. It took place in Olivehurst, California. He walked into his former high school to kill four people and wound ten others. He wanted retaliation for a failing grade he had gotten. The court gave him a death sentence.[73]

Certainly this is not a conclusive list of the entire episode of violent terror that took place in the American school during the period 1970 to 1992. Just how partial it is will not be known until someone draws up a meticulous list such as the National School Safety Center has done for the years from 1992 through the 1990s. But it certainly demonstrates that many schools in the United States, and hundreds, if not thousands, of students and teachers have had their work disrupted by those who would inflict terror, often for no real reason. If this was not the beginning of a dark season in the history of the American school, it was an era when deadly, mindless terror intruded itself upon the sanctuary of the school with greater fury than ever before.

NOTES

1. "The Texas Killer: Former Florida Neighbors Recall a Nice Boy Who Liked Toy Guns," *New York Times,* August 2, 1966. http://groups.yahoo.com/group/TexasTower/message/12.

2. In order not to confuse the violent activity discussed in this chapter with the racially inspired violence of the Civil Rights era, this chapter covers the period 1945–1992 but leaves out much of the 1950s and all of the 1960s, when most violent intrusions were motivated by racial animosity. These are discussed in Chapter 6. The main thrust of the chapter is from the 1970s on. Also, events discussed in earlier chapters are generally not repeated here.

3. "Boy Stabbed in School," *New York Times,* February 20, 1945, pg. 21.

4. "Boy Fires at Teacher," *New York Times,* March 1, 1947, pg. 17.

5. "Policeman's Shot Kills Crazed Man Who Invades 46th St. Girl's School," *New York Times,* June 5, 1951, pg. 1.

6. This chapter, whose purpose is to show that violence inflicted itself on the schools, makes no claim that it is a comprehensive list of school shootings. It involves a series of selected intrusions into the school by persons—often other than students—who killed or wounded other people in the schools. Our point is that the systemic violence that characterizes the greater culture frequently inflicted itself in a way that is detrimental to the schools and their functioning. We are certain that this selective process omits several important violent events that are discussed in the Secret Service study.

7. "An Interim Report on the Prevention of Targeted Violence in Schools," October 2000. http://www.ustreas.gov/usss/ntac_ssi_report.pdf.

8. "Study Calls Public Schools 'Oppressive' and 'Joyless,'" *New York Times,* September 20, 1970, pgs. 1, 70.

9. "High School Disruptions Put at 5,191 Since Fall," *New York Times,* May 31, 1972, pg. 24.

10. "Crime and Violence Rise in City Schools," *New York Times,* March 19, 1972, pg. 1.

11. "3 Hold Illinois Pupils Hostage; One Theft Suspect Slain, 2 Held," *New York Times,* May 1, 1973, pg. 50.

12. "U.S. Explosives Experts Testify in West Virginia Textbook Case," *New York Times,* April 17, 1975, pg. 33 and "2 Found Guilty in Dynamiting Schools in Protest on Textbooks," *New York Times,* April 19, 1973, pg. 21.

13. "Sniper's Classmate Says Guns Were 'Whole Life,'" *New York Times,* January 1, 1975, pg. 1.

14. "1,000 Attend Funeral For Jersey Priest Murdered by School Intruder," *New York Times,* March 1, 1975, pg. 29.

15. "Home of School Board Aide Bombed," *New York Times,* March 14, 1975, pg. 46.

16. "A Soiled Apple for the Teacher," *New York Times,* May 28, 1976, pg. 38.

17. "Crime in Schools Reported on Rise," *New York Times,* March 9, 1976, pg. 38.

18. "U.S. Study Finds Violence Rampant in Nation's Schools," *New York Times,* March 19, 1976, pg. 66.

19. "Warrants Issued for 3 in Abduction of Coast Students," *New York Times,* July 22, 1976, pgs. 1, 32. "Town Hoped and Prayed for the Missing Children," *New York Times,* July 17, 1976, pgs. 1, 13. "26 Children Safe After Coast Abduction," *New York Times,* July 17, 1976, pgs. 1, 13.

20. "Firecracker Blast in Glass Case Kills a Jersey Schoolgirl, 14," *New York Times,* May 28, 1976, pg. 5.

21. "Pupils See Teacher Shot to Death," *New York Times,* November 11, 1976, pg. 33. "Detroit Class Still Bears Scars of Teacher's Slaying," *New York Times,* February 17, 1977, pgs. 1, 55.

22. "Shots Fired at School Bus; 3 Children Are Injured," *New York Times,* November 11, 1977, pg. 18.

23. "Boy Hijacks School Bus; Police Shoot Him Twice," *New York Times,* March 15, 1978, pg. 17.

24. "8 Children Wounded Riding in School Bus," *New York Times,* May 20, 1987, pg. 8.

25. "Teen-Ager in Philadelphia Held in Bus-Sniping Case," *New York Times,* May 27, 1978, pg. 6.

26. "Boy Arrested in Teacher's Killing," *New York Times,* May 9, 1978, pg. 12.

27. "Youth Shoots Himself at Graduation Ceremony," *New York Times,* June 12, 1978, pg. 16.

28. "San Diego Girl Slays 2 With Rifle And Wounds 9 on School Grounds," *New York Times,* January 30, 1979, pg. 10.

29. "Farragut Player and Coach Shot," *Chicago Tribune,* September 12, 1979, pg. 2–1.

30. "Student Shot At Suitland High School," *Washington Post,* October 2, 1979, pg. B1.

31. "Teacher, Wife Indicted in Kidnap, Torture Case," *Washington Post,* August 1, 1979, pg. A14.

32. "Gunman Kills 5 at Texas Church and Shoots Self: Suspect's Condition," *New York Times,* June 23, 1980, pg. 14.

33. "Assistant Principal Given Probation for Shooting," *Washington Post,* February 21, 1981, pg. B3.

34. "Manslaughter Charges Filed in Death at Spingarn," *Washington Post,* September 12, 1980, pg. B1.

35. "Another D.C. Pupil Charged With Carrying Gun," *Washington Post,* September 24, 1980, pg. C3.

36. "3 Guilty of Trying to Kill Teacher," *New York Times,* June 8, 1979, pg. 14.

37. "A Failure to Report Sex Case is Checked," *New York Times,* June 7, 1980, pg. 23.

38. "Student a Suspect in Teacher Slaying," *New York Times,* March 20, 1982, pg. 8.

39. "Teacher Shot in Classroom," *New York Times,* December 18, 1983, pg. 44.

40. "Teacher Convicted in Slaying," *New York Times,* October 29, 1983, pg. 21.

41. "Hostages at Long Island School," *New York Times,* May 17, 1983, pg. 1.

42. "Sniper Firing at School Kills Child, Injures 13 Before Shooting Himself," *Washington Post,* February 25, 1984, pg. A3.

43. "Gunmen Wound Three Students Near Yeshiva U.," *New York Times,* June 23, 1983, pg. B1.

44. "Student Opens Fire in School, Kills Principal," *Los Angeles Times,* January 22, 1985, pg. 16.

45. "15 Year Old Held in Attack on Students: Caustic Spray Injures 14 on School Bus," *Los Angeles Times,* June 20, 1985, pg. 10.

46. "Terrorism Fears Cancel School Trips," *New York Times,* February 16, 1986, 11LI, pg. 1.

47. "Couple Take Over School But Die After Bomb Blast," *New York Times,* May 17, 1986, pg. 6.

48. We have included this story about a technical college because we regard it as a secondary school. Normally, this book has not dealt with problems at colleges and universities.

49. "Five in Brooklyn Shot at College; Student is Held," *New York Times,* August 13, 1986, pg. 1.

50. "Departing in Fear: 35 Students Pull Out of Fairfax High After Fatal Shooting," *Los Angeles Times,* September 28, 1986, Part 9, pg. 1.

51. "2 Killed, 3 Wounded in Shooting at East Harlem Christening Party," *New York Times,* September 29, 1986, pg. B4.

52. "Gunfire at Football Game Wounds 2; Fans Stampede," *Los Angeles Times,* October 5, 1986, Part 2, pg. 3.

53. "High School's Image Hurt by Shooting," *Los Angeles Times,* October 9, 1986, Part 9, pg. 1.

54. "Failing Grade is Linked to Shooting of Teacher," *New York Times,* December 6, 1986, pg. 34.

55. "Berserk Gunman Kills 14," *San Diego Union-Tribune,* August 20, 1987, pg. A-1.

56. "School Open After Deaths," *Washington Post,* January 5, 1988, pg. A7.

57. "Teenage Gunmen," July 26, 2000. http:/www.mystickunicorn.freeservers.com/custom3.html.

58. Ibid.

59. "Slayer Found Dead After Attack on School Kills Boy, 8," *New York Times,* May 21, 1988, pg. 6.

60. "Gunman in S. Carolina School Kills 1 and Wounds 10 Others," *New York Times,* September 27, 1988, pg. 24. Robert S. Watson, Janice H. Poda, C. Thomas Miller, Eleanor S. Rice, and Gary West, *Containing Crisis: A Guide to Managing School Emergencies* (Bloomington, IN: National Educational Service, 1990), pgs. ix–x.

61. "Rifleman Slays Five at School; 29 Pupils, Teacher Shot in California; Assailant Kills Self," *Washington Post,* January 18, 1989, pg. A1. "Motive Sought for School Massacre; Drifter Matter-of-Factly Blasted Pupils," *San Diego Union-Tribune,* January 18, 1989, pg. A-1.

62. "'Festering Hatred' Fueled Stockton Killer," *Los Angeles Times,* October 7, 1989, pg. 26.

63. Ibid.

64. "Man Shoots Wife, Rapes Teachers at School," *San Diego Union-Tribune,* December 1, 1989, pg. A-10.

65. "Man Shoots Wife to Death at School, Kills Himself," *Courier-Journal,* May 11, 1990, pg. 1A.

66. "Teenage Gunmen," July 26, 2000. http:/www.mystickunicorn.freeservers.com/custom3.html.

67. "San Fernando Girl, 14, Wounded in Drive-By Shooting Near School," *Los Angeles Times,* June 7, 1991, pg. B-3.

68. "Boy, 14, Fatally Shot by Friend," *St. Petersburg Times,* June 8, 1991, pg. 6B.

69. "Security Tightened After Bus Shooting," *Los Angeles Times,* September 28, 1991, pg. B1.

70. "Gangs Send a School Back into Mourning," *Los Angeles Times,* October 1, 1992, pg. A1.

71. "Shooting at D.C. School Kills One," *Washington Post,* May 31, 1992, pg. B8.

72. "School Associated Violent Deaths," The National School Safety Center, June 12, 2001, pg. 2.

73. "School Violence in America," *Indianapolis Star,* March 30, 2001. http://www.starnews.com/library/factfiles/crime/school_violence/ school_shootings.html.

Chapter 10

The Paradox of the Clinton Era (1993–2001)

A prominent sociologist noted toward the end of the decade of the 1990s that it seemed to be a paradox that in the midst of a strong economy, declining national crime rate, and sense of economic well-being—during the Clinton administration, which was proactive on school reform and improvement, and when many middle-class people were prosperous and living better than ever—that incidents of school violence featuring middle-class student killers came into the national consciousness in a regular and most dramatic way, changing public perception of school safety drastically.[1] In the latter half of the decade, it seemed that one American small town after another experienced the shock of student killings, usually in suburban high schools. By the end of the decade an attitude of "it can't happen here" had been replaced in the popular mind by a generalized paranoia about the absence of safety and the latent potential for violence existing in a dormant but potentially volatile state in all high schools and even some elementary schools. Fear itself had become the pervasive mind-set for students, parents, teachers, and concerned citizens, in spite of the fact that school crime was lower than it had been several years before.

GOVERNMENTAL EFFORTS TO IMPROVE SCHOOL SAFETY

Measures already taken at the national, state, and local levels have probably saved many lives in our schools. The U.S. Office of Education under Secretary Richard Riley gave national leadership during the 1990s to several important initiatives dealing with the safety of schools. In some of the states, bureaucracies were set up to provide assistance on a statewide basis to local school systems. The Safe and Drug Free Schools and Communities Act (Title IV of the Improving America's Schools Act of 1994) had the avowed purpose of helping the nation's schools provide a disciplined environment conducive to learning by eliminating violence and preventing illegal drug use in and around schools. The very fact that the act was passed indicated concern by the U.S. Congress about the safety of American schools.

Alarm was expressed at 1) increasing use of alcohol and drugs; 2) approximately 3,000,000 crimes and acts of violence a day in the schools; 3) violence linked to prejudice and intolerance; 4) alcohol and tobacco use by young people; 5) lack of safe, disciplined, and drug-free learning environments. Grants are given to the states on the basis of public and private school enrollment.[2]

Among other ways to make schools more secure, school security officers were installed in many schools. These persons, usually trained policemen, relieved teachers and administrators of having to serve a police function in the schools and gave them an added measure of safety.

The states and local governmental jurisdictions have also set up laws and mechanisms to improve the safety of schools. In almost every state, "zero tolerance policies" have been installed. These policies, conceived to keep drugs and weapons out of high-crime schools, have gotten more controversial as they have spread. Indeed, like the criticisms of airport type security and "penitentiary-like" buildings, critics have pointed out the harm closely monitored schools do both to the children and to the academic environment:

> Since the mid-1990s, every state and the District of Columbia have adopted some form of zero tolerance, to be interpreted by local districts. Some have led to excesses. A 2000 report by the Civil Rights Project at Harvard University and the Advancement Project, a nonprofit legal-assistance group, documented abuses. A 6-year-old in Pittsburgh, for example, was suspended last Halloween for carrying a plastic axe as part of a fireman's costume.[3]

The individual states passed a rash of new legislation in 1999 to complement the school safety bills passed by the federal government. A few are representative. In Michigan, Governor John Engler signed three bills aimed at improving school safety. The bills amended the Michigan codes and dealt with suspension of students by teachers, expulsion of students who assault school district employees, and procedures for dealing with assaults by or against students in school.[4]

California passed the School Safety and Violence Prevention Act in June 1999. The bill provided $100 million to create programs that provide a safe learning environment.[5] South Carolina passed at least five separate laws related to school safety.[6]

In the state of Washington, a legislator sponsored House Bill 1153, which required the notification of schools when a juvenile committed a sexual or violent offense or was convicted of drug or alcohol violations. Schools were also to be informed when a violent juvenile was released from prison or paroled and returning to the school district.[7] In Alaska, legislation requiring crisis response planning for schools was passed.[8] Virginia's General Assembly passed four school safety laws, including one that requires schools to have a written school emergency and crisis management plan and one that requires schools to conduct a written assessment of the safety conditions.[9]

AN EXPLOSIVE DECADE[10]

In spite of progressive initiatives by federal, state, and local governments, the 1990s from a personal and institutional point of view were an explosive decade for schools. For instance, in what might have been another New London, Texas, a junior high school in Morton Grove, Illinois, experienced a boiler room explosion in February 1993 that fortunately killed no one. One teacher, who must have been rather strict, told her students, "The school blowing up is no excuse. I want that book report on time." One student had to have six stitches when flying glass hit her in the head.[11] In June 1994, three students in Palo Alto, California, thought they would pull a senior prank, so they set off an explosion that injured 18 other students. Needless to say, the three did not graduate with their class.[12]

An electrical explosion at an elementary school near Columbus, Ohio, raised the potential that deadly polychlorinated biphenyls, a poisonous, cancer-causing chemical, had been spilled in December 1995. A hazardous materials team was called to the school, and a custodian and a firefighter were taken to the hospital as a precaution, but no chemicals were found. The school staff said that they heard the explosion inside an electrical transformer around 11:00 A.M. after they began smelling burning odors.[13]

In 1999, an explosion took place in an unused locker in a high school in Missouri, injuring 11 students. After the explosion, the school's 1,110 students were evacuated and bused home.[14]

In November 2000, a gas explosion tore apart a school in Plankington, South Dakota, and ignited a fire, which killed two men and injured a third. A propane gas leak somehow ignited and blew the old wing and the new wing of the school apart. School officials had smelled the gas at about 5:20 P.M. and evacuated the school. Two hours later, only the three men were inside the school. The roof of the school was completely blown off, and most of the rest of the building was nothing but debris. One firefighter, in addition to the two custodians, was hospitalized in serious condition.[15]

Perhaps even more menacing were explosions, bombs, and bomb threats set off by students or intruders in schools around the country throughout the 1990s. For instance, in March 1995 an 18-year-old and four 15-year-olds were arrested when a copper pipe bomb blew up in the first floor lavatory of a junior-senior high school near Buffalo. A similar pipe bomb was confiscated from another boy. No one was injured in the explosion.[16]

In September 1995, a pipe bomb blew up inside a boys' restroom in Brandon, Florida. "It potentially could have been fatal," said a sheriff's deputy about the bomb that went off just after the school's last bell at 2:50 P.M. There were some boys in the room at the time, but no one was hurt.[17]

In Farmington, Minnesota, in March 1996, two boys, 13 and 14, called the town's two elementary schools and said that bombs would go off on Monday. The schools were evacuated, but no bombs were found.[18] In Kansas City in March 1997, an explosive charge caused an explosion that started a fire in a large physical education equipment room, where thin foam rubber mats gave off a noxious black smoke. When the students were herded into the auditorium, a fight broke out and security guards sprayed the students with pepper spray.[19]

In 1998, two boys in Ryan, Oklahoma, were arrested for allegedly threatening to bomb their high school and kill a teacher. Police at the home of one of the boys found the material for the bomb.[20]

Two incidents in 1998 demonstrated that authorities no longer took threats lightly. Unlike some of the bomb threats of the past, no threat was taken to be a joke. In Racine, Wisconsin, in 1998, three teenage boys were charged with plotting to take over their high school to kill students and teachers. The boys intended to carry out a shooting spree with two other boys who backed out of the plot. One of the boys' fathers had a box full of guns they intended to use.[21] When word spread that a sixth-grader had threatened to bring a gun to school to kill several classmates in Waleska, Georgia, more than 200 students stayed home, teachers locked their classroom doors, and a sheriff's deputy patrolled the halls. Police arrested a 13-year-old boy. "There's no such thing as an idle threat anymore," a school spokesman said.[22]

A school explosion in Massachusetts almost happened when an 11-year-old planned to bomb his parochial school and kill a few students with a knife. The Lynn boy told a group of friends that he had a hit list and would plant a bomb that would kill everyone in the school. When the word reached school authorities, they contacted the police, who found enough substance to the story to charge the boy.[23] In Medina, Ohio, at about the same time, a 13-year-old junior high school student wrote two threatening notes, saying that the school would blow up, and another giving the names of seven students he planned to kill.[24]

In Cleveland, Ohio, authorities closed a school after they discovered that several South High School students planned an attack with guns and explosives, similar to the Columbine incident. A student who learned of the plot alerted authorities. Documents found by the police implicated eleven students. All of the 11, dressed in black, showed up at the school with the intention to carry out the plot. The students planned to begin the massacre just before noon.[25] The seriousness of this case was underscored by reports that at least 350 students nationwide had been arrested on similar charges. In Florida alone, Broward and Miami-Dade prosecutors brought cases against 47 students for making alleged threats against classmates, teachers, or schools.[26]

In Hastings, Minnesota, in March 1998, six eleventh-graders faced expulsion and possible criminal charges after they admitted setting off a homemade bomb at the front door of their vice principal's house, where the vice principal and his wife and six children were awakened by a 4:00 A.M. blast that could have injured someone. Metal fragments were imbedded in the front door.[27]

A less serious incident occurred when fireworks caused a school explosion at Arlington High School in March 2000. A custodian who heard the evening explosion evacuated all of the persons in the gymnasium who were participating in a girls' basketball banquet on the other side of the school.[28]

Bombs and the threat of bombs continued into the next year, 2001. In New York, officials closed seven schools in March because of "vague" phone threats. The Westchester town of Harrison closed all six public schools and one Catholic school after police received the threats. Schools were also closed in Edgemont, New York, because an 18-year-old man was making computer threats against the town's schools.[29] CNN reported at least ten other bomb threats to schools in New England in the month of March 2001.[30]

Perhaps the most unique of the bomb-threat cases came when the athletic director of a Catholic high school in Coon Rapids, Minnesota, was accused in 2000 of leaving six bomb-threat notes in the school in the fall. The 52-year-old coach also taught seventh-grade social studies at the school. School was canceled only once.[31]

Since bomb threats increased greatly after the Columbine incident, some states passed laws ordering a convicted person to pay police and fire response costs and pay the schools for damages. If a juvenile could not pay the costs, the parent or guardian must pay. This was the substance of a Michigan law passed in 1999 after the Detroit area had over 20 bomb threats. The preventative measures seemed to be working in that state, where bomb threats were on the downturn.[32]

SOME SCHOOL FIRES

At a time during the decade of the 1990s when civil behavior and courtesy seemed to be breaking down, as people were shooting each other on freeways and animosities of all other sorts seemed to be at a fever pitch, it was little wonder that many of the school fires were either arson or were in some way related to the human propensity for meanness. For instance, the city of San Jose experienced arson attempts in two serious school fires within a few months in 1994 and 1995.

Many of the hundreds of cases of arson in the 1990s involved school-age teens. In December 1994, five teens were charged with starting a school fire in San Jose, whose cost to an elementary school was estimated to be $2.5 million. In addition, the fire hurt two fire fighters. Three girls, ages 14, 14, and 16, and two boys, ages 15 and 16, apparently ignited the fire outside of the Santa Teresa Elementary School while playing with cigarette lighters. When a plastic window panel ignited, the fire entered the building and quickly engulfed the sprawling wood-frame edifice. One fire fighter fell through a fire-weakened roof, and another suffered second-degree burns to his face and neck. A county official said that the roof over one wing was completely caved in and totally gutted: "There's nothing left. Other classrooms are severely smoke-and-water damaged, and the library's computer room is most likely a total loss."[33]

Among the other acts of arson in schools during the Clinton era were those committed in Arizona in 1995; Boston in 1995; Montgomery, Alabama, in 1995; Compton, California, in 1999; Staten Island in 2000; Berkeley High in California in 2000; Freemont, California, in 2000; St. Petersburg, Florida, in 2000; Tampa, Florida, in 2001 (girls); and Gilbert, Arizona, in 2001.[34]

Possibly the worst school fire of the decade happened in March 1999 at Clay Elementary School in St. Louis, where six children died. The building was set on fire by an arsonist. The two-story building was gutted. The school system called in grief counselors to meet with the entire third grade.[35]

In May 1995, a six-alarm fire at Yerba Buena High in San Jose raged through four classrooms, the library, and the cafeteria. The fire started in a metal trash can in a courtyard next to the school snack bar and spread rapidly through the attic. The school is on a sprawling campus, so all of its buildings were not affected, but four buildings surrounding the courtyard were severely damaged. More than 80 fire fighters battled the blaze, and one fire fighter was hurt. The computer teacher lost much of the equipment he had spent 22 years gathering for the school. He had just finished replacing equipment stolen during the Christmas break of 1993. The school had been plagued with discipline problems all during the year. A month before, the door of an office containing attendance records was burned.[36]

The District of Columbia schools had a series of problems meeting fire codes in the 1990s. In September 1994, schools were prevented from opening because a judge refused to accept an interim plan to open 47 school buildings that had failed to meet fire codes. A spokeswoman said, "We have 126 schools that have now been approved for opening and another 39 schools still await her approval." Officials looked for places near their homes where students could be placed and parents frantically looked for day care for their children. School officials said that the failure to meet fire codes was because the school system was underfinanced.[37]

THREATS TO THE ENVIRONMENT

Increasingly in the 1990s, schools were faced with chemical and biological dangers from the environment. One mother in Phoenix in 1995 withdrew her two sons from school because officials decided to stop using air filtration systems and the boys had chemical sensitivity, she said. The school's principal had the units installed after a summer renovation sent paint and carpet glue fumes through the halls. The parents of the boys filed discrimination suits through the Department of Education's Office of Civil Rights, and the school was put under a compliance order. The principal did not comply, however, because she said that the boys could not prove they had a disability.[38]

In 1997, a Florida high school became infested with spiders. Apparently, the highly poisonous arachnids were successfully eradicated and no one was bitten.[39] In November 1998, a letter claiming to contain anthrax bacteria was opened at a Catholic parish in Indianapolis, sending all of the pupils in the parish school home. An anti-abortion group in Chicago and a Roman Catholic Church in suburban Buffalo received similar letters. Nine people were decontaminated after the letter was received at the school.[40]

An old problem still hounded school officials in Denver when a school security officer warned that there were asbestos deposits at Fort Morgan High School. When they finally checked into the matter, authorities thought that the asbestos contamination was so serious that state health officials shut the school for the year, forcing the 850 students to finish the school at a nearby middle school. It was to cost $2.8 million to fix the problem. The school security guard who discovered the problem apparently met scorn: "My life has been hell," she said. "Teachers won't talk to me. Friends won't talk to me. They think asbestos is nothing to worry about."[41]

Another danger reappeared in Los Angeles, where children may have been exposed to peeling, lead-based paint. In times previous, lead poisoning had been linked to neurological and behavioral problems, reduced IQ, and tooth decay. Although lead-based paint was outlawed in California, thousands of older schools were shown in a 1998 study—in fact as many as 78 percent of the elementary schools—still to have lead in their paint.[42]

A tornado hit Jarrell, Texas, in 1997 and killed 27 people, more than half of whom were of school age. Nine high school students were killed. Five more middle school and elementary children and an elementary school teacher were also killed in the disaster. The toll was devastating on a high school that had only 150 students. The football team of 18 lost four players, and a popular cheerleader was killed. "When you come into a small community like this, you are family," the superintendent of schools said.[43]

In the summer of 1997, Grandview's High Grove Elementary School in Kansas City was flooded by a water main break, and water and mud washed through the classrooms. The building had already been cleaned and was ready for the fall opening.[44] Another kind of flooding hit southern Kentucky after severe storms in April 1998. Three people were killed in the severe storm. Hail demolished the roof on a high school in Bowling Green. Three elementary schools were damaged, and the basement of Bowling Green Junior High School was flooded.[45] A bizarre accident created another kind of flooding in a high school in Avon, Indiana, in the summer of 1999. The stage of the auditorium was flooded with hundreds of gallons of water when a piece of rigging snapped, sending a boom toward the ceiling. It struck four pipes that were part of the sprinkler system, breaking all four and sending water gushing onto the stage. Electricity in the area had to be shut off for safety reasons.[46]

Another bizarre and potentially dangerous incident happened in suburban New York when 3,000 students at Sheepshead Bay High School had to be evacuated because 3,000 gallons of heating oil accumulated in the basement of the school. Students began to notice a suspicious odor about 8:45 A.M. Staff members and students were sent home for the day.[47]

But perhaps the greatest danger posed in the 1990s was the spread of the AIDS virus. New York City discovered that for every teenager with AIDS, 10 had the human immunodeficiency virus. Nearly 1 percent of teenagers giving birth were H.I.V. infected.[48]

THE HORSEPLAY FACTOR

Sometimes children's horseplay turns deadly. In Oak Hill, Ohio, in December 1995, two boys were engaged in horseplay in school when one of the boys was injured. He had a ruptured spleen and died after he was taken to the hospital.[49]

A third-grader at Cheetowaga's Cleveland Hill Elementary School was playing in a school lavatory, trying to swing from the door frame of a stall, when she fell backward and hit her head on the edge of a toilet. She died from injuries she sustained. Three other girls were present when the accident happened. A police spokesperson said, "It looks like it was one of those things where kids were being kids, playing and never thinking anything like that would ever happen."[50]

One bit of horseplay was nearly fatal for 15 students. A student brought a 60 mm military shell to Charlton County High School in Folkston, Georgia, and took it to the band room, where 15 students were passing it around when someone dropped it. It went off and injured all of the students, three critically, and four seriously. Others had shrapnel wounds and burns. The area "looks like a war zone," someone remarked.[51]

COMBATING THE ANCIENT RITUAL

One of the things magnified by the violent events of the 1990s was a new awareness of an age-old problem: the bullying of younger and weaker people by older or stronger ones. For the millions of people who had, at one time or another in their lives, experienced the bully's foul menacing, this was good news. That schools had finally become aware of the dangers of bullying was reflected in the fact that new laws outlawing bullying were being legislated. One ironic legacy of the Columbine incident was the law Governor Bill Owens signed in Colorado in May 2001 designed to prevent bullying in schools. The law requires school districts to adopt policies against bullying and provide yearly progress reports to the state. The bill was brought about by the Columbine shootings.[52]

New laws in Georgia, New Hampshire, and Vermont require anti-bullying policies in schools. The National Threat Assessment Center, run by the U.S. Secret Service, found that in more than two-thirds of 37 recent shootings, the attackers had been persecuted, bullied, threatened, attacked, or injured. The National Association of School Psychologists say bullying is the reason why 160,000 children skip school every day.[53]

Education experts, seeing the bullied child syndrome acted out in the rash of killings, began to suggest ways that bullying could be curtailed. One mediation expert suggested that the school culture influences bullying. "If the school culture is one of civility and tolerance and one where emotions and differences are addressed, discussed, and treated as problems to be solved, kids will understand that teasing and bullying are inappropriate," said Ellen K. Wayne. Just punishing bullies may only make them madder, she suggested, because children bully others to increase their own power or because intimidation and force are the only ways they know. "These are aggressive strategies, learned from observing others in our culture, like the adults around them or the people they see on TV."[54]

Some schools are trying other ways to reach children about bullying. In Stone Mountain, Georgia, a professional production company put on a skit for the entire student body. And in other states, other measures are being taken.[55]

SUICIDES IN SCHOOLS

Attempted homicides were not the only plague to schools in the 1990s. It began to dawn on school officials somewhere along the line that bullying had a correlation with teenage suicide. Suicides in school buildings and on school grounds came to national attention as a major problem in the 1990s. Of the 62 fatal shootings at school in 1993 listed by the National School Safety Center, six were suicides, most often 14- and 15-year-olds.

Take a small town in New Hampshire, for instance. In 1993, the tiny hamlet of Goffstown realized that five school children had killed themselves in the two and a half years just past. The state, too, took notice: New Hampshire teenagers were dying by suicide at a rate almost double the mid-1980s rate and 40 percent above the national average of 12 per 100,000. In a nearby town, Kearsarge, the problem was almost as bad, so they devised a peer counseling system. One psychologist blamed the state's problem on the recession. Others thought it had more to do with teens' hazing, harassment, and violence. One parent said, "High school cliques have been around forever, but not like this. If kids don't wear brand names on their behinds, they get picked on. If you're the one who gets singled out, there's no limit to how low your self-esteem can go." One of the girls who killed herself left a note saying that she could no longer endure the harassment by a clique of classmates. She had been beaten up and threatened with harm. In response to criticism of the school for the suicides, the principal pointed to broken marriages, violent movies, and TV images.[56]

A respected sociologist points to social stratification in high schools as the root cause of school violence. She said suicide victims "are at the bottom of the social hierarchy. The jocks were on top and their great claim to fame were these idiot games." Donna Gaines also says, "It's freedom of expression. If it is rewarded, it's very good. But if the school doesn't recognize it or punishes it or dismisses it, then we have this outcast thing." Gaines, who wrote the book *Teenage Waste-land: Suburbia's Dead End Kids,* says that high schools often give differential treatment to jocks who bully others. Schools not only condone stratification, they encourage it, she believes. She calls high schools "breeding grounds of homophobia, racism, and sexism." The easy fix is to pass gun control legislation. It would be better to change the culture of high schools.[57]

LITIGATION

Several cases dramatized and epitomized what schools would have to do to improve their approaches to safety by the middle of the decade. In Renton, Washington, in April 2000, the father of an 11-year-old boy who died after slipping on milk in the school cafeteria sued the school district for negligence. Shortly after the incident, the boy was treated by a school nurse and sent home; later he collapsed and underwent two surgeries before dying of massive internal bleeding. "It's not about the money," the father said.[58]

In Simi Valley School District in California, parents of a boy who had been stabbed filed a wrongful death lawsuit against the school, alleging that school officials failed to protect the student. Another boy knifed their son in the chest while he was waiting for a school bus. The lawsuit contended that the school authorities failed to prevent knives from being brought onto the Valley View Junior High School campus. In addition to the school, the lawsuit named the boy who had committed the stabbing. He was sentenced to four years in a California Youth Authority prison. The parents claimed that the school knew there was conflict between the boys.[59]

THE SCOTTY BAKER CASE

Another situation, in what became a sensational Kentucky case in which two women went into a school, obtained early dismissal for a child, and took him in a car, was more portentous for school systems. In fact, it may have been one of the most important cases ever as far as the safety of children in schools is concerned. The body of ten-year-old Donald Scott "Scotty" Baker was found on December 1, 1992, in a strip mine pit in Laurel County, Kentucky, right on the edge of eastern Kentucky's coal fields. Scotty Baker was a fifth-grader at Paces Creek Elementary School in Manchester, Clay County.

Scotty's stepmother, Stephanie Genean Baker, 22, and her friend, Susanne Baker (no relation) came to the school to pick the boy up the day before Thanksgiving, telling the school secretary they were taking him to see his father.

The boy's parents, Ruth and Donnie Baker, who had been divorced five years before, waited for the six days that the boy was missing. Donnie Baker, 33, later said that his wife, who was pregnant, had always been cold toward Scotty and may have felt the boy would prevent him from spending time with her baby when it arrived. During the time of the boy's disappearance, the F.B.I. and state police told the parents not to confront Stephanie. Besides, Stephanie pretended that she was concerned, helping in the search, crying with the family, and was even going to do a TV interview with the parents.[60]

Police then charged Stephanie Baker with Scotty's murder. They said that a woman who identified herself on a school sign-in sheet as "Patricia Smith" took the boy from school. The stepmother and her friend took the boy away from school as other children were preparing to eat a special Thanksgiving meal. The stepmother apparently strangled Scotty as the other woman drove the car.

The principal of Paces Creek Elementary School said the woman produced no identification but told a school secretary that she was the boy's cousin and that she was taking him to meet his father. When children were taken from Paces Creek, they had to sign a sheet stating their name, the child's name, and the reason for taking the child. The sheet did not list the woman's reason for taking Scotty.

Meanwhile, when state education officials learned of the murder, the education commissioner said that he would ask all school districts in the state to review their policies concerning how children can be picked up from school. Thomas Boysen said that policies on releasing children from school were strictly a local matter. A statewide policy would require action by the general assembly or by the state school board.[61]

The state prosecutor asked for the death penalty for the stepmother who had strangled the boy and then mutilated his body. The accomplice, Susanne Baker, said that she was duped into helping kill the boy and then intimidated into keeping quiet about it. Stephanie Baker told her to wear a wig, say she was a cousin, and check the boy out of school. She said the stepmother, who was in the back seat, strangled the boy from behind as she drove the car. The two women set the body on fire after they dumped it.[62]

In the civil court case that followed the murder, the boy's parents were awarded a $4.2 million dollar judgment in January 1997, which said that the Paces Creek Elementary School principal, Caleb Collins, and the school secretary, Charlotte Smith, were negligent in letting a stranger sign Scotty Baker out of school. Ms. Smith said, "He knew her. He wanted to go with her, because I asked him if he wanted to eat first or did he want to go. He didn't hesitate in any way. He didn't show any fear. He was ready to go." But the secretary acknowledged she had never read the policy book that requires a parent, guardian, or designated person to sign a child out. She admitted that it was a common practice not to ask for identification. Stephanie Baker pleaded guilty to kidnapping, murder, and abuse of a corpse and was sentenced to life in prison without parole for 25 years. After this nationally known case, schools across the country, and especially those in Kentucky, began to examine their policies for releasing children from school and other measures protective of children's best interests.[63]

SOME EPISODES OF VIOLENCE, 1990s[64]

In the 1993–1994 school year, there were 53 killings with one or more fatalities each in American high schools. All but eight of them were shootings, and eight were gang related.[65]

In that year, at East Carter High School in Grayson, Kentucky, a senior student at a small, rural high school took a class, its teacher, and a custodian hostage and then shot both of the adults dead.[66]

Trauma is inflicted on a school and its program is seriously interrupted even when no one from the school is killed. For instance, a group of middle school children were in gym class in Sheridan, Wyoming, when a man carrying a rifle and a handgun walked onto the school's football field and began firing at the children in the class. Kevin Newman apparently fired at everyone in the class because he discharged between 23 and 26 rounds of ammunition. Four children were wounded, two of them not seriously. As soon as the teacher realized what the gunman was doing, she waved the children off the field. After he had discharged the bullets, Newman shot himself in the head. He was taken to a hospital, where he died about four hours later.

The shooter had recently received a less than honorable discharge from the navy. He wore a backpack that contained an unopened whiskey bottle and boxes of ammunition. Authorities said that the gunman left a suicide note that did not explain why he went to the school, which enrolled about 550 sixth- and seventh-graders. School was dismissed for the day.[67]

By September 1994, violent episodes were becoming so frequent in New York City that school officials decided to install airport-style, walk-through scanners, which cost about $20,000 each. In addition, they would put bars or heavy screens on all first floor windows and doors. Also, some schools planned to install complicated systems with electromagnetic door alarms.[68]

No wonder. Better incident reporting showed that violence was rising in New York schools. Between July 1, 1993, and June 30, 1994, there were 17,000 incidents in the city's 1,100 schools, ranging from vandalism to robbery. This was a 25.5 percent jump over the previous year. The good news was that there were no homicides reported in the city's schools for the first time since 1990. A school safety official said, "When I read the list of weapons we have seized, I wonder if we shouldn't start handing out medals for valor instead of report cards." More than 3,300 weapons were seized in the schools.[69]

But the city school chancellor rejected that report, saying a month later that new statistics he had found revealed that 400 schools had failed to file reports, meaning that there was 30 percent more crime and violence than had previously been reported. Of the 1,300 incidents that were not reported in the first survey, 375 were assaults, robberies, and other serious incidents.[70]

One of the New York incidents happened in the Bronx in March 1994 when a group of high school students, playing softball on school time, were fired upon by a gunman, who killed a 20-year-old woman and a 17-year-old boy and wounded another student. Dominican and Puerto Rican youngsters made up the two teams. The woman who was killed was a bystander who was sitting watching the game.[71]

In September 1996, a 16-year-old boy shot and killed his teacher in a DeKalb County, Georgia, school. The teacher was shot several times and died on the way to the hospital. The teacher had taught in the county for 21 years and was then teaching in an alternative school.[72]

In January 1998, a 52-year-old man walked into a middle school in Mississippi looking for his estranged wife, a cafeteria worker. About 15 students were in the cafeteria when the man confronted his wife. All of them fled, including his wife, who hid in the office area of the school. The man returned to the cafeteria office, where he stood outside and then put his gun to his head and killed himself.[73]

A *St. Louis Post-Dispatch* story in November 1996 looked back on violence in area schools for the previous three years and made the following list:

November 1996: A student shoots and critically wounds another student.

November: An eighth-grade girl suffers a knife wound to her face.

November: Two female students, 15, are stabbed in a St. Louis high school.

September: A 13-year-old girl hit by stray bullets as she rides school bus.

May: A 17-year-old points a scoped .22-caliber rifle at a school bus while his brother fights with two other students on board.

February: A man gets on a bus and fatally shoots a pregnant student. Her baby dies later. The gunman also wounded the driver.

October 1995: A boy standing behind a school bus shoots a pistol inside the bus.

October: A substitute teacher collapses and dies after scuffling with fourth-grade boy, age nine.

October: Student, 15, punches a teacher in the eye, strikes her head, and kicks her in the abdomen.

February: A senior at St. Louis High School is shot repeatedly in a crowded hallway.

January: A student, 15, is sexually assaulted and fatally beaten in a girls' bathroom at a high school in Florissant. The killing prompts Missouri to tighten school safety.

February 1994: A gang of 20 terrorizes an English class in a high school.

January 1994: A student, 15, stabs another student and collapses his lung.

December 1993: A seventh-grade girl, 13, stabs another girl in a middle school.

March 1993: A 17-year-old girl at a high school stalks her former boyfriend, 17, for a week before fatally shooting him in the head.[74]

In Fort Worth, Texas, in November 1996, two former military cadets, a boy and a girl, shot and killed another 16-year-old girl because of a sexual encounter she had had with the male killer. The shooters were high school seniors at the time. The boy went on to the Air Force Academy and the girl to the Naval Academy. The slaying went unsolved until September, when the two were enrolled in the academies.[75]

In May 1999, a boy upset over a broken romance shot six other students in his Georgia high school. The 15-year-old boy brought a rifle and a handgun to school. After shooting the six schoolmates, he intended to take his own life but was talked out of it by the school's assistant principal. Shortly after this shooting episode, Vice President Gore broke a tie by casting his vote as the U.S. Senate passed new gun-control legislation.

The school day was just beginning on the last day for seniors, and everyone expected pranks. Suddenly, the laughing was interrupted by a popping sound as the sophomore standing in front of the girl's bathroom began shooting. He seemed to be aiming below the waist so as not to kill anyone. Students took cover wherever they could. After wounding the six students, the boy dropped the rifle and walked outside. He aimed the pistol at a senior briefly and then dropped to his knees and put the pistol in his mouth. That's when the assistant principal came over and persuaded him to give up the gun. The most seriously wounded student was a girl who was hit in the buttocks with the bullet passing through to her intestines. The gunman was described as a quiet boy.[76]

On March 30, 2001, a 16-year-old student was shot to death in the parking lot of a Gary, Indiana, school by a 17-year-old boy. The gunman just walked up to the boy, put a gun to his head, and fired, witnesses said. The shooter was a former student at the school who had been expelled.[77]

At Santana High School in Santee, California, on March 5, 2001, Charles Andy Williams shot two students, then went from the restroom to a quad where he fired randomly, stopping to load at least four times, shooting at least 30 more times. He killed two students and wounded 11 others. Also wounded were two adults. Williams was thought to have been bullied frequently by other boys.[78]

One of the few female school shooters of the era was a 13-year-old girl who opened fire inside the cafeteria of her Catholic school just three days after the Santee incident, injuring one student but causing no deaths. Police in Williamsport, Pennsylvania, said that the victim had been hit in the shoulder by the outburst, which occurred about noon at Bishop Neumann High School.[79]

On March 23, 2001, for the second time in three weeks a California high school cancelled classes, as four students—including the shooter—and two teachers were wounded at Granite Hills High School in El Cajon. An 18-year-old senior was the suspected gunman who received wounds in his buttocks and jaw in a gun battle with a campus police officer. Granite Hills is in the same school district as Santana High School in Santee.[80]

After the Santee shooting, numerous threats of violence were made by children around the country, including:

- A 16-year-old pulled a gun in class in a high school near Seattle.
- Two California 17-year-olds were arrested on charges of conspiracy to commit murder after authorities found a "hit list" of 16 students.
- In Perris, California, a 15-year-old was arrested for boasting he could outdo the Columbine massacre.
- In Savannah, Georgia, a 15-year-old was arrested when he brought a BB gun onto the school campus.
- In Williamsport, Pennsylvania, a 14-year-old girl fired a single shot at another student in the cafeteria, hitting her in the shoulder.
- In southwest Philadelphia, police arrested a 12-year-old in an elementary school. He was carrying a .22-caliber pistol.
- Another Philadelphia student, 8 years old, threatened a "bloodbath" with a loaded shotgun.
- An honor student in Camden, New Jersey, was arrested for threatening to shoot members of a clique.
- In Bradenton, Florida, a high school sophomore, 17, was suspended after he carried a semiautomatic handgun to school.
- In St. Petersburg, a 17-year-old carried a revolver with a sawed-off barrel into his former middle school.
- In Davenport, Iowa, a 15-year-old threatened to get a gun and kill everyone in the school.
- A Harlingen, Texas, freshman had a hit list.

- In Arizona, three teenagers were arrested for threatening to kill others.[81]

And so the violence continued.

15 SECONDS OF FAME—THE LITTLE BIG MEN

The 1990s will be famous for a series of shootings perpetrated by middle and high school students, persons sick with some sort of rage, persons who seemed to become more numerous as time went on and as media fever seem to take them in, individuals who would commit the most heinous of crimes against their fellow students and teachers. Since some of the shootings are now known to virtually everyone, we have chosen to list the cases with multiple victims rather than discuss each individually. Unlike ordinary criminals, almost all of the killers wanted to get caught, and almost all did not act impulsively. Most were like Anthony Barbaro (Chapter 9) who wanted to kill the person he hated most, himself. Probably most of them also had serious mental problems. The *New York Times* did a profile of 102 killers in rampage attacks, including the one at Columbine in 1999. About half the killers had a prior diagnosis of mental illness. The mentally ill are no more violent than average people, except when they are off their medications. Rampage killings represent only one-tenth of one percent of all killings, but they did increase in the 1990s. Whereas these kinds of killings once took place most often in the family setting, it is now most often in the workplace or school that the killers inflict themselves on others. There is also some evidence that the killers are "feeding off each other"—a copycat element—because of the media coverage of such events.[82]

LOOKING FOR REASONS

At least nine of the multiple shootings occurred in towns with populations of less than 46,505 (Jonesboro, Arkansas). Boys committed all of the school shootings with multiple fatalities in the 1990s (except those listed by estranged husbands and school employees). All of the schoolboy shooters had some sort of precipitating event such as social rejection, school expulsion, disciplinary action, or bullying. All were isolated, rejected by peers, and considered social outcasts. All were fascinated with violent music, movies, videos, and usually weapons. All had antisocial and narcissistic features.[83]

MULTIPLE VICTIM SCHOOL SHOOTINGS IN THE U.S. FROM 1993 TO 2001[84]

Year	School	Location	# Killed	Method	Reason	Shooter
1993	East Carter High	Grayson, KY	2	shooting	unknown	Scott Pennington
1993	Weatherless Elem.	Washington, D.C.	2	shooting	gang-related	unknown
1994	Lee County, Fla.	Fort Myers, FL	2	shooting	hatred	school employee
1995	Olathe N.H.S.	Olathe, KS	2	shooting	random	student
1995	Blackville-Hilda	Blackville, SC	2	shooting	suspended	student
1995	Richland H.S.	Lynnville, TN	2	shooting	random	student
1996	Frontier Jr. H.S.	Moses Lake, WA	3	shooting	bully-related	student
1996	Beaumont H.S.	St. Louis, MO	2	shooting	unknown	young man
1996	Smedley Elem.	Phila., PA	2	shooting	est. wife	est. husband
1997	Bethel H.S.	Bethel, AK	2	shooting	bully-related	student
1997	Pearl H.S.	Pearl, MS	2	shooting	random	student
1997	John Glenn H.S.	Norwalk, CA	2	shooting	jilted	ex-boyfriend
1997	Heath H.S.	Paducah, KY	3	shooting	bully-related	student
1998	Hoboken H.S.	Hoboken, NJ	2	shooting	delusional	husband
1998	Westside Middle	Jonesboro, AR	5	shooting	planned	2 boys
1998	Philadelphia Elem.	Pomona, CA	2	shooting	gang	gang member
1998	Thurston H.S.	Springfield, OR	2	shooting	unknown	student
1998	Stranahan H.S.	Ft. Lauderdale, FL	2	shooting	jilted	ex-boyfriend
1999	Central H.S.	Carollton, GA	2	shooting	suicide	boyfriend
1999	Columbine H.S.	Littleton, CO	15	shooting	hate crime	2 boys
1999	Lynwood H.S.	Lynwood, CA	2	shooting	unknown	gunman
1999	Guyan Valley H.S.	Branchland, WV	2	shooting	mur-suicide	bus driver
2000	Beach H.S.	Savannah, GA	2	shooting	unknown	student
2000	Carmichael H.S.	Sierra Vista, AZ	2	shooting	mur-suicide	ex-husband
2000	Valley View Elem.	Glendale, CA	2	beating	murders	boy, 16
2000	Santana H.S.	Santee, CA	2	shooting	bullying	student

For the many commentators who blamed the media for the fact that so many of the shootings seemed to be of the "copycat" variety, Ishmael Reed reminded them that there was no television in the nineteenth century when gangs of white ethnics killed many people in northern cities. For those who blamed the parents of the shooters and for those who seemed shocked that the shootings happened in predominantly white suburban schools, he pointed out that as early as 1994 a major public opinion research firm had pointed out that violence among teenagers was the worst in the west and that schoolchildren in smaller rural areas were twice as likely to carry weapons as students living in large cities.[85]

The Report of Governor Bill Owens' Columbine Review Commission is an important document because it makes numerous recommendations based upon the tragedy at Columbine High School. Among the conclusions was that the incident was badly handled by just about everyone in authority who was concerned with it, including the SWAT team that was so slow to try to take out the killers. The commission's recommendations fell under the following categories:

A. Recommendations relating to crisis-response actions.

B. Recommendations for improved communications for critical emergencies.

C. Recommendations for advance planning for critical emergencies.

D. Recommendations bearing on interaction with media representatives.

E. Recommendations concerning tasks of school resource officers.

F. Recommendations concerning detection by school administrators of potential perpetrators of school-based violence and administrative countermeasures.

G. Recommendations concerning medical treatment for attack victims.

H. Recommendations concerning reuniting attack victims and their families.

I. Recommendations concerning identification of victims' bodies and family access to bodies.

J. Recommendations concerning suicide prevention in the aftermath of incidents like Columbine.[86]

In spite of attempts by school officials, police, and legislators to prevent the reoccurrence of such vile acts as those perpetrated at Columbine, the real legacy of that atrocity and others is the fear that such violence will happen again. Also, perhaps attention should be paid to the strong argument that public schools have grown too large, that in those huge schools "there is inevitably a critical mass of kids who are neither jocks nor artists nor even nerds, kids who are nothing at all, nonentities in their own lives."[87] Perhaps modern society makes nonentities of too many people.

FULFILLING THE PURPOSES OF THIS BOOK

In Chapter 1, the authors stated that the purposes of this book were first to provide a balanced view of school safety so that public opinion would be based in facts as well as impressions. By providing an extensive number of selected examples, we have tried to make our argument that social forces determine to a great extent what happens in schools. Our intention was to make the concept of the vulnerability of schools a reality for the reader. Our second purpose was to present an historical basis for analysis of the school safety question. We have tried to show, by using a large number of factual illustrations, that schools can be threatened in a multitude of ways. Third, we wanted to provide a basis for future scholarly inquiry. There are thousands of incidents and questions raised in this book that require further study. Since we have only used incidents that serve to prove our points about large social forces, there are thousands more details needed. Our fourth goal was to show what states are doing to make schools safer, and we think we have done that in several places throughout the book. Fifth, we wanted to show what impact historical disruptions of the schools have had in shaping laws and regulations that govern safety in the schools, and we believe the cases cited do that. Last, we wanted to show how complicated it has become for school teachers and administrators to respond to all of the burdens of school safety, and we have tried to illustrate that in a number of places throughout the book, and most particularly in Chapters 7 and 10.

What is the impact of each chapter and why have we arranged the chapters in the order found here? In Chapter 1, we wanted to begin with the prevailing notion of the school by presenting the metaphor of the school as a safe haven. In Chapter 2, we wanted to show that schools immediately after World War II were perceived differently from the way they are perceived today. In Chapter 3, we began to tell about one of the threats, juvenile delinquency, which had an impact upon school safety for the era covered by the book. In Chapter 4, we wanted to show how devastating school fires have been and how important fire safety is to schools. Chapter 5 demonstrates that natural forces can devastate a school environment. In Chapter 6, our desire was to show how the most important American social movement of the twentieth century has had such an enormous impact upon the well-being of schools. In Chapter 7, we argued that the burden upon teachers is not one-dimensional, that it is not merely that this has become a litigious society, but that other factors have made the role of disciplinarian difficult if not impossible. Chapter 8 presents some of the darkest aspects of contemporary society's most menacing problems: sexual misconduct, drugs, and gangs. Chapter 9 shows perhaps overwhelmingly that violent intruders in schools did not begin with the 1990s, that precursors to Columbine were numerous. Chapter 10 tries to complete the historical story line of the book by discussing some events of the 1990s. By having each chapter cover a period of time (which admittedly is somewhat arbitrary at times), we have tried to tell a story in a cumulative and natural way. It is clear to us at this point that although a great deal of good work has been done in improving the safety of schools, there is much more to do. We feel that educators and aspiring educators, especially, can benefit from the lessons our illustrations have taught, but all of us, as citizens, can find the information provided here to be informative and useful as we support and provide leadership for our nation's schools.

NOTES

1. Dr. James Hoagland of the University of Kentucky in an undated informal note to Rollin J. Watson. We are indebted to Dr. Hoagland for his encouragement and advice on this project.

2. "Goals and Purpose of Safe and Drug Free Schools and Communities Act," Center for Effective Collaboration and Practice, July 26, 2000. http://www.air.org'cecp/resources/safe&drug_free/goals_and_purpose.html. "Safe and Drug-Free Schools Act," Indiana Prevention Resource Center at Indiana University, July 26,2000. http://www.drugs.indiana.edu/laws/dfsc.html.

3. "Zero Tolerance Policies Change Life at One School," *New York Times on the Web*, July 27, 2000. http://www.nytimes.com/learning/students/pop/010409snapmonday.html.

4. Michael W. Roskiewicz, "New Safety School Legislation," *Violence*

in Schools, January 26, 2001. http://www.dickinson-wright.com/web2/dweb.nsf/htmlmedia/dw_vpw00_school.html.

5. "Governor Davis Signs Legislation to Implement School Safety Program," News release, June 30, 1999. http://old.ca.gov/s/governor/063099.html.

6. "School Violence Prevention," *A Guide to Safe Schools,* July 29, 2000. http://www.sde.state.sc.us/archive/educator/safeschl/html.

7. Lisa Stiffler, "School Safety a Thorny Issue Confronting the Legislature," *Northwest,* February 2, 1999. http://seattlep-i.nwsource.com/local/legi02.shtml.

8. "Knowles Signs School Safety Bill, Other Legislation," Office of the Governor, Press Releases, June 24, 1999. http://www.gov.state.ak.us/press/99136.html.

9. "School Safety in Virginia," Virginia Center for School Safety, July 29, 2000. http://www.vaschoolsafety.com/schoolsafety.html.

10. As has been our practice throughout this book, we have selected a few examples from each category of threat to the schools. Many other instances can be documented.

11. "Morton Grove Jr. High Blast Injures Pupil," *Chicago Sun Times,* February 5, 1993, pg. 37.

12. "3 Accused in Blast Expelled," *San Francisco Chronicle,* July 1, 1994, pg. A22.

13. "Mentor: Grade School Reopens After Explosion Caused Evacuation," *Columbus Dispatch,* December 14, 1995, pg. 4D.

14. "School Explosion in Missouri Injures 11," *Milwaukee Journal Sentinel,* January 6, 1999, pg. 3.

15. "Two Killed in Gas Explosion," *Anderson Independent-Mail,* November 19, 2000, pg. 1.

16. "Youth Charged in School Explosion," *Buffalo News,* March 10, 1995, pg. 1.

17. "No One Injured in School Explosion," *Tampa Tribune,* September 22, 1995, Brandon-South Bay, pg. 1.

18. "Farmington Boys Charged in Bomb Threats," *Minneapolis Star Tribune,* March 2, 1966, pg. 3B.

19. "Fire at Metro High Follows Blast at Paseo," *Kansas City Star,* March 13, 1997, pg. C1.

20. "2 15 Year-Olds Accused to Threat to Bomb School," *Buffalo News,* April 12, 1998, pg. 9A.

21. "3 Wisconsin Teens Charged with Conspiracy to Kill," *Minneapolis Star Tribune,* November 19, 1998, pg. 4A.

22. "Cherokee School Acts on Threats," *Atlanta Constitution,* May 30, 1998, pg. 01D.

23. "5th Grader Charged with Bomb Threat," *Boston Globe,* May 22, 1999, pg. B4.

24. "8th Grader Accused in Bomb Threat," *Plain Dealer,* September 24, 1999, pg. 1B.

25. "Officials Say School Massacre Foiled in Ohio," *Atlanta Constitution,* October 29, 1999, pg. 1A.

26. "Courts Pursue School Threats," *Miami Herald,* August 27, 1999, pg. A1.

27. "6 Hastings Students Accused of Bombing Vice Principal's Home," *Minneapolis Star Tribune,* March 25, 1998, pg. 7B.

28. "Fireworks Suspected in School Explosion," *Seattle Times,* March 24, 2000, pg. B1.

29. "'Vague' Phone Threats Close 7 N.Y. Schools," *CNN.com,* March 27,2001. http://www.cnn.com/2001/US/03/27/school.threat/index.html.

30. "School Bombarded by Student Threats," *EagleTribune,* March 20, 2001. http://www.eagletribune.com/news/stories/20010320/FP_002.html.

31. "Teacher Is Accused of Bomb Threats," *Minneapolis Star-Tribune,* March 28, 2000, pg. 2B.

32. "Schools Fight Fake Bomb Threats," *Detroit News,* March 1, 2000. http://detnews.com/2001/schools/0104/20/a01-21485.html.

33. "5 Teens Charged in School Fire," *San Francisco Chronicle,* December 23, 1994, pg. A21.

34. "Fire Destroys 2 Classrooms," *Arizona Republic,* October 9, 1995, pg. B1; "Prom-Threatening Principal Denies He Burned His School," *USA Today,* October 20, 1995, pg. 3A; "Compton Declares State of Emergency for Schools," *Los Angeles Times,* August 4, 1999, pg. B1; "Graffiti Leads Police to 2 Boys, Who Are Charged With Arson at a School," *New York Times,* March 15, 2000, pg. B3; "Fires Force Tighter Security, Relocations at Berkeley High," April 21, 2000, pg. A21; "5 Teens Arrested in Fremont School Fire," *San Francisco Chronicle,* July 29, 2000, pg. A19; "Student Accused of Setting Four Fires," *St. Petersburg Times,* November 11, 2000, pg. 3B; "Girls Charged with Arson," *Tampa Tribune,* February 17, 2001, pg. 1; "High School Arson Tab Put at $100,000," *Arizona Republic,* March 15, 2001, pg. 1.

35. "Grief Counselors Help Pupils Discuss Deaths of Six Children in Fire," *St. Louis Post Dispatch,* March 16, 1999, pg. A6.

36. "6 Alarm Fire at Yerba Buena High," *San Francisco Chronicle,* May 23, 1995, pg. A13.

37. "With Washington Schools Delayed for Week, Officials and Parents Look for Alternatives," *New York Times,* September 7, 1994, pg. B11.

38. "Mother, School Clash Over Air," *Phoenix Gazette,* April 7, 1995, pg. A1.

39. "School's Spiders Eradicated," *Tampa Tribune,* October 2, 1997, Pinellas, pg. 1.

40. "Anthrax Letters Sent to School, Church," *Los Angeles Times,* November 10, 1998, part A, pg. 21.

41. "Asbestos Whistle-Blower School Security Officer Warned of Problem in Fort Morgan But Was Ignored," *Denver Rocky Mountin News,* July 9, 2000, pg. 7A.

42. "Children at 2 Elementary Schools May Have Been Exposed to Lead," *Los Angeles Times,* November 4, 2000, part B, pg. 5.

43. "Youths Deaths Tear at a Town's Heart," *Seattle Times,* May 30, 1997, pg. A1.

44. "High Grove School Cleaned Up, Ready After Summer Flood," *Kansas City Star,* August 21, 1997, pg. 11.

45. "Southern Ky. Starts Cleanup After Violent, Deadly Storm," *Courier-Journal,* April 18, 1998, pg. 1A.

46. "New School Mopping Up After Its Latest Mishap," *Indianapolis Star,* August 26, 1999, pg. C04.

47. "School Out After Oil Spill," *New York Daily News,* December 13, 2000, pg. 3.

48. "Why Everyone Needs to Get AIDS Message," *New York Times,* January 18, 1994, pg. A22.

49. "News Around Ohio," *Columbus Dispatch,* December 14, 1995, pg. 4D.

50. "Horseplay in School Kills Girl, 8," *Buffalo News,* October 27, 1999, pg. 1A.

51. "School Explosion," *USA Today,* November 4, 1994, pg. 3A.

52. "Colorado Governor Signs Bully Bill," *San Diego Union Tribune,* May 3, 2001, pg. A7.

53. Nadya Labi, "Let Bullies Beware," *Time,* April 2, 2001, pg. 46.

54. "School Culture Influences Bullying," *CNN,* July 25, 2001. http://fyi.cnn.com/2001/fyi/teachers.ednews/07/25/bullies.ap/index.html.

55. Labi, pg. 46.

56. "N.H. Teens Cry for Help/Suicide Rates Surge Above National Average," *USA Today,* October 22, 1993, pg. 2A.

57. "The Real Root Cause of School Violence," *Washington Post,* May 28, 1999, pg. C11; Donna Gaines, *Teenage Wasteland: Suburbia's Dead End Kids* (New York: HarperPerennial, 1992).

58. "Dad Sues School District After Son's Fatal Fall," *Northwest,* April 20, 2000. http://seatlep-i.nwsource.com/local/suit20.shtml.

59. "Parents of Slain Student Sue Simi Valley School District," *Los Angeles Times,* February 2, 1995, pg. B4.

60. "Slain Boy's Parents Cope With Anger and Anguish," *Courier-Journal,* December 3, 1992, pg. 1A.

61. "Murder Leads State to Have Schools Review Child Pickup Policies," *Courier-Journal,* December 3, 1992, pg. 1B.

62. "Woman Testifies She Was Tricked Into Role in Murder," *Courier-Journal,* January 25, 1994, pg. 1B.

63. "Jury Awards $4.2 million in Pupil's Death; Clay Jury Finds School Secretary, Principal Negligent," *Courier-Journal,* January 10, 1997, pg. 01B.

64. The National School Safety Center has a comprehensive list of "School Associated Violent Deaths" which covers the 1992–1993 school year to the present of which we have made use. In this chapter, we will discuss some of the shootings on that list, but by no means all of them. Though that list is very helpful, carefully and meticulously comprehensive, it certainly cannot be emulated here, nor is there any desire to. One of the purposes of this book is to chronicle facets of school threats and intrusions, including selected shootings, but we devote only a portion of the chapter to the decade's most sensational stories. "School Associated Violent Deaths," The National School Safety Center, June 12, 2001, 32 pages. http://www.nssc1.org.

65. Ibid.

66. Ibid.

67. "Children Attacked in Gym Class," *Houston Chronicle,* September 18, 1993, pg. A7.

68. "Guns in the Schools," *New York Times,* September 17, 1994, section 1, pg. 22.

69. "Violence Grows in New York Schools," *New York Times,* June 11, 1994, section 1, pg. 25. See also "Report Shows Violence Rising in Schools," *New York Times,* August 13, 1994, section 1, pg. 25.

70. "Report Finds More Violence in the Schools," *New York Times,* July 7, 1994, pg. B1.

71. "Gunfire Kills Two Students After Fight at a Bronx Park," *New York Times,* March 24, 1994, section B, pg. 3.

72. "Shoot at Dekalb Alternate School," *Atlanta Journal and Constitution,* September 26, 1996, pg. 08C.

73. "Gunman Hunts his Wife at School, Then Kills Himself," *Times-Picayune,* January 16, 1998, pg. A1.

74. "A Look Back at Violence in Area Schools," *St. Louis Post-Dispatch,* November 1, 1996, pg. 12A.

75. "Cadets Won't Face Death in High School Killing," *Milwaukee Journal Sentinel,* November 12, 1996, pg. 6.

76. "Shooting in Georgia," *Boston Herald,* May 20, 1999, pg. 001.

77. "1 Killed in Gary, Indiana, School Shooting, Police Say," *CNN,* March 30, 2001. http://www.cnn.com/2001/US/03/30/shool.shooting.02/html.

78. Information obtained from "School Associated Violent Deaths," The National School Safety Center, June 12, 2001, 32 pages. http://www.nssc1.org.

79. "Student Shot as Girl, 13, Opens Fire in School," *Independent (London),* March 8, 2001, pg. 13.

80. "Again, A School Shooting Stuns California Community," *CNN*, March 23, 2001. http://www.cnn.com/2001/US/03/23/school.shooting.01/index.html.

81. "An Epidemic of Violence," *CNN*, March 8, 2001. http://www.cnn.com/2001/US/03/08/alarming.incidents/ index.html.

82. "Rampage Killers," *New York Times*, April 9, 2000. http://groups.yahoo.com/group/Texas Tower/message/9.

83. "Violence Goes to School," July 27, 2000. http://www.n-fa.com/schoolhome.html.

84. This list is derived mostly from the National School Safety Center's "School Associated Violent Deaths." The National School Safety Center, June 12, 2001, 32 pages. http://www.nssc1.org.

85. "The Pundits Misfire on School Shootings," *Baltimore Sun*, May 30, 1999, pg. 5C.

86. *The Report of Governor Bill Owens' Columbine Review Commission,* State of Colorado, May 2001, pgs. x–xx.

87. Anna Quindlen, "The Problem of the Megaschool," *Newsweek*, March 26, 2000, pg. 68.

Postscript:
Forging a New Paradigm

Work on this book was completed well before the events of September 11, 2001, but the acts of terrorism committed on that fateful day had a bearing on almost every aspect of American culture, tending to intensify some things and make others seem irrelevant. Regarding the subject of school safety, we could see a new intensity of concern develop among our colleagues in the public schools as the unimaginable acts of terror brought forth the specter of new and dreadful possibilities such as bioterrorism, chemical, nuclear, and all manner of other environmental contamination.

Perhaps most people working with schools had begun to think before that time that the pendulum of public opinion had swung too far toward the negative side regarding the safety of schools, with far too much attention being paid to student-initiated violence as a factor in overall school safety. When September 11th happened, a new dimension in the human capacity for evil seemed to dominate most Americans' thoughts.

We retain our belief in the strength and resiliency of the American school and its ability to remain one of society's safest institutions. What has brought life to this book is that schools have weathered more storms than most think while still retaining the overall integrity of their mission to provide a safe place to learn for America's children. It was our hope that if the book had any "message," it was that the story it tells reinforces the need for schools—like every other institution in our culture—to take more care, to be more meticulous and circumspect, to refuse to allow themselves to be insouciant or careless about little things, as they often have been in the past. Truly, this book is about little things that got away from schools and became big things. Hopefully this glimpse at history helps us see that most of them can be prevented without a great deal of additional expense.

Americans at all levels are now surveying the expense and time that will be required to adequately protect our institutions in the new world of international terrorism. The price will have to be paid. School systems and state, federal, and local governments will have to find ways to do things they have never done before.

We think that schools have learned, at least since the time of Columbine, that they will have to be bolder and more assertive about measures necessary to protect themselves, including the necessity of forging closer relationships with police, fire, and other emergency responders in the community. We have emphasized throughout this book our belief that schools emanate from the community while nurturing the community's lifeblood—its human resources—and in turn they depend on the community to help preserve their safety and fight for their success. The events of September 11th gave this imperative for community unity a new urgency.

This book has not focused solely on violence—in fact, violence has been only a small part of the overall concern about school safety. But unfortunately, again, we focus on violence as it intrudes itself upon the school. As Robert L. Maginnis said, "the school violence epidemic is rooted in larger societal problems."[1] Of course, international terrorism has become American society's problem in this time and no one can overlook it.

The scope of threats has broadened since September 11th. Etiological, chemical, and even possible nuclear threats have expanded our response necessities. School principals and faculties are learning how to secure a site that is thought to be or actually is contaminated with a life-threatening man-made hazard. Schools have been the recipients of numerous anthrax threats.

The extensive reiterations of the subject of terrorism by the media have made schools and communities rethink the unthinkable. Communities are participating in exercises to respond to mock water supply contamination events. Weapons of mass destruction that may be directed at the community at large will certainly have an impact upon the schools, just as the New York City schools near ground zero had to evacuate when the World Trade Center towers were attacked.

In the old—and perhaps in some places prevailing—worldview of school safety, the range of threats to safety and security in any school depended on a host of conditions. Some were under the school's control and some were not. A variety of remedies for identified threats were employed to offset vulnerabilities; some of these were barriers, alarms, locks, procedures, personnel, technology, and training, to name a few. In many cases the school ignored threats because they did not believe disasters could happen to them. Unlocked doors, poor mechanical and technical safeguards, and especially the failure to observe procedures—such as happened in the Scotty Baker incident—have resulted in suffering or even tragedy.

A new paradigm has evolved over the past decade, exacerbated by the school killings of the 1990s and escalated greatly by September 11th. No coruscating illumination has brought about this new way of looking at school safety, however, for there is no panacea for the problems schools face. The new paradigm involves an integrated set of responses based on knowledge and appropriate resources.

The apathy and indifference to safety that characterized a past era, when people believed in the myth of the school as a safe haven, is no longer acceptable. The range of threats in safety and security has widened because of the potential for use of weapons of mass destruction directed at the community or at the school. The school's response to threats that arise from terrorist acts will depend on the nature and extent of the threat. The school will have to be prepared to fit into the larger community response. It will have to have trained staff with the means to communicate efficiently with the emergency community and to the general population that it serves.

By expanding the basic crisis response training to include teachers and office staff especially in the areas where international terrorist acts using weapons of mass destruction are used whether they are biological, radiologicial, or chemical may serve to mitigate many problems that arise from these threats. In the future, school personnel will require training in crisis response, threat assessment, and threat containment. Threat assessment involves systematically identifying and managing threats in a timely manner.

It will be necessary for safety and security procedures to be well known and religiously followed. School personnel will have to be equipped with appropriate communications devices and security technology to protect the staff and students under its direction. Most of all, the school will have to be included in emergency community crisis response training.

The myth of the school as a safe haven was not a bad thing, nor was it a dangerous concept. It was just an inadequate way of thinking about the school—it was a myth. And it is time to forge a new paradigm about the safety of the American school, one that takes into account what has happened in the past to help prepare for future realities.

In the preface to this book, we said that we wanted to show that there had been a subtle incremental increase in the dangers and threats to the American school from the time right after World War II to the present. We also wanted to demonstrate that most threats to the school are derived from the greater culture of which the school is a part. Some threats to the school cannot be eliminated until some of society's problems are adequately dealt with, while others can be handled at the level of the local school. The environment around the school is never static; it is constantly changing, and schools must continually adapt to new realities. A neighborhood that was once occupied by middle-class people becomes run down and is taken over by drug dealers, for instance. Or perhaps a new plant moves near a school, and the landscape changes as the demands of the plant change traffic patterns, pollute the air, or modify other things that can affect the school. Or perhaps a town simply grows until a school that once served a small population of students has to meet new demands made by a larger and more diverse population.

It is sometimes easier to write about grand devastating events than it is to focus on individual struggles with life and death. It is easier in some ways to objectify things from a distance than it is to look at them up close. The basis for a new safety theory has to take into account all of the things that can happen to individuals and institutions, and it has to study the lessons of the past, including the threats faced by individuals and the threats posed to the entire institution. It can never allow reason to be jeopardized by fear. It always has to consider what has been done in lieu of fear and consider whether those actions have made a difference. Even if certain of the recent legislation amounted to little more than political posturing in some quarters, some measurable good at least was accomplished by the effort. Unfortunately, good theory, good practice, and good law often evolve from what has gone wrong in the past. The history of our country is the story of people who faced up to threats, applied reason to solve them, and then stood courageously for remedies that overcame their vulnerabilities.

NOTE

1. Robert L. Maginnis, "Violence in the Schoolhouse: A Ten Year Update," Family Research Council, July 10, 2000. http://www.frc.org/insight/is94e5cr.html.

Index

About the Authors

ROLLIN J. WATSON has held a number of teaching and administrative posts in higher education and served as president of two colleges. In 1999, after eleven years as president of Somerset Community College in Kentucky, he retired to teach and write full time.

ROBERT S. WATSON is a retired school superintendent and F.B.I. agent. He has co-written *Containing Crisis*, which grew out of the 1988 school shooting in Greenwood, South Carolina, where he was then superintendent of schools.